T0283395

Slow Noodles

Slow Noodles

A Cambodian Memoir of Love, Loss, and Family Recipes

CHANTHA NGUON

with Kim Green

ALGONQUIN BOOKS
OF CHAPEL HILL
2024

Published by
Algonquin Books of Chapel Hill
Post Office Box 2225
Chapel Hill, North Carolina 27515-2225

an imprint of Workman Publishing
a division of Hachette Book Group, Inc.
1290 Avenue of the Americas
New York, NY 10104

Printed in the United States of America.
Design by Steve Godwin.

Portions of the epilogue by Clara Kim were first published in the
Nashville Scene's Vodka Yonic column.

The publisher is not responsible for websites (or their content)
that are not owned by the publisher.

Cataloging-in-Publication Data for this title is
available from the Library of Congress.

ISBN 978-1-64375-349-2 HC
ISBN 978-1-64375-602-8 E-book

10 9 8 7 6 5 4 3 2 1
First Edition

To my children, Clara and Johan,
for listening to my stories.
And to Ann Walling,
for encouraging me to share them with the world.

———————

CONTENTS

————◆————

Slow Noodles

PROLOGUE

———————

IN 1975, THE Khmer Rouge informed the Cambodian people that we had no history, but we knew it was a lie.

Cambodia has a rich past, a mosaic of flavors from near and far: South Indian traders gave us Buddhism, an alphabet, and spicy curries; China brought rice noodles and astrology; and French colonizers passed on a love of strong coffee, pâté, flan, and a light, crusty baguette.

We lifted the best tastes from everywhere and added our own: sour pickled fruits and vegetables, the famous Kampot peppercorn, and the most distinctive flavor of all: prahok, Cambodia's (in)famous fermented fish paste.

Even now, I can taste my own history, in shimmering sense-memories of my mother's homemade fish sauce, the soup noodles she rolled out in her hands, and the pâté de foie she served to guests.

One occupying force tried to erase it all. The Communist Party of Kampuchea stole our name: today, people hear "Khmer," and they think "Khmer Rouge." A word describing our identity now evokes horror and mass murder. But the Khmer language and Khmer people, native to Southeast Asia, preceded Pol Pot's communist guerillas by more than a thousand years.

Cambodians were a new generation, starting from "Year Zero." That's the phrase Pol Pot invented to describe the annihilation of Cambodian culture and the birth of a new, revolutionary society, as his soldiers emptied the cities of people to replace civilization with an "Agrarian Paradise." He mixed together some borrowed ideologies and added his own genocidal flavor; his cadres freed us from the burdens of pâté de foie and soup noodles, and also education, medicine, cinema, books, money, cars, and religion. In return, Cambodians won the right to dig canals and harvest rice, to starve and be executed. By those and other methods, Angkar—Pol Pot's "organization"—liberated nearly two million[1] people from life itself.

I fled to Vietnam as a little girl of nine, five years before the liberation began.

The ideologues were busy there, too, setting everyone "free" and turning back the clocks. At political meetings, they cried into their megaphones about past-life indulgences that must be disavowed: Down with old ballads; up with fervid songs of blood and sacrifice. Down with pâté and pastries; up with watery rice mash cut with cassava. Everything mushed together in one pot. It tasted like a gray nothing.

Fourteen years later, as a young woman alone in Saigon, I thought my past had been erased, too. My family was gone. My country had drowned in its own blood. All I had left were memories: the smell of a charcoal fire in my mother's kitchen, the perfume of my father's pipe. Only smoke remained.

Pol Pot restarted time at Year Zero. When did he intend for Year One to begin? When the dead rose from the ashes? Was it his ambition to erase the future along with the past? His cadres murdered everyone whose job it was to plan for tomorrow: doctors, engineers, teachers, scientists. The Khmer Rouge buried them all and ground the schools and hospitals to dust. They remade a civilization into a vast forced-labor camp and turned eight million Cambodians into six million emaciated inmates and beggars. Not even the eternal pagodas survived.

---

1   Estimates range from 1.6 to 3 million dead, from one fifth to more than a quarter of the population.

When I finally made it home to Cambodia after more than two decades as a refugee, I found a country with no idea of tomorrow. During the Khmer Rouge regime (or, as we Cambodians say, during "Pol Pot Time"), and for years afterward, lives slipped away so easily—by torture, hunger, and disease; by land-mine blast; by guerrilla fighting that never seemed to end—people could scarcely imagine growing old. Every bowl of rice might be the last.

I understand this mindset. When you are hungry, the past and future darken, until only the present is visible. Many nights I, too, dreamed only of rice. Hunger focuses the mind but shrinks one's hopes.

In a way, I was lucky. Though I'd lost my home and my family, there was something no one could take away: a happy childhood, rich with the flavors of my mother's cooking. In the kitchen, she cared for people by feeding them wondrous soups and curries, spring rolls and stir-fries. When I look back on the first nine years of my life, in the light of what came later, that time seems magical, a perfection. Those memories became recipes for building a future. They gave me strength to fight for a life I knew could be better, because I had tasted it before.

Maybe the years of loss were also a gift. They taught me this: Once you have learned how to lose everything, there's nothing left to fear. A poor woman's heart grows stouter as her options narrow. She has no choice but to make bold moves, take wild chances, tempt fate.

A fortune teller in Saigon told me that in my darkest hours of life, cooking and sewing would carry me. That prediction came true in unexpected ways: I have worked as a cook in a brothel and a suture nurse in a refugee camp, a tofu maker and a silk weaver. I have been through poverty and back to relative security—and even, you might say, success. I know how to show other women the way, and that has become my life's work.

There's a saying in Cambodia: "Men are gold; women are cloth." It implies that men are a treasure, and women can be thrown away. But more than that, it means that when a man falls into the dirt, he can be polished clean, whereas a woman will be soiled forever.

I believe the saying misjudges so much, including the value of fabric. Cloth can be delicate, yes; but it can also be strong and light, tough and resilient. And some textiles can even be priceless.

Still, I am no longer pliant or delicate. I've become as hard as diamond—there was no other choice. In Cambodia, who has time for being whisper-soft? There is too much work to do. Women cannot wait for a man's permission to survive. They have to sparkle and cut like diamonds. That is what I have always told the women at our women's development and weaving center in Stung Treng Province. And they have started to believe it. They can see, from my example, how my mother's "Slow Noodles" philosophy in the kitchen has become a philosophy for life: from her, I learned that the best dishes require extra time and patience to prepare. Later, I discovered that the path from hunger and poverty to economic self-reliance is long and hard, if it is even possible. And I see now that rebuilding a traumatized society after genocide takes many generations of investment—there are no quick fixes. That's what Slow Noodles means to me.

WE CAMBODIANS DO not like to bare our scars. We share an unspeakable history, so we rarely speak of it. But I will tell my story in these pages, if only to prove that the past cannot be extinguished. I have done my best to remember it all, but some months have gone dark in my mind. This is the truth of my story as faithfully as I am able to render it.

Now that I finally have a kitchen of my own, I've found a sweeter way to resurrect the past: rekindling the aromas of my mother's cooking. When I stoke the charcoal grill for roasting pork ribs, or stir coconut milk into fish amok, I revert to the age when I tasted the dish for the first time. And my mother's image comes flooding back.

When I'm cooking or eating, it's less painful to remember. And so, in working on this book, my cowriter and I came together in our respective kitchens. At her house in America, and at mine in Phnom Penh, where I live now, I cooked and remembered, and she scribbled in a notebook (and ate). The stories poured out in their own order, according to whatever I was craving. If I saw a lovely fresh fish in the market, I told her a fish story. Over a Pimm's Cup with lime, I spoke of starved malarial sugar-and-lime cravings. The same memory might bring laughter or tears, depending on the taste of it that day.

I will tell you my story, but I insist on telling it with hands busy and the kitchen full of enticing aromas. I'll cook for you throughout the telling. You'll see for yourself that the past cannot be erased so easily. You'll taste for yourself the way that history can be carried forward, borne on the smoke from a long-gone mother's charcoal fire.

PART I

———

Young Rice Is Fleeting

1. Soft Like Pâté de Foie

When the water rises, the fish eat ants.
When the water recedes, the ants eat fish.
—Khmer proverb

I SPENT MY first nine years in my mother's kitchen in Battambang, Cambodia. Sometimes I wish I could have stayed there forever, helping her chop onions and garlic, running to fetch wood and water, and falling asleep in a hammock as she rocked me to sleep.

My mother—"Mae," as I called her in Khmer—left me nothing but her songs and recipes, and aromatic memories to last the rest of my life.

I was always happiest in that open, airy kitchen. I remember it as being made up of pure light. A large window high in the pale blue walls framed the bright, tropical sky—so much blue that the walls and sky seemed to merge. Sunlight streamed into the doorway, which opened onto a narrow staircase leading down to my father's ground-floor auto repair shop. A folding table for eight fit into a nook by the door. Municipal water came from a tap in the wall in a cement washing area, where we did dishes and laundry and sometimes showered. My oldest sister, Chanthu, sat on a low stool by a drain in the floor to do the washing chores.

Next to that was a smaller window, a portal for leaning out and chatting with our neighbors—the street-food vendors, laborers, and farmers who lived in wood-stilt huts arranged around a clearing. We always had plenty to eat; many of them did not. So my mother and Chanthu usually prepared extra, then lowered pots of leftovers out the window, by a string tied to the handles, to our closest neighbor family—I called her Oum, or "Auntie," and her daughter, Srey.

Our soup pot was so huge, I could not wrap my arms all the way around it. Once, after I climbed the shelves of a high cupboard to look for something to eat, I fell backward—right into the pot, where Mae was marinating meat for her famous tamarind stew. She laughed as she helped me climb out, her naughty little daughter marinated in tamarind and stained bright red.

I was five or so when Chanthu finally let me put a pot of water on the wood fire to boil. I was ecstatic! And then, when I was eight, it became my job to pour the hot water into a glass thermos twice a day for my father's tea. Mae cautioned me never to do this alone. The metal thermos case was cracked, which meant you had to hold on to the bottom to keep the glass thermos inside from falling out and shattering. I don't know why my mother never replaced the broken case.

Most of my early responsibilities were more related to kitchen maintenance than food preparation. My mother cooked over wood and charcoal fires, in three big clay braziers on a table topped with gleaming white tile. The cooking fire left pots coated with a stubborn black slag, and it was my job to scour soot from the cooking pots until they shone. Black smoke from the braziers poured out the big window right next to the cooking area and into the sky, but the fire still left its mark—we were always scrubbing the white tile table, kitchen walls, and ceiling.

For my mother, the extra trouble of cooking on a real fire was worth the reward. To her, food prepared on an electric burner tasted like nothing. She loved the richer flavors that wood and charcoal imparted. I feel the same way. But my present-day kitchen is not as open to the sky as hers was, so when I'm inside the house, I cook on a gas burner. And when I have time, I build a charcoal fire on a small clay brazier in my little courtyard and squat over it, boiling bones for soup stock or grilling beef pierced with bamboo skewers. I can even bake bread and pastries on it.

For me, rice simmered over a charcoal fire tastes better than rice from a rice cooker, and the smell of a charcoal fire is the smell of home and family. My favorite kitchen memories are steeped in that aroma.

EVERY DAY AFTER school, I went straight to the kitchen to shadow Mae and Chanthu while they cooked, begging them to feed me a bite of something tasty. Between meals, there was always some delicious snack to be found: a crunchy, sweet green mango dessert, ice-cold from the thermos, or dried lotus seeds from a tin box high on a shelf. In the rare moments when the kitchen was empty of cooks, I hunted for some tasty morsel to devour on the sly. I'm sure my mother knew which ingredient had gone missing, but she pretended not to notice.

Once, I stole a bite from the bony belly of a big fried fish that was cooling on the counter. To avoid capture, I swallowed it whole, without chewing. But my mother and sister found me coughing and made me swallow a thumb-sized bite of rice, our remedy for dislodging a stuck bone. After ten rice-thumbs, the fish bone had not moved, and my throat started to bleed.

Chanthu hailed a remork (a passenger carriage towed by a bicycle or moto) and rushed me to the provincial hospital. I was terrified that she would shout at me for sneaking the fish, but instead she only asked, "How are you?" every minute or so, looking alarmed. At the hospital, I stretched out on a long metal table, where a doctor gently slid long forceps into my throat and extracted the belly bone of a fish.

I did not learn my lesson. In most ways, I was an obedient child, but I couldn't resist plundering any delicacy left unguarded in the kitchen. My nose was always leading me toward temptation and trouble.

I have an acute sense of smell—my mother always said so. I can detect a tiny trace of bitterness in a dish brightened with lime; when the juice touches the peel, it carries the bitter taste along with it. That's why I always peel limes before squeezing them. People tell me they can't taste any difference. But for me, the lime-peel sharpness can ruin an otherwise perfect dish.

My nose has been a gift and a curse. I was forever poking it into my mother's kitchen business, inhaling everything and absorbing the nose's lessons, like the before- and after-tastes of adding charred scallions to simmering pork stock—it softens the more disagreeable aromas of pig fat.

Mae laughed that I was just like a puppy, with my voracious, curious nose. "Puppy" became her pet name for me.

In my defense, I submit that my mother's fried fish, when left alone in a kitchen, would make a thief of anyone.

Irresistible Fried Fish with Green Mango Salad (Trei Chien Sab Svay)[2]

A whole white fish like branzino (a type of bass) with skin on works well for frying—the skin will turn golden and crisp. A fishmonger can gut and scale it for you. For the salad, look for green, unripe mangoes that are firm but not rock-hard.

Serves 4 fish thieves

Ingredients:
2 tablespoons fish sauce
4 cloves garlic, minced
1 shallot, thinly sliced
1 red Thai chili, thinly sliced, plus more for garnish
1 tablespoon lime juice (optional)
1 teaspoon sugar (optional)
1 unripe green mango, cut into matchsticks

---

2   For more detail about many of the ingredients in this recipe and in all the recipes that follow, see relevant entries in *"Notes on Ingredients, Techniques, and Supplies,"* at the end of the book.

2 pounds firm, whole white fish, such as branzino, tilapia, catfish, snapper, or bass (you can use fillets if you prefer, but it's trickier to get them crisp)
Salt
At least 2 cups neutral oil

In a medium bowl, stir together fish sauce, garlic, shallot, and chili. Add lime juice and sugar (if using). Toss with mango.

Rinse fish and pat it thoroughly dry. Make 3 shallow, diagonal slits in each side (if using a whole fish) and rub a pinch of salt over fish. In a large skillet or wok, heat enough oil over medium-high heat to shallow-fry fish. Fry until golden, crisp, and very enticing—the time varies by fish size and thickness. Remove fish from skillet and drain. Do not leave it unguarded!

Serve fish on a large platter for sharing, with the spicy green mango salad on top and a side of jasmine rice. Garnish with more chilies—for decoration and to serve as a visual warning for the spice-averse.

———

MY EARLIEST COOKING adventures were somewhat inauspicious. The first time I cooked rice by myself, I burned it to a tarry blackness. I was maybe six years old. My mother saw how much I loved to "help" her in the kitchen, so she bought me my own clay pot and a small sack of rice to play with.

I ran to visit my friend Yet, who lived in the village behind my parents' house. I call it a "village," but it was really a small settlement of mud-and-straw huts, built by the same landlord who rented us the land where our house stood—near the Battambang train station and market. A mere hundred yards away, past the huts, were rice fields. I loved to play with the village children. We picked wild fruits by the railway or caught fish along the rice fields.

That day Yet and I gathered branches and stones and built a fire in front of her house, a simple structure of bamboo and grass mixed with elephant dung. As the rice simmered, we sat together on the sharp rungs of the steep, ladderlike entry stairs to watch and wait, stoking the fire while we clapped our hands and sang. I left the rice on the fire for a long time, to be sure it was well done, then ran home and presented it to Mae. The rice was inedible, but she smiled and took a bite as if it were cooked perfectly. "This is tasty!" she exclaimed. "The best I've ever had!" The truth of the charred, smoky rice wasn't lost on me, but it didn't matter: I had cooked something, and my mother had praised me. For the rest of the day, I floated above the ground.

It amazes me to remember a time when we had so much rice to spare, we could afford to let an inept little girl blacken it, just to amuse herself. Even now, when there's plenty to eat, I cannot bear to waste food. I would have scolded my daughter, Clara, for such a thing when she was little.

The memory of hunger is a curse that never leaves you.

THE MEMORY OF happiness also lingers—I will never forget its flavors and aromas. It smelled like cloves, cracked pepper, and pâté de foie. On special occasions, Mae spent hours cranking chicken liver, pork, and pork fat through a grinder until it was velvety smooth. She stirred in garlic and cloves, wrapped the ground meat in a translucently thin slice of pork belly fat, and steamed the mixture in a square tin that had once held French cookies. She carved the vegetables into roses to decorate the plate, and we ate the pâté like a sandwich, with a Khmer baguette, and pickled carrots and daikon. I loved the holiday feeling that filled the kitchen whenever she made her pâté de foie.

Happiness also tasted like the street food at the Phnom Penh Central Market: rice wrapped in a lotus leaf, and charcoal-roasted chicken on a bamboo stick. It tasted like anticipation: the lullaby *chick chick chick* of the night train from Battambang to Phnom Penh, rocking me to sleep as I dreamed of the pâte à choux (cream pastry) we would buy upon our arrival, just by the station. My mother always ordered two of them for me, and I sank my teeth into their soft creaminess immediately.

The most perfect happiness of all tasted like the wind, when I stood on the front of my oldest brother's Vespa as he raced around Phnom Penh, where he lived and studied. He told me to open my mouth wide and drink in the warm night air. "AHHHHHHH!" I cried, as my brother laughed, zooming north along the river toward the Cambodia-Japanese Friendship Bridge. That feeling was my heaven, a snapshot of fleeting perfection.

I will always remember the recipe for little-girl heaven. It is a simple one, but difficult to replicate.

Recipe: Little-Girl Heaven

Ingredients:
One older brother
A moto
A carefree girl, small enough to stand on the front
A beautiful city
Night wind

Combine one spoiled little girl, a shiny Vespa, and a worshipped older brother. Weave through the bustling streets of prewar Phnom Penh at night. Grin like mad into the onrushing wind and drink the night air through your teeth. Savor this feeling, as all the ingredients will soon be extinguished, save the night wind.

2. House of Rice

Don't let an angry man wash dishes.
Don't let a hungry man guard rice.
—Khmer proverb

IN KHMER, THE phrase for kitchen is *ptaeh bai*, which translates as "house of rice." For Cambodians, rice is gold. In ancient times, before the riel—the modern currency of Cambodia—rice was used as legal tender. But then, in the time of Year Zero, rice became the only currency that mattered.

If you want to ask a Cambodian whether they've had anything to eat, you say, "Ta neak nham bai?" The literal translation is, "Have you eaten rice?"

When we are rich, rice is part of a complicated menu of daily dishes. When we are poor, rice is sometimes the entire menu, with a little salt, chili, or MSG for flavor.

When Khmers say we are hungry, we say, "klean bai," or, "hungry for rice."

Rice is what you eat when you have nothing and when you have everything. In one Khmer proverb, it is the "blood and sweat" of the farmer; another rice saying delivers a lesson about pride: "The immature rice stalk stands upright. The mature stalk, heavy with grains, bends over." In other words, a willingness to bend with changing winds is a valuable trait, especially when the winds become fierce and destructive.

AMID THE GENTLE breezes of the years we lived in Battambang, my mother spent her days in the kitchen with Chanthu. As the oldest of four daughters, Chanthu was the one expected to stay home and do most of the cooking and cleaning, but my mother was always right beside her.

Every morning after breakfast, Mae went to the market, then set a kettle to boil and began preparing lunch. The cooking didn't pause for long after lunch was eaten. At five in the evening, Chanthu revived the leftovers from lunch to feed my father's employees in the auto shop. After they had eaten, Chanthu and Mae made dinner for themselves, my father, and me. (My other two sisters and three brothers, all much older than I, were by then grown and married, in convents, or in school in Phnom Penh. One brother, Tung, lived in Battambang with his wife, Nary, and her family. He worked in the auto shop with my father.)

A traditional Khmer lunch or dinner can easily cover the whole table. A proper meal consists of three dishes served all together, with rice and an assortment of tasty condiments. My mother's table usually featured a cha, or "stir-fry"; a more elaborate protein dish involving pork, chicken, beef, fish, or shellfish from Mae's vast mental archive of recipes; and a soup, such as a delicately flavored s'gnao or a rich and complex samlor.

Mae might sometimes omit the vegetable cha or the meat dish, but a samlor had to appear at every meal. The category of samlor is not one thing, but many: rich or sour soups with beef, chicken, and/or fish; soups with vegetables, lotus, bamboo shoots, or even pineapple; highly spiced stews that resemble Thai red or green curries.

A very typical Khmer samlor, loved by rich and poor Cambodians alike, is samlor machu kroeung. *Machu* is Khmer for "sour," a flavor Cambodians adore. *Kroeung* (which literally means "ingredients") refers to several pounded herb/spice mixes that add a distinctively Khmer flavor to many soups, noodles, and curry-style dishes.

For us, samlor machu kroeung is the flavor of village life, of catching fish in a pond and children playing by a rice field. We love to add any number of vegetables, greens, and blossoms, like morning glories, water lily, banana flower, Thai basil, and raw garlic. But you can use whatever protein, vegetables, greens, and herbs you have on hand.

ONE OF THE few meals my mother and sister did not prepare from scratch was kuy teav, a noodle soup introduced by Cambodia's Teochew (southern-Chinese immigrant) community—and a national breakfast staple. From dawn to late morning all over Cambodia, you'll see street stands, market stalls, and open-air shops full of eaters happily slurping kuy teav, accompanied by strong coffee, hot or iced, sweetened with condensed milk.

Every morning, we bought kuy teav from a neighbor who produced miraculous quantities in his tiny kitchen. His was simpler than most restaurant versions: broth, chopped pork, a slice of meat, and chive flowers. Instead of rice noodles, he made mee—yellow noodles of wheat flour and egg. Whenever I had a day off from school, I loved to drop by and watch him kneading, rolling, and cutting the noodles by hand.

And every afternoon at 3 p.m., we listened for the soup-vendor neighbor's son clacking bamboo sticks and hailed his soup cart for a snack—of kuy teav. On trips to the market on my days off from school, my mother went straight for—you guessed it—the kuy teav stall. I could barely stand the sight of it. I craved variety and would cast greedy glances at the vendor selling num banhchok—a traditional Khmer rice vermicelli noodle (and also the name of several dishes made with it), so universally loved in Cambodia, we call it "Khmer noodles."

But in 1960s' Cambodia, children were not asked their preferences. So if my family was having kuy teav for breakfast or a snack, so was I, whether I liked it or not. My mother would quiet my resistance by mixing the kuy teav with rice and hand-feeding me a few bites.

The recipe for kuy teav comes later in our story. It never crossed my mind to learn to make it until many years later, when I had to become a kuy teav street vendor myself.

THE DISHES I loved best when I was small were the ones that took the longest to make. My puppy sense told me that time equaled love, and love equaled deliciousness. On the time continuum, instant noodles tasted careless, like nothing at all; the kuy teav noodle-maker's hand-cut mee were far superior. But the slowest and best noodles of all came from my mother's kitchen. They went into Mae's bobor bánh canh, a comforting, thick soup with chewy handmade rice flour noodles. In Vietnamese, *bánh* can mean "cake" or "bread," and *canh* means "soup." But in Khmer we call the dish bobor bánh canh—essentially, "cake soup porridge." The base can be pork or chicken stock, and you can add your choice of protein, from pork knuckle to shrimp or crabmeat. But the springy, thick rice noodles play the starring role.

If you want to prepare bobor bánh canh the way my mother used to make it, you'll need to clear your schedule. First, soak white rice overnight. In the morning, grind the rice into a cotton bag and place a stone on it to force the water out. When the dough becomes thick and a little bit sticky, cook it in a large frying pan. Keep stirring the dough until it's half cooked through, then smash and mix the "cooked" and raw dough together. The dough is hot, but you have to squeeze it with your hands for more than an hour to make it soft, smooth, and very fine.

Next, shape the noodles. Tear off blueberry-sized chunks of dough and roll them one by one into identical cylinders. Nothing less than perfect will do. This will most likely take several hours, depending on how many soup-eaters you plan to feed and how many hands are available to roll noodles. Devouring the noodles will take a tiny fraction of the time required to prepare them.

I am joking! I know that you have no intention of grinding the flour yourself. Even I don't do it that way anymore. And what's worse, I cut the noodles with scissors instead of rolling them each by hand.

Mae would strongly disapprove. My mother despised the flavor of shortcuts.

I suspect that bobor bánh canh was Mae's favorite, not despite but
because of the investment of both time and effort. Cooking something complicated took longer, which meant more togetherness, more devotion. More
love. Those were my favorite times—those special-occasion days when Mae
and Chanthu prepared something extra difficult, dishes that took them
many hours, or even days, to prepare.

ONE OF THE most unforgettable special-occasion tastes of the year comes
at the beginning of harvest season, when a strange kind of water magic
happens in Cambodia: as the rainy season wanes, the swollen Tonlé Sap,
a great freshwater lake and river system, reverses direction and flows back
toward the sea.

Bon Om Touk, the Water Festival, signals a time of plenty, when those
receding waters leave behind fertile fishing grounds and richly silted fields
along this lake that feeds a nation. Cambodians mark the occasion with
dragon boat races, fireworks, and concerts. It is a tradition to make small
boats out of banana or lotus leaves, laden with candles, to send onto the
water.

What I remember best about the water festivals of my childhood is
light: the river glittering with a full-moon sparkle, hundreds of tiny candle-
lit boats on the water, and paper lanterns afire, floating up into the silver
night sky.

At the end of the monsoons, there is no more beautiful place on earth
than Cambodia. In the final moments of day, sugar-palm silhouettes shim-
mer like mirages above a silver-green sea of rice, and flooded paddies glow
with the dying sun's fire. In all the years I was in exile, that is how I would
remember autumn in Cambodia. Sunset on the rice fields, the aroma of my
mother's fish sauce, and young green rice fresh from the paddies.

Young rice is something you can *only* enjoy in its season. Before the rice
is mature enough to harvest and dry for storage, we collect the sticky, milky
green rice. The tender grains smell like the color green: fresh and alive, like
grass, river water, or a cool wind carrying a suspicion of rain. My mother

would mix it with coconut juice, tender coconut meat, and sugar. The taste of it reminded me of my mother's fine French perfume.

The green rice has a very special flavor, nutty and sweet, and it does not keep for long. You cannot warehouse or export it.

The green-fresh fragrance of young rice is as lovely and fleeting as childhood itself.

———

Slow-Noodles Porridge with Chicken and Pork (Bobor Bánh Canh)

My mother's version is slightly different from traditional Vietnamese bánh canh, in which the chewy noodles are usually made with rice and tapioca flours. In her preparation, the soup is thicker, like porridge, and she uses only rice flour, which makes the noodles softer and less springy. For this recipe, I replace some of the rice flour with unbleached all-purpose flour—this helps bind the noodles.

In Cambodia, we love to include the bone-in cuts of meat right in the soup bowl. But you can pull meat from the bone to serve the soup, if you prefer.

Serves 4 (*and* keeps them busy before dinner)

Ingredients:
For the noodles:
1½ cups rice flour
Boiling water (up to ¾ cup)
½ cup unbleached all-purpose flour

For the soup:
¼ to ½ cup neutral oil
2 heads garlic, minced
1 pound chicken pieces, such as thighs and drumsticks (or boneless thighs)

1 pound pork ribs or neck bones, separated (or pork shoulder)
Salt
1 teaspoon sugar (optional)
2 cubes Knorr chicken bouillon (optional)

For serving: 3 scallions, thinly sliced; ¼ pound bean sprouts; a few
sprigs cilantro; Thai red chilies, sliced; Asian-style ground chili-
garlic oil; freshly ground black pepper

Make the noodles: Place rice flour in a large bowl. Slowly add
boiling water, mixing well with a spoon until the dough just comes
together. (You may not need the whole ¾ cup.) Incorporate all-
purpose flour with your fingers until dough is sticky and tough,
then knead with your palms until smooth and elastic, about 5
minutes. (If the water isn't hot enough, the dough will be brittle
instead of stretchy.)

Line a baking sheet with parchment paper and dust with flour.
On a lightly floured clean surface, divide dough evenly into golf
ball–size portions, then use a rolling pin to gently roll into small,
thin ovals (slightly less than ¼ inch thick). Use scissors to cut
into thin strips about 2 to 4 inches long, transferring noodles as
you work to prepared baking sheet, taking care not to crowd the
noodles. If you want your noodles a little bit slower (and more
noodlelike), roll strips into cylinders about the width of the small
end of a chopstick. Toss a little flour over noodles and set aside in a
cool, dry place.

Or roll them Mae's slow-noodles way: Mix the dough as
described above, then lightly oil a clean wooden surface (and your
fingers) with canola or vegetable oil. Pull off blueberry-size pieces
of dough and roll them out with your palm on the oiled surface
until they are about 2½ inches long and about the width of the
small end of a chopstick. Recruit lots of assistants. Laugh and talk

for hours as you roll noodles together. Maybe make a cocktail. Lay out noodles on a parchment-lined baking sheet as described above.

Make the soup: In a medium skillet, heat oil over medium heat and fry garlic until golden and crisp, about 2 or 3 minutes. (Don't let it get too dark, or the garlic will be bitter.) Remove garlic from skillet and set aside. Do not wipe skillet.

In the same skillet, sauté chicken and pork in garlic oil over medium-high heat until the exterior is light golden on all sides, about 2 minutes each side. Add a pinch of salt.

In a stockpot, bring 3 quarts of water to a boil. Add chicken and pork. Reduce heat and simmer gently, periodically skimming foam, until the meat is cooked through, about 25 minutes. Remove meat, pull from bone, and set aside for serving. If you're using sugar and/or chicken bouillon, add them now. Season with salt.

Add noodles gently into the simmering broth, including 2 tablespoons of flour from the baking sheet. Do not stir. When broth resumes bubbling, reduce heat and simmer, stirring very gently from the bottom once or twice, for 3 to 5 minutes. When the noodles float, they are most likely cooked through—they should be tender and slightly chewy.

Serve in a large, deep bowl. Top with fried garlic, scallions, bean sprouts, cilantro, and chilies. Drizzle with chili oil and season with freshly ground black pepper.

3. Chicken-Lime Soup for the Village Soul

My dearest daughter, no matter how
poor you are, follow the women's rules.
—*Chbab Srey,* the "Rules for Women"

MY MOTHER WAS stunning; everyone said so. I didn't look like her. When my sister and I went into town, people asked, "Is she your stepmother? You didn't get her beauty, did you?"

I often stared into the mirror, wishing I had her straight nose and willing my skin to become as pale and milky as hers. Mae was tiny, with delicate bones, and she looked so graceful in the long, white áo dài tunic she wore to church. Her soft, low voice soothed me like a gentle rain when she swung me in the hammock at naptime and sang old Vietnamese ballads.

After lunch, Mae would relax with a book and listen to the radio. Mae's favorite song became my favorite: "The Smile of the Mountain Girl," about a boy who pines for a lovely young girl after spying her in the forest. She wears a white scarf and a shiny ring, and he never forgets her dazzling smile. People said the artist had written that song to freeze her image in his memory forever. Now the song is frozen in mine.

Mae did not need big muscles or a loud voice to intimidate people; her eyes did that well enough. She spoke quietly but looked straight into people's faces, her eyes blazing, whenever she heard a cruel comment or a nasty bit of gossip. She despised meanness; she said it made people ugly.

"If you say mean things," she often warned, "people will call you 'Badmouth Girl.'"

I was afraid of that searing glare, so I kept my unkind thoughts to myself.

I don't know where my mother acquired her regal gaze. Her nobility didn't come from privilege. She fled Vietnam with her family when she was eight years old and grew up in a poor neighborhood in the northern outskirts of Phnom Penh—a cluster of stilted wooden shacks in a lowland flood zone, settled by ethnic Vietnamese. I never met my maternal grandparents, but the stories my mother told fueled my love for them. My grandfather was a carpenter, and my grandmother bought roots, herbs, and berries from the Chinese medicine shop and concocted traditional remedies.

People said Mae had the hands of a healer. She often treated our burns with an ointment her mother taught her to make. She would dissolve a bit of slaked lime in water overnight, then pour the clear liquid slowly into coconut oil until it was soft and creamy, like a salve. We always had a jar of it on hand. Once, when my father was working in his mechanic shop, a gas explosion burned his hand and knees terribly. My mother's ointment healed his wounds, leaving no scars.

I nearly forgot it after Mae died. But later, in the refugee camps, I resurrected the recipe and it proved useful.

Mae told me that her mother had saved the lives of many children, including one French baby whose desperate parents came to her after doctors failed to help him. Somehow, my grandmother rescued the little boy. Every Lunar New Year afterward she feasted like a queen, thanks to that grateful French family, who always brought her delicacies for the holiday.

Mae's brothers attended the Lycée Français René Descartes in central Phnom Penh. (I'm not sure how they afforded the fees, but some poor families received financial aid.) But my mother was a girl, so she went to school just long enough to learn to read and write.

Still, Mae was a literate woman. She spoke and read Khmer and

Vietnamese. In her spare hours, she loved to swing in the hammock, her nose buried in a kung fu novel.

According to family lore, my mother was the loveliest girl in the district where she grew up. Somehow, my parents crossed paths: him at thirty-one, from a rich neighborhood, and her at eighteen, living in a flood-prone shantytown. Although his well-heeled mother had no use for my mother's have-nothing family, it was Mae's mother who opposed the marriage. His family was too rich, she said. She was a proud woman and did not want her daughter to suffer under the tyranny of a scornful mother-in-law.

My father had already eroded his mother's opposition by threatening her with his own disappearance. He'd spent years in Vietnam training to become an auto mechanic. If he couldn't marry this girl, he warned his mother, he would move back there permanently.

My father earned a good salary as a senior mechanic in Phnom Penh for Peugeot, the French car company, before the Second World War. He was a magician with any kind of engine. But he could never repair what was broken between his mother and his wife. My grandmother had no kindness in her heart for Mae. Early in the marriage, she warned her son to guard his money carefully, because his wife might steal it to support her own impoverished parents.

My father—I called him Puk, which is "Father" in Khmer—obeyed his haughty mother. Every month, he allowed Mae just enough money to buy food for us. He gave the rest to his mother to save for him.

I didn't know how terribly she had treated my mother until many years later, when Mae told me stories about her mother-in-law's cruelty. I learned that my grandmother was a nasty, puffed-up woman, the kind of person who donated large sums to the church to ensure herself a place in heaven but gave not a single riel to poor people on earth. But even as a small girl, I sensed my grandmother's contempt, and I had no love for this particular grandmother. Once, she came to visit while my mother was cooking a chicken. She told Mae that she had no right to the same food my father ate.

"You are a dependent housewife," the old woman spat. "You deserve nothing better than his leftovers."

Mae held her tongue. In Cambodia then, mothers taught their daughters never to show anger to a husband (or his spiteful mother), no matter what he may have done. In public schools, Khmer girls studied a collection of classical didactic verses called the *Chbab Srey* ("Rules for Women"):

> My darling daughter, don't ever forget:
> You must serve your husband
> Don't make him unsatisfied . . .
> Remember that you are a woman
> Don't say anything to suggest you are equal to him.

Those poems, handed down through many generations, defined how Cambodian women were expected to behave: According to the *Chbab Srey*, a proper Asian woman was supposed to shine dimly, like a moon, and reflect her husband's sunlight. Her skirts could not rustle when she walked. Even her laugh had to be quiet and demure.

"Lower the fire," the saying went, "so the rice doesn't get burned"—a warning to women to control their temper. In Catholic school, I didn't study the *Chbab Srey*. And I never understood why the burden of fire-lowering was placed on the wife's shoulders alone.

WHEN WORLD WAR II came, my father lost his job at Peugeot. The Japanese military had garrisons in French Indochina, which comprised Vietnam, Laos, and Cambodia, but still allowed Vichy France to govern its protectorates; in Cambodia, they installed a young Cambodian prince named Norodom Sihanouk as monarch. Puk was caught between occupiers, afraid that working for the French might bring reprisals from the Japanese, and vice versa, so my mother became the family breadwinner. Her poor parents had taught her to fend for herself. She used those skills to eke out a living by any means necessary. Mae was very resourceful: She raised pigs to sell in the market. When she bought the rice for pig feed, she would sieve the rice, sell the larger grains for people to eat, then feed the smaller grains to her pigs. She used the raw-cotton rice sacks to sew casual knee pants that my father wore inside the house.

My mother's industriousness awakened in her a dream of freedom.

According to Cambodian tradition, the matriarch rules over the extended family. Her daughter-in-law must serve and obey her. And even as the family's status suffered during the wartime hardships, Grandmother retained her imperiousness and was feared by her children and their families—including the men.

She abused her power and treated my mother with scorn. On the surface, my mother was compliant and docile—she kept her fire low. But quietly, she plotted an insurgency.

One day she asked for a small loan from my grandmother. Mae used the money to buy a chheu keo—a rickshaw pulled by hand—to rent out. Her business savvy and hard work slowly began to soften her mother-in-law's mistrust. Once she'd proved herself capable of making a living, my mother then asked Grandmother to "loan" her the entire sum of my father's earnings that he'd given his mother over the years. With that money, she bought nine more chheu keo.

Once her budding business had earned enough, Mae sold all ten chheu keo and convinced Puk to move the family to Battambang, a busy trading town near the Thai border. By working to earn a living for herself, Mae won her freedom—and I like to think perhaps my grandmother's grudging respect, however fleeting. It was nothing less than an act of insurrection, a "silken rebellion" masquerading as moonlight deference.

I knew nothing about Mae's act of defiance until those later years, when she told me the story during our lunches together, two lonely refugees in postwar Saigon. I was shocked: To me, she had always represented a feminine ideal that I knew I could never achieve: an elegant, demure, and steadfast wife who managed money like an accountant and cooked like a chef. She did not work outside the home once she arrived in Battambang, but her outfits were perfect: She wore a clean, ironed dress every day, even during our hardscrabble Saigon years.

All that time, I'd thought she was the very model of *Chbab Srey* womanhood, only to learn that the heart of a rebel pounded in her breast. I adored her all the more for it.

LONG BEFORE I tasted hunger for myself, my mother and sister were quietly shaping my ideas about poverty and power, wealth and charity. And so was my horrid paternal grandmother.

Grandmother was a wealthy woman. Whenever anyone talked about her, they spoke with hushed reverence. Like my grandmother, I was the youngest child. I had ten older siblings, six of whom survived past infancy. In Khmer culture in those days, birth order determined your future. We have a saying: "The youngest child inherits a rich family's wealth and a poor family's suffering."

As far as I could tell, our shared status as youngest was the only thing we had in common, but she made out far better in that arrangement than I did. Grandmother inherited most of the family's property where her parents' stately old wood home had stood—near Phsar Chas, the old market in Phnom Penh, by the Tonlé Sap River. She married a rich man who built a huge, French-style brick villa on the family compound.

I dreaded my visits to that house, and not only because I didn't like my grandmother. In fact, she was usually absent until late in the evening: right after breakfast, Grandmother grabbed her umbrella and disappeared to play mahjong all day. But the quiet house didn't feel peaceful; it felt lonely, with a foreboding silence and an all-white, haunted emptiness. I was afraid to go into the ghost house alone; the place pealed with fearsome echoes. Whenever a plane crossed the sky, the roar ricocheted inside like the cry of a beast, sending me fleeing to the garden, where chompu (Malabar plum) and custard apple trees grew. Grandmother had caged the fruit trees with bamboo to keep children from picking the fruit, so I salvaged the ripe plums that had fallen and sank my teeth into their sweet flesh. I never touched the custard apples, though—those were for my father. Yet during the day, I often had the garden all to myself and spent long mornings picking leaves and pretending to cook them on the steps, as if the staircase were my very own outdoor kitchen.

I preferred my great-auntie's house to the cavernous, empty one belonging to my grandmother. I called my great-aunt Yiay Thom, and thought of her as my "poor grandmother." She was Grandmother's sister, but her home wasn't grand; it was a humble house with palm-leaf walls and a thatched roof. I loved how the rain tapped the thin leaves, a soothing melody that lulled me to sleep.

Yiay Thom was permitted to live on Grandmother's compound, but the two women lived very different lives. Rich Grandmother had servants and did not share food, or anything else, with her sister. Poor Grandmother couldn't afford much meat or fish, so she learned to make magic from simple ingredients. The delicious aroma of her homemade fish sauce drew me to her kitchen. I once tried to sneak a taste of it from her fish sauce pot, but I spilled it all over me and was betrayed by the fishy smell that lingered on my clothes.

Her green papaya pickles were the best I have ever eaten. Whenever we planned a trip to Phnom Penh, my mouth watered in anticipation of that sour-fruit crunch and salty-vinegar fire. Green papaya pickles are a delicious snack, and they can elevate a simple bowl of rice to an exquisite meal.

In my years of forced exile from Cambodia, I dreamed of those pickles. When I returned home decades later, I experimented with recipes, but the taste wasn't quite as I remembered. Then one day I found just the right fish sauce, and there it was—the intense flavor of fermented saltiness, of river fish cured in the sun. One bite of pickle, and I was five years old again, on Poor Grandmother's front kitchen stairs, my senses flooded with the sour-sweet spice of pickled papaya.

I eat those pickles almost every day now. Whenever I serve them at dinner parties, the pickle jar empties quickly, and my guests' happiness fills me with pride. Those green papaya pickles made me feel rich then, and they still do.

———

Poor Grandmother's Spicy Green Papaya Pickles

Ingredients:
1 large green papaya
3 tablespoons salt
3 large cloves garlic, minced
6 Thai red chilies, minced
5 tablespoons fish sauce
3 tablespoons rice vinegar
4 tablespoons cane sugar (or light brown sugar)

Day 1: Peel papaya as you would a cucumber or apple. Cut it in half lengthwise and scrape out the seeds and fibrous interior. Halve again crosswise, and slice into wedges about the width of two fingers. In a bowl, toss wedges with salt, cover, and refrigerate for at least 3 hours (or overnight, if possible).

Day 2: Rinse papaya well. Cut the wedges into pinkie-size pieces (about 2 inches long) and return to bowl. In a small bowl, combine garlic, chilies, fish sauce, rice vinegar, and sugar. Add to papaya, cover, and refrigerate for at least 3 more hours.

Taste the pickles and adjust seasoning. Store in a sealed container and keep refrigerated. (Papaya pickles can last for several weeks in the refrigerator, but probably won't—because you'll eat them all.) These pickles pair well with anything grilled—and with memories of beloved auxiliary grandmothers.

———

THOSE VISITS TO my rich and poor grandmothers' houses instilled in me a wariness of wealth. There seemed to be an inverse relationship between status and generosity, and I could not understand why.

Here is an image that seared itself into my little-girl mind: a traffic jam on a hot afternoon. A man pedaling a rickety bicycle-remork knocks into a big, shiny car. The boom-voiced owner of the car leaps out and shouts at the terrified remork man. He is stick-thin and dark-skinned, and he shakes with fear as the big man screams. Even as small as I am, I'm desperate to help the poor man somehow, to step between him and this storm of fury. To take away his powerlessness and make the rich man *pay*.

Why do I remember that moment so clearly, more than fifty years later? I let go of my too-simple ideas about rich and poor, good and bad, long ago, because I've come to know many people with both money and charity to spare.

But those early impressions don't die easily. As a little girl, I saw my rich grandmother disdaining people she considered beneath her and showering attention on anyone with influence, or the promise of it. A perfect example is how she treated my sister Chanthu and my oldest brother, Jean Pierre Phan. Chanthu was the number-one daughter, not a lucky number for a girl. In Cambodian tradition, the eldest girl inherits only hard work but the first son is the family's gold.

Jean Pierre Phan was his school name, but everyone called him Noh. He was a year younger than Chanthu but he was a son, not a daughter—almost a different species. He understood his importance and behaved accordingly. He wasn't callous, like my grandmother, just pretentious and vain. To little me, back then, he was like a god.

At various times, four of my older siblings lived on my grandmother's compound and attended secondary school in Phnom Penh. Noh studied law and economics at a university. My parents said he deserved this because the firstborn son heads the family when the father dies. He was my grandmother's golden grandson. She wouldn't let the maid clean his room or do his wash because she wanted to do those things for him herself.

In my mind, this meant Noh was someone momentous. I worshipped him from a great distance. He was much older, and I only saw him on our occasional visits to Phnom Penh. But I have a clear memory of watching him with fascination as he peeled an apple. He did it the French way, peeling toward your body, whereas we Khmers peel away. To me, this was more evidence that Noh was a superior person, above and apart from the rest of us.

It was on his Vespa that I rode that perfect, little-girl-heaven night, drinking from the evening sky. For me, that was as impossible as a dream of flight, to weave through the city with the Golden Brother.

Chanthu was the opposite of a dream; she was real, the one who was always there, sweating over the washing or helping Mae in the kitchen. She was big-boned and tall, with my father's prominent nose.

Chanthu left school after fifth grade to help Mae care for the younger children. No one gave her a choice in the matter. Eventually, she seemed to stop caring about her own desires—she always put herself last. My mother loved beautiful things, so Chanthu made her a new outfit nearly every week. She also delivered food to our neighbors and visited patients in the Providence Convent medical clinic, acts of charity she somehow worked into her busy schedule. I remember seeing her buy bandages with her own money, to replace the soiled dressings on a patient's bedsores. Chanthu wanted to join the Providence Convent. But Sister Celeste, the most powerful nun at the convent, told her no, it was her job to take care of our parents, and she could never leave them.

Many Cambodians believe that serving your parents is a divine act—"better than building a temple," as one saying goes. So even though Chanthu gave up on becoming a nun, she still lived a life of service and selflessness. She never married, even though a man—one of my father's young trainees in the garage—wanted to marry her. As the groom, he would have moved into our family's house with her.

She said no, and my parents didn't press the issue. "I've taken care of children my whole life!" Chanthu protested. "I don't want more." It was true: She took care of us all. She was like my second mother and could be a formidable maternal figure. She dressed me and fixed my hair for school and cared not at all when I protested the hideous topknot she sculpted on my head, or the hand-me-down boys' shoes I had to wear. Once, when my teacher, Sister Leonore, wrote to inform her that my class ranking had dropped, Chanthu commanded me to lie on my belly, and then lashed me ten times with a stick. I remember the number because Chanthu always notified me in advance of how many times she planned to strike me on the bottom, and with what object.

Even worse was the coining treatment she gave me whenever I got sick. It took her and Mae both, plus a hired helper, to hold me down while my sister scraped in long lines down my back, neck, shoulders, and arms with brass coins until linear bruises appeared. The darker the bruises, the sicker I was—or so they believed. And that meant she would have to scrape me even longer to let the sickness out. I always fought to escape the painful "cure" and screamed from start to finish.

But Chanthu was equal parts ferocity and gentleness. I loved it when she washed my face at night. Her fleshy hands felt as cushiony as pillows against my baby-soft skin. And her fingers moved so lightly at her sewing machine, where she worked late into the night making clothes for hire. Whenever she had scraps left, she sewed them into a colorful new dress for me—sometimes of many fabrics artfully stitched together.

I was always confused by the disparity in how my eldest sister and brother were viewed in our family. In wartime Saigon, Chanthu's resilience would prove a far more valuable survival skill than Noh's vanity.

My thinking on poverty and status has evolved, but I still turn loud and fierce when I see a bully abusing his power. I've been known to vocalize my contempt for a neighbor who hits his wife or a village policeman who demands a bribe. This defies my instincts for self-preservation. But so far, I've survived these outbursts—if only because the victims of my tirade could not believe they were being dressed down by a woman.

My grandmother exercised her voice on behalf of no one except herself.

She seemed to care more about money than people. I feared her, but I did not love her. Once, when I was six years old, she tried to make me accept a kiss, but I squirmed away. "I'll give you ten riels," she called after me. I considered the offer: Ten riels could buy a great many afternoon snacks, I reasoned. So I let her kiss me, accepted the money, and then ran outside to wipe the kiss off my face.

As a girl in Battambang, I never understood whether we were rich or poor; I only knew that we never wanted for anything. My mother indulged both herself with elegant clothes and her guests with extravagant meals. Her growing collection of dresses drove my father mad.

"Another one?" Puk would exclaim. "You already have too many!"

But he never said a word about having too much delicious food on the table.

Mae's heart seemed divided: She was kind to our poorer neighbors and never treated them as inferiors, and she was careful with the family budget. But I wonder whether my mother's new outfits and lavish cooking signaled a need to prove her worth to my father's wealthy family—or to herself.

When Puk's business associates or our priest came to visit, Mae always made something extra impressive, like her pâté de foie. It was as if she were performing in a play or a dance, with the table as her stage.

Once, when she served some visiting French priests khor trei roh— slow-cooked fish with garlic and chili—they came dangerously close to blasphemy in their invocations of how delicious the meal was. My mother beamed. I would not have been surprised to see her take a bow.

For foreign guests, my mother often made fish amok—a gorgeous, rich dish that highlighted her artistry and brought forth gasps of awe in her guests.

To prepare the amok, she marinated the fish for three hours or more in a rich red kroeung, then steamed the fish in a banana leaf. The final dish was an exquisite art installation—a banana-leaf-bowl sculpture decorated with crimson curried fish, drizzled with pearlescent coconut cream, and topped with a lacework of sliced chilies and slivered Thai basil. The fresh, green aroma of steamed banana leaf added depth to the delicate amok flavor. Mae's secret ingredient was a bed of morning glories hidden under the fish.

Mae refused to skimp on guests because she loved that her cooking made people so happy. I believe she loved cooking more than she loved eating. And despite her secret rebellious spirit, she enjoyed pleasing my father—and amok was his favorite dish.

I MAY HAVE been oblivious to my family's status, but I could see (and taste) that we were different from our neighbors. We were Catholics who owned a car, studied French, and ate pâté de foie at Christmas, in a village of Buddhist farmers and fishermen who were lucky to have anything more than rice and fish for dinner. Still, my notions of rich and poor were vague. I never made the connection that people often called my grandmother Rich Lady and that my siblings were sent to school in Phnom Penh so we must also be rich.

The war came before I had a chance to study in the capital. But when I was four, I enrolled at the Providence School, a Catholic institution we kids called the "nun school." (It was associated with the convent that Chanthu had hoped to join.) My first teacher was a dictatorial sister who forced me to skip lunches at home until I could draw a stick-straight letter *I* in French. Instead of walking home to eat with my mother, I had lunch with the children from the convent's orphanage. I assumed that the burned-smelling food—nothing like the delicious lunches my mother made—was my punishment for all those wavy *I*s, but I soon became close friends with the orphans.

I felt like I was one of them, even though I had an allowance and they usually had nothing. If they had any riels at all, it was because a few of them performed as apsaras ("celestial beings") in a dance group and would receive ten riels a year. Whereas every morning, my mother sent me to school with five riels; and every day, I spent it on my daily remork ride to school and all the snacks I could eat: a cookie or a salty, sun-cured shellfish from a street vendor. Sometimes I gave a riel to one friend one day, to another friend the next day, taking turns among my three closest schoolmates. One day they opened their notebooks to show me all those gift riel notes pressed between the pages.

They had saved them all. I was amazed by their discipline. It would be many years before I learned to value every coin, as they did.

After school, Mae gave me another riel to visit the noodle vendor's wife, who sold a delicious fruit cocktail made of longan, jackfruit, shaved ice, condensed milk, and syrup. When my father came home and emptied his pockets before his evening bath, I sometimes stole a riel from his nightstand and ran to buy another fruit drink.

My snack budget could buy a good dinner for an entire family—an equivalency I learned one day when I went to buy a grilled banana from our neighbor, the older woman I called Oum, who supported her family as a street vendor. Her husband had died of malaria while digging rubies in Pailin Province, by the Cardamom Mountains near the Thai border. While chomping down on the grilled banana, I asked Oum how much she spent on pork for dinner.

"Five riels," she said. When I told Chanthu this, she was astonished. We spent sixty to a hundred riels a day on food, she told me.

On Sundays after church, my parents often stopped by their friend's orange plantation for a picnic and let me play with the children from the adjacent fishing village. I never thought of myself as superior in any way, even though I wore fine dresses and they wore the same soiled, threadbare clothes day after day, and no shoes at all. Among the fishing-village children, or the orphans at the convent, I felt like I belonged. We spoke the same language and loved the same things: the freedom to roam the fields as we pleased, the feeling of sunshine on our faces. But I could also sense their sadness.

On my Thursdays off from school, and any other time I had free, I played with Yet, my best friend. She was a girl my age whose mother lived nearby and worked at a guesthouse. Yet did not go to school. Her mother

often came home drunk, with her hands shaking. Many nights I heard her
shouting at Yet and her four-year-old brother, Tee, and I also heard slaps
and cries of pain. One day I ran to Yet's house to visit after school, and she
wasn't there. Instead, I found Tee and his Chinese father. Soon the mother
came home. I had never seen the father strike Tee, but suddenly his mother
slapped the little boy hard on the back. He fell to the floor, and she kicked
him again and again. I watched silently, in horror, and quietly slipped away.

Soon after that, the father took Tee away and never returned. From
then on, Yet played alone in the street, a wild girl with a pack of feral dogs
tagging along behind her. Besides me, they were her only companions.
Occasionally, she would gather her few clothes in a bundle and tell me
that she was running away to find Tee in Phnom Penh. Her mother always
brought her home. And then one day, Yet and her mother were gone. I
missed her terribly.

Another friend was six or seven years old and lived with a family three
doors down, as their servant. I don't remember her name. She wore torn
clothes and had an empty face. No one had taught her to brush her teeth, so
they were dark yellow. Her job was to carry the family's youngest on her hip
all day long and feed him when he was hungry. When the baby slept, she
helped the mother with housework and cooking. Once after school, I went
to her house while the owners were eating dinner. The family ate tralach
(wax gourd) soup and a fried fish. But when it was my friend's turn to eat,
they poured their leftover soup and rice into the baby's remaining porridge,
then served the slop to her as if she were a pig.

I was shocked and disgusted. I saw how my mother and sister prepared
extra food to share with the village families. I wanted to be like Mae and
Chanthu, so I did my best to follow their example: If I had candy or an
orange, I shared it with my village friends, or with the orphans at school.

But when my friends' families invited me for dinner, I was torn. I
wanted to sit with them, but something told me I shouldn't partake of what
little they had. Instead, I went home and asked Mae to fry the tiny river fish
I saw in those families' kitchens. Only very poor people eat such small fish,

all bones and no flesh. We usually ate bigger fish, prepared more elegantly. But I asked Mae to cook small fish the simple, "village" way, fried and pickled with some sour vegetables, and dipped in soy sauce. I insisted on sitting on the floor while I ate it, to copy my friends' dinnertime ritual exactly. My mother smiled and served me the fish, then left me to eat it alone on the kitchen floor.

I WAS AMAZED at how families in the settlement behind our house could make do with so little. They cooked soups using whatever they had on hand. If my mother had leftover fish heads from a meal she had prepared, the village women would carry away the heads in a basket and use them as a base for soup. For flavor, they added sour tamarind leaves from the trees and a little prahok—salted, fermented fish paste.

Prahok is both a poor man's food and a guilty pleasure of kings. In the village, it's a staple for hard-working rice farmers and fishermen, who preserve surplus fish during the rainy season, to secure a steady protein source for when the skies dry and the rivers and lakes recede. In the palace, it's a simple, flavor-packed delicacy—although usually made from bigger, choicer fish than the village version. And for Khmers of all backgrounds, it is a taste of home we crave when we are far away.

There are various methods for making prahok. Generally, you start with a humble small river fish like a mud carp or gourami fish. (In Khmer, the ubiquitous mud carp is called trei riel; some people believe the riel, Cambodia's post-colonial currency, is named after it, but it's more likely named for the real, a Mexican silver coin widely used in the 1800s by merchants from other parts of Asia. Still, trei riel are so vital to village economies and food security in the Mekong River Delta, you could think of the tiny fish as currency.) Some people step on the small fish to crush it, or they may grind it by machine. And the salted, sun-cooked fish will ferment in a large clay jar or concrete vat for anywhere from three weeks to three years, depending on the quality desired. The runoff is often collected to make fish sauce.

Prahok is everywhere. You cannot miss it. You'll see fishermen and their families on the shore of any river in Cambodia, stomping on baskets full of small, bony fish, or squatting on the ground to cut off the heads. And if there is prahok for sale in the local market (there usually is), your nose will find it easily.

When a Khmer mother calls her child foul-mouthed, she says "moat si prahok," or "the prahok-eating mouth." This is not a compliment.

But when a Cambodian says, "No salt, no prahok," after taking a bite of something, she means that the dish is bland and needs more seasoning. For Khmers, prahok is as essential an ingredient as salt—and is a vital part of the Khmer diet, especially for families who can't afford fish or meat. It's also a method for spicing up plain rice: Just add a little prahok, MSG, and chili, and you have a tasty meal. Or, a typical village snack: a salad of green banana, star fruit, raw prahok, and chili, all crushed and mixed together. That's a very special taste: bitter, sour, salty, and spicy.

My mother didn't serve raw prahok at our house. I don't know why. But I have a strong memory of following my sister as she joined a circle of people who were eating that prahok salad in the village behind our house. She spied me and shouted at me to go home. From that incident, I deduced that I was not allowed to eat raw prahok in the village, or anywhere else. I didn't question this, and I never learned to crave it. But I did love my mother's more refined adaptation: a cooked prahok dish, delicately spiced and grilled. Mae chopped the pungent fish very fine and added minced pork, garlic, and lots of lemongrass, then wrapped it in a banana leaf and grilled it on charcoal. Even a Western, non-prahok-eating mouth would enjoy it. You would not recognize the prahok in it.

THE VILLAGE DISH I loved above all (and was actually allowed to eat) was s'gnao chruok sach mouan (sour chicken soup) made from an extraordinarily fresh chicken—organic, you might say, the kind that runs free and sleeps in a tree. I still can't stand store-bought chicken, raised in cages and fed with chemicals. A village chicken tastes like freedom—tough and muscled from running wild, but much more deeply flavored. Once you taste its freshness, you'll never want the industrial kind again.

Chicken soup may sound like a humble dinner, but for many rice-farming families, a whole chicken is a rare treat. I loved that village version even more than my mother's sour chicken soup. Mae never used lime leaf in her soup; her dishes were more delicately flavored. But I once asked Chanthu to make it that way, shimmering with lime, herbs, and lemongrass. "It's a little too strong for my taste," she said. But I make it now with lime leaf in my own kitchen, and I crave it whenever I'm traveling in the countryside.

For most Cambodians, prahok is the taste of the village and of the past. But my village memory tastes like chicken-lime soup, sunshine-bright with lemongrass, lime leaf, and a generous squeeze of lime.

Sour Chicken-Lime Soup, Village Style
(S'gnao Chruok Sach Mouan)

S'gnao refers to a range of simple, brothy soups—the word means "to boil." The extremely fresh village chicken soup of my childhood requires a recently chased and slain bird. If you can't lay hands on one, find a small organic chicken from a nearby farm and cut it into pieces. Of course, grocery-store chicken will also suffice. As you adjust this soup to taste, try to balance the sour taste of lime, the saltiness of fish sauce, a hint of sweetness, and the heat of chili.
Serves 4

Ingredients:
For the soup:
1 small whole chicken (about 3 pounds) or 4 chicken thighs
2 stalks lemongrass, cut into thirds and bruised
3 makrut lime leaves
Juice of 1 to 2 limes (3 to 5 tablespoons, or to desired sourness)

¼ teaspoon sugar

1 to 2 tablespoons fish sauce (optional)

½ teaspoon salt

For serving: Thai basil; handful of culantro (sawtooth herb, or ngò gai; optional); 2 scallions, thinly sliced; Thai red chilies, thinly sliced; lime wedges

Fill a large pot with 10 to 12 cups of water, then add chicken, lemongrass, and lime leaves. Bring to a boil, reduce heat to low, and gently simmer until chicken is cooked through, about 25 minutes. Skim foam from the surface.

Remove and set aside the solids, then strain the broth through a fine-mesh sieve. Add lime juice, sugar, fish sauce (if using), and salt; adjust to taste.

Pull chicken from bone, arrange individual portions of chicken in medium bowls, and ladle in broth.

Serve as an accompaniment to a protein dish (such as Irresistible Fried Fish, p. 12), or on its own with a side platter of the herbs, sliced scallions and chilies, and lime wedges, and a bowl of jasmine rice. Squeeze lime juice over soup and top with fresh herbs—and as much chili as your palate will allow.

4. Farewell to Fish Amok

With water, make rivers.
With rice, make armies.
—Khmer proverb

WHEN THE BAD things started to happen to us, my mother and Chanthu said it was because I was born in the Year of the Buffalo.

In the Vietnamese zodiac, the second year of the cycle belongs to the water buffalo (the ox, in Chinese astrology). The buffalo is born to a hard life. It works in the rice fields every day, plowing land whether the sun shines or the rain falls.

A child born in the buffalo year is industrious and stubborn, as she must be, for her toils will likely take many years to bear fruit. No saviors will magically appear, so she must learn to depend on herself. That, according to the prophecies, is a Buffalo Girl's inheritance.

As Chanthu liked to point out, it was even more inauspicious that I was born at four-thirty in the morning, the hour a buffalo begins its labor. "At least the farmer feeds his buffalo before he puts it to work," Chanthu added, trying to be helpful. To her, this meant that even though I would have to work very hard, I would always have enough to eat.

Everything that happened fit perfectly with our beliefs about luck and fate: Our family lost everything, including each other. I toiled like the buffalo, just to survive. The bad-luck part of my life lasted nearly a quarter century. It began just before I turned nine years old.

Maybe you don't believe that our fortunes are written into the night sky, or that a little girl can be cursed by her birth sign. But our family did believe it—sometimes, at least. We were Catholic, so we placed our faith in God. But for situations that the Bible did not expressly address, we looked to a more ancient faith for counsel: the Chinese zodiac. Of late, I call this "lunatic fate"—the moon's madness reinterpreted as foreshadowing, after the fact.

A Christian cannot blame God when disaster strikes. But she can blame the moon and stars.

ALTHOUGH PUK TOOK pride in his beautiful wife and her skills in the kitchen, his stomach often prevented him from enjoying the rich samlors and amoks she prepared for their guests. Every year or so, my father was hospitalized for another stomach hemorrhage. Mae never seemed to worry about my father's ulcers. I assumed his illness wasn't a serious one, just an ordinary (if painful) ailment.

My last memory of him is from the day I finished the third grade. When I brought my graduation certificate home, my father smiled and said, "My youngest daughter has received her first certificate!" Puk wanted to frame it right away. But he wasn't feeling well that day, so Mae took him to the doctor in Phnom Penh. He never came back.

He might have lived if my grandmother hadn't refused to allow the doctor to treat his ulcer. Her permission was the only one that counted. Mae had no authority to sign the legal papers, and Grandmother did not believe in surgery.

"Let my son die without a cut," she declared to my mother. "And if you go through with it and he dies, I won't permit you to have his funeral in my house."

Even my brother, Noh, my grandmother's favorite, could not change her mind. Mae was forced to abide by her mother-in-law's edict, but she never forgave her for it.

One Sunday when I was nine, after morning Bible study, I heard the church bell ring to signal that someone had died. My sister came to take me home early but wouldn't tell me why. When we passed the priest on our way out, he said, "Tell your mother we'll come to Phnom Penh for the service."

The bell had rung for my father.

So many people brought flowers to Puk's funeral, the blooms obscured his body. He was buried in white lilies, a blossom I have hated ever since. For me, the white lily is the flower of death.

MY EARLIEST MEMORIES of my father were of his hands gently massaging me awake for morning prayers. Every morning and evening, our family gathered before an altar decorated with statues of Jesus, Mary, and Joseph in a glass cabinet bursting with fresh flowers and glowing with candlelight. Even at four years old, I was expected to pray with the family. Every morning before first light, Puk rubbed my back and legs so lovingly, I couldn't be annoyed with him for rousing me from sleep.

"Baby daughter, wake up to pray," he whispered. Then he'd carry me into the living room and put me down by the altar, next to my mother. I leaned on her while the family prayed, sometimes falling asleep against her arm.

Puk had a gentle side, but he could also be fearsome. One Khmer New Year, when I was six years old, I was walking along a street where people were celebrating the holiday by playing kla klok, a gambling game using three dice each printed with six identical pictures—usually of a crab, a fish, a chicken, a squash, a prawn, and a tiger. Players lay their cash down on any of six pictures on a grid, then the dealer shakes the dice in a bowl and tosses them. If your picture comes up, you win.

I threw my riel down onto a picture, and one of the dice came to rest with my animal on top—I had won one riel! I ran home shouting, "Puk, Puk, I won a riel in kla klok!" Puk whirled around on the staircase and glared down at me. "If you ever play that game again, I will beat you to death."

I don't have many memories of Puk, but I do remember now he and Mae laughed together at night, listening to music or football on the radio. And after he was gone, I remember how much I missed his laugh and the smell of tobacco from his pipes. They were gifts from the Italian bishop, who lived in Phnom Penh and visited my parents any time he was in Battambang. He'd bought my father those pipes during a visit home to Italy.

Mae buried Puk's beloved pipes with him, but she kept a can of his tobacco on the shelf, a burgundy-red can with a picture of a black cat on it. Perhaps it was inevitable that I would become a smoker myself later in life. Now I have a painting of a pipe in my kitchen. The floating memory of sweet pipe smoke still hangs there, smoke from more than fifty years ago.

My strongest memory of that time is of how our happiness ended with Puk's death. The day after his funeral, our house felt desolate. I lingered in the kitchen, as always. As I entered my school years, I awoke before morning prayers and turned up sleepy-eyed in the kitchen to boil water for Puk's tea—my daily task. That morning, Mae woke me to say that there was no need for me to prepare the water. Then she left for early-morning mass.

Of course, I disobeyed her. I heard her coming home just as I was pouring the boiling water into the heavy thermos. I was afraid that she would catch me, so I took off running with the thermos, just as her feet touched the steps. But I forgot to hold the cracked case from below, the way she had instructed me. The thermos slid from the case and shattered, and the boiling water splashed onto my foot. I was so terrified that she would be angry with me for breaking the thermos—and for disobeying her—that I didn't even dare to scream.

"Oh, my daughter," she said, her eyes on my burned foot.

She treated my burns with her mother's burn ointment. That burn cream was like a magic potion.

After my father died, no ointment in the world could soothe Mae's heartache. I watched her grow dimmer, like a shadow at sunset, as grief began to consume her little by little. Every evening after dinner, she went straight to bed and turned her face toward the wall. I never heard her crying, but I could see her shoulders shaking from the sobs. We rarely saw her smile; she even stopped calling me Puppy.

After that, our luck only seemed to grow worse. A few weeks after Puk's funeral, my brother Tung, who took over the garage after Puk died, repaired a car that belonged to the deputy governor of Battambang and then took it out for a test drive that evening. It was a quiet backstreet, so when he saw a single headlight shining out of the darkness, he assumed the moto would easily pass by. Instead, he drove straight into a truck with one burned-out headlight. Fortunately, the truck was moving slowly, so Tung suffered only a bump on the forehead and a minor shock. But the front of the car was a ruin. Mae and Tung begged the deputy governor to let him repair the car instead of buying a new one, which would have ruined us financially. He agreed, but the repairs still cost Mae a huge sum—our garage fixed engines, so she had to pay a body shop to do the work.

This was our second round of misfortune. Believing that bad luck strikes in threes, we braced ourselves for a third.

Chanthu would sometimes say, "If Puk were alive, we wouldn't have it so hard." My mother, though, never spoke of her sadness. We Khmers rarely discuss our feelings. To talk about pain is to lose face.

Much later, in the leanest Saigon years, when Mae and I had nothing left but each other, she nourished me with her stories about the past. She attributed our dire situation to magic and stars, which gave her some comfort. And she infused in me a belief in the ill-fated buffalo birth year.

IN 1970, NOT long after Puk died, Chanthu, my brothers Tung and Noh, my sister Hua, and I left behind the only lives we'd ever known and fled Cambodia, leaving our mother and brother Phuong behind to sort out the family's affairs.

It had finally come: our third piece of dreadful fortune. Only this time, the bad luck fell upon all Cambodians.

The wars all around us were spilling across our borders. The 1954 Geneva Accords ended colonial rule in French Indochina and partitioned Vietnam, but the struggle for power in Vietnam continued, and flared into war— between the communist North and the corrupt South Vietnamese government and their American allies. North Vietnamese fighters infiltrated eastern Cambodia and used our territory to move armies and arms; in response, American B-52s pockmarked the Cambodian countryside with "secret" bombs—driving the fighters further into our country and causing immense destruction and loss of life in the villages.

Meanwhile, the Khmer Rouge gathered strength in the forests and villages.

Our head of state, Prince Norodom Sihanouk, had long struggled to maintain Cambodia's neutrality, stuck between great powers fighting a Cold War that, in Vietnam and Laos, now burned very hot indeed. Prince Sihanouk's attempts to placate all sides satisfied none of them. And in March of 1970, he was ousted in a coup headed, in part, by his own prime minister, Lon Nol, a general and a politician—who claimed to be an anti-communist and promised to eject the North Vietnamese from Cambodian soil. This vow, though impossible to fulfill, switched on a flood of American aid.

However, Lon Nol was also a superstitious nationalist who dreamed of restoring Cambodia to a mythic past, and of purging the country of non-Khmers and non-Buddhists. He was skilled at shifting alliances and rekindling ancient resentments. And one of Cambodia's favorite ancient resentments was held for our nation's more powerful neighbors, the Vietnamese. Some Khmers called ethnic Vietnamese by a racial slur: *yuon*.

Lon Nol's campaign to rid the nation of Vietnamese Communists quickly mutated into a sort of holy crusade against anyone of Vietnamese descent living in Cambodia. His soldiers rounded up ethnic Vietnamese civilians and murdered thousands. And his rhetoric inflamed these older racial hatreds and incited pogroms against Vietnamese people and their homes and businesses.

Lon Nol's violence, and his obsession with racial "purity" and restoring a glorious Angkorian past, augured tyranny and genocide. But as it turned out, he had these tendencies in common with the man who would soon overthrow him: Pol Pot, his Marxist mirror image. And in 1975, after five years of fighting, Pol Pot's Khmer Rouge would win the Cambodian civil war and launch a genocide so horrific and vast in scale that Lon Nol would become a historical footnote.

At the time, however, Lon Nol seemed plenty scary to us; we had no idea that something worse was coming. All we knew was that my mother was Vietnamese, so the blood in our veins had suddenly become poisonous, a danger from which we could not hide.

One day not long after my father died, I walked a classmate home from school. Her family was Vietnamese and operated a bike shop out of the first floor of their house. As we reached the entrance to their home, we noticed a pile of ruined bicycles littering the road. Her family huddled inside the shop, their faces darkened with horror. There was a murmuring in the street that some boys from the high school had formed a mob and vandalized the shop.

People said that most of the Vietnamese-owned businesses in town had been destroyed. I rushed home, only to find a group of boys riding bicycles up and down the street in front of our house. I was shocked to see that one of them was the postman's son, a tall boy I knew from church, who went to a high school nearby. I was terrified that they would attack our house, too.

While the boys performed their menacing circles, our neighbors pushed the cars from our family's auto shop into the street and moved into the garage to keep watch. Seeing that our "pure" Khmer allies had moved to protect us, the boys rode away and left us alone.

I still remember the postman's son very clearly. We called him Bee, and ironically, he was Vietnamese himself. When I look back, I still believe that he led that mob in order to protect himself. As it turned out, it was only a temporary salvation. He would soon meet his end by the hand of a new authority entirely.

A DARK CLOUD of dread fell over our family. My mother was afraid that one mob or another would soon come back for us. The next day, she, Chanthu, and I went to hide in an upstairs room at our church. I barely recall that time, how long we stayed there or what we ate, only that Chanthu disappeared downstairs every day to cook, and I wasn't allowed to play on the balcony. This time is a black hole in my memory. All I remember is a quiet, like deafness, and no smiling faces. No one spoke to me or looked in my direction. My mother no longer teased me like she used to. It was as if I weren't there at all.

Then one day we left the church and went home, with no explanation from Mae or Chanthu. Later, I overheard my sister say that the priest asked us to leave because someone at the boys' high school across the road had seen Vietnamese people upstairs in the church. Some of the students at that school were the same ones who had circled our street on their bicycles.

It was decided that I would go to Phnom Penh to stay in Grandmother's compound. My rich grandmother had died not long after my father did, but several family members still lived in the compound, and Noh had taken over her big brick villa. During this unrest, I would be safer in Phnom Penh with my older siblings.

Mae and Chanthu stayed behind to sell the contents of our Battambang home. Because the house was on rented land, the only things my mother had to sell were a few pieces of furniture, including the heavy wood table from the living room, some china, my father's cabinet, and a stately wooden clock that he had climbed onto a chair to wind every night. We loved to watch it tick and waited giddily for its chimes.

All she could get for those possessions, which had been so valuable to us, was a hundred riels—the amount my sister might spend on food in a single day. I pictured crowds filing through our house and carrying away our things. They might as well have stolen it all. They knew we had to run and that we would accept any price.

MAE SENT ME to Phnom Penh with Oum—our neighbor, the grilled banana vendor—for the scary taxi ride to the capital. The countryside had become dangerous. I lay in the back seat, my stomach pulsing with car-sickness. Every so often, soldiers would stop the car to look for Vietnamese males. "Are there any yuon here?" they shouted, their angry faces filling the taxi window. If they saw someone who looked Vietnamese, they demanded that he speak; many ethnic Vietnamese living in Cambodia spoke Khmer very poorly, so if the suspected yuon spoke fluent Khmer, he was allowed to pass.

I cried all the way to Phnom Penh, where Noh waited for me. He carried me inside and put me to bed.

The sun rose over a city transformed by unrest. The population of Phnom Penh had swollen with refugees, who streamed in from the surrounding forests and villages. In the countryside, bombs[3] rained down (unofficially, but lethally) from American planes, in a covert campaign to destroy the Vietnamese Communists' operations in Cambodia. The destructive shelling fanned the flames of a civil war between government troops (backed by US aid) and Khmer Rouge revolutionaries, who—with the help of North Vietnamese fighters—were suddenly gaining territory and strength very quickly.

Cambodia's neutrality was shattered.

Phnom Penh's graceful boulevards were packed with soldiers and refugees and ringed with barbed wire, and the three rivers that flow through the capital were full of boats.

Chanthu and Mae soon joined us in Phnom Penh. One day my sister and I took a ferry across the Tonlé Sap River to the strict Carmelite convent in Chroy Changvar, to visit my sister Yen one last time. We called her "Marie Thérèse" after she became a nun. I had visited her once before, when I was small. I remember how quiet the place was, and that we spoke with Yen through a barred window.

I remember almost nothing of this farewell visit, except that on the way across the river, we noticed many rice sacks floating in the water. The sacks

---

3   Between 1965 and 1973, the US dropped more than 2 million tons of bombs on Cambodia. Nixon's secret 1969–70 bombing campaign in the border zones was called Operation Menu, which included missions nicknamed Breakfast, Lunch, Dinner, Dessert, and Snack.

bulged with round objects, like peeled coconuts. I heard Chanthu ask the ferryman what was in the sacks.

"We pulled one out and opened it," he said in a low voice. "It was full of human heads."

In a single night, the ferryman claimed, all the Vietnamese men in a fishing village across the river had been massacred; their heads filled those sacks.

After my mother heard this, she begged Noh to stay inside his room upstairs. He didn't even leave for meals—someone delivered him food, and the door otherwise stayed closed.

My mother did not seem to worry for herself as much as she did for her children. But the danger felt amorphous and incomprehensible. It was hard to know who would be targeted and who passed over. Mae's children all spoke fluent Khmer, which might have protected us. But my mother spoke Khmer with a Vietnamese accent. So after Mae sold the contents of our house, she went to the deputy governor (whose car Tung had damaged) and asked for permission to travel to the capital. She hoped that document— evidence of her connection to an important official—would be enough to protect her if a mob stopped her vehicle, looking for yuon, as she tried to travel to join us in the city.

Those were unsettled days in Phnom Penh; I'm not even sure how long we were there—a few weeks at most. I just remember a feeling of constant dread. I felt unwanted, a stranger in a country I'd thought was home. The teenage daughter of my grandmother's former cook walked the streets with me; she was my bodyguard. We stood at the gate of a beautiful old church, where the soldiers had set up a refugee camp for thousands of ethnic Vietnamese waiting to board freighters out of the capital. I wept to see them living in ramshackle shelters of plastic sheeting, cooking and eating out in the open—people who only weeks before had had homes, jobs, and hopes for the future. I will never forget that refugee-encampment smell: a pungent stew of spoiled food, urine, sweat, and shit.

Much later, in Thailand, I would come to know that smell quite intimately.

UNDER LON NOL, thousands of ethnic Vietnamese were slaughtered. Thousands more fled, or were forcibly expelled, from Cambodia. Here is what Mae knew: Vietnamese businesses were in ruins, families turned out of their homes. The corpses of murdered Vietnamese men floated down the Mekong River. Mae was Vietnamese. And her children were fatherless and half-Vietnamese.

Mae made it safely to us in Phnom Penh but she now had an agonizing decision to make: She chose for Chanthu, Noh, Hoa, and me to join that flood of refugees pouring into South Vietnam, to a "homeland" we had never seen. Our brother Tung had already left with his family. (Yen stayed at the convent; she and the other nuns at the convent would later be evacuated to Belgium before the Khmer Rouge marched into the capital in 1975.)

But Mae was not coming with us—at least, not yet. As she had done when we left Battambang, my mother stayed behind, this time to sell my grandmother's Phnom Penh house. She would send us the money to buy a place in Saigon. My eighteen-year-old brother Phuong stayed with her to help with the sale. A woman could not sell property then without a man's signature on the official documents, even if the man was really just a boy.

Mae was a woman without a husband, in a country that had suddenly become hostile to people of her heritage. She was alone with Phuong and vulnerable in that atmosphere of chaos and menace. All I knew at the time was that I was in anguish about leaving my mother. When my siblings and I said goodbye to Mae and Phuong, we shed many tears together. My mother planned to join us as soon as she could earn enough to make us safe.

We didn't yet grasp that safety was a ghost, a shadow, a child's lullaby. Or that leaving Cambodia would soon become nearly impossible.

If I was cursed by the stars, as my mother and sister said, why did an entire nation seem to share so much ill fortune? Were we all born in the buffalo year, we displaced and diminished Cambodians? We half-Khmers and ethnic Vietnamese or Chinese who had lived in Cambodia for generations? The artists of the Angkor Empire must have known something we didn't about the peaceful Khmer people: On those ancient temple walls, tucked in amongst the Hindu deities, dancer-goddesses, and impassive

Buddhas, are bas-reliefs of battles and massacres, and barbaric scenes of sinners tortured in hell.

Were those stone-carvers historians or fortune tellers?

AT NINE YEARS old, at the Pochentong Airport in Phnom Penh, I said goodbye to my mother and brother Phuong, to my childhood in that sunlit Battambang kitchen, and to Mae's fish amok and pâté de foie. I was bidding farewell to some of those things for more than two decades, and to others, forever. We were luckier by far than the thousands who stayed: five years later, Pol Pot's Democratic Kampuchea would begin to purge the country of Vietnamese with grim finality.

I would have to become our family's memory keeper. I would be the one responsible for gathering and safeguarding the old recipes, and one day, resurrecting them.

The Saigon years were to be my years of gathering. Chanthu and Mae saw to that.

—————

Mae's Fish Amok (Amok Trei)

Amok trei is a rich and vividly colored special-occasion dish. To be authentically "amok," the dish should be steamed in banana leaves; otherwise, it's technically a fish curry. Mae made her amok with a coconut cream so thick, it wouldn't leak through the banana-leaf bowl. She layered the dish with morning glory at the bottom. Turmeric, annatto, and dried chili paste give this dish a deep scarlet color.

Note: To make the optional banana-leaf bowls, see instructions in "Notes on Ingredients, Techniques, and Supplies."

Serves 4

Ingredients:

6 tablespoons amok paste (see below)

1½ pounds flaky white fish such as tilapia, catfish, sea bass, or cod (you can also use tofu or shrimp)

1 (13.5-ounce) can full-fat, unsweetened coconut milk
½ teaspoon sugar
4 to 8 banana leaves (optional)

For the amok paste:
3 stalks lemongrass (white part only), thinly sliced
1 (1-inch) turmeric root, grated or minced (or 1 teaspoon powder)
5 to 6 slices galangal
4 makrut lime leaves, thinly sliced
6 cloves garlic, smashed
3 shallots, roughly chopped
4 tablespoons neutral oil
1 teaspoon annatto seeds
1 (4-ounce) package mild dried red chilies (to make 2 tablespoons chili paste—see instructions in "Notes on Ingredients, Techniques, and Supplies")
1 teaspoon shrimp paste (optional, but recommended)
Salt

For serving: 4 sprigs Thai basil or 4 makrut lime leaves, thinly sliced; Thai red chilies, sliced

Make the amok paste: Using a mortar and pestle, pound lemongrass, turmeric, galangal, lime leaves, garlic, and shallots to a fine paste (or grind in a food processor). Begin with the tougher ingredients, then add the softer ones one by one.

In a medium skillet, heat oil over medium heat. Drop in annatto seeds, stirring until oil turns golden red, about 1 minute. Remove and discard seeds. Add 2 tablespoons chili paste to oil and fry for 1 minute. Reduce heat to medium-low, add amok paste, and sauté for 3 minutes more. Reduce heat to low, add shrimp paste (if using) and a pinch of salt, and sauté for 2 to 3 minutes. Remove from heat and let cool.

Prepare the fish: Cut fish into 1½-inch pieces. Thoroughly coat each piece in the amok paste and refrigerate in a sealed container for 3 to 4 hours (or overnight).

Reserve ¼ cup coconut milk for topping the fish. In a bowl, combine the remaining coconut milk with sugar. Add about half of this mixture to the marinated fish and mix gently.

Transfer fish to small, single-serving heatproof bowls (or the banana leaf bowls, if using). Steam gently over medium-low for 15 to 20 minutes—ideally, in a bamboo steamer. (If you use a metal steamer, wrap each bowl individually in foil to prevent lid condensation from dripping into the bowls.)

Pour remaining sugar–coconut milk mixture around the fish and steam for 10 minutes more. Meanwhile, in a saucepan over medium-low, gently warm reserved ¼ cup coconut milk.

Remove bowls from the steamer. Drizzle warmed coconut milk over fish and top with sliced Thai basil or lime leaves and Thai chilies. Serve with jasmine rice.

PART II

———

The Rules for Ration Queues

5. Fish Soup Lessons

One worm will spoil the whole pot of soup.
—Vietnamese proverb

OUR FIRST FIVE years in Saigon were turbulent and uncertain. Those years blur together in my mind. It would be 1975 before I saw my mother again; even after she sold Grandmother's house, she stayed behind in Cambodia. I still don't understand why. Chanthu said only that business was good under Lon Nol's corrupt regime, and that Mae could earn money more easily there—selling fruit in the market, or any kind of work she could find—and send it to us in Saigon.

Still, what money we had initially insulated us from the squalor and misery so many of our fellow exiles suffered. Thousands ended up in refugee settlement villages on an arid mountain in Long Khánh Province, a few hours east of Saigon. Before the refugees arrived, there wasn't much there except a big banana plantation. Everyone called the place Banana Mountain.

A few months after we arrived in Saigon, my sister took me to one of those villages to visit Mae's cousin. The refugees slept on simple bamboo floors under plastic sheeting, with sandbag-reinforced trenches under the floor that served as makeshift bomb shelters. They survived by scraping cassava out of the rocky soil, planting cashew trees, and digging wells twenty meters deep into the ground. The cloudy, hard well water left a white film on everything they washed: clothes, plates, bodies. These were city people who had worked as artisans and cooks. Now they had to become farmers.

Our family's slide into poverty was less precipitous. When we first arrived in Vietnam, Chanthu, Noh, Hua and I stayed with Chi Nam (*Chi* or *Jae* is an honorific derived from Chinese, meaning "older sister"), a relative of my mother who lived in a working-class district, in a small wooden house by a canal.

We shared quarters with Chi Nam and her family—around twenty of us in a tiny place without a proper kitchen or living room. My brother curled up on the kitchen floor. Chi Nam and her husband slept in one bed with their youngest, and Hua and I shared the other with four or five other children. We stretched out crosswise along the mattress, with my arm dangling off the edge against the mosquito netting. The mosquitoes were adept at piercing my arm through the net, so every morning I woke up covered in bites. I slept very little and cried for Mae every night, harder still whenever Chanthu tried to console me.

Chi Nam was a skilled cook. She often prepared feasts for weddings and festivals. But with so many people to feed and so little money, she had to stretch a few paltry ingredients very far. She cooked giant pots of vegetable soup with little or no meat, or sometimes with blood added to make the soup heartier. And she ruined (in my opinion) her gỏi su hào—a shredded kohlrabi salad with julienne carrots, daikon, and chopped herbs—by adding a disgusting sausage stuffed with pork fat and blood. It was inedible. I could not help but compare it to my mother's beautiful banana-flower chicken salad.

I had to force down the strange, repulsive food; every bite made me miss Mae even more.

One day, a well-dressed family distantly related to us, with two teenage daughters, came by and offered to let me stay with them for a few weeks. That time was like heaven. They drove me across Saigon in their car to a neighborhood that looked wealthy to me after being at Chi Nam's. The family lived on a posh row of three-story apartments—so much space, all for just four people. The sweet couple spoke in quiet voices and wore constant smiles, and the food was marvelous—just like in Battambang, with three dishes of soup, meat, and stir-fried vegetables at every meal. One night, we had a jambon, a whole pork thigh, rolled up and tied with a string. The round slices of salty pink meat marbled with lacelike fat and spirals of skin were beautiful and elegant, and I was allowed to eat as much as I liked. And I could even have ice cream from the shop next door!

The peace of their household was a welcome counterpoint to the noise, close quarters, and thin soup at Chi Nam's, where her little son always cried, the older siblings argued, and Chi Nam shouted at them all. No one had any free space whatsoever, like at a refugee camp. In a sense, her home *was* a refugee camp. Certainly, it was a refuge; it was profoundly selfless of Chi Nam to take us all in during our time of extreme need. And there was less of everything to go around with our family packed in. But I was a child and could barely see beyond my own nose. All I knew was that I was sad to leave that beautiful, quiet apartment with its abundant meals and delicious jambon.

WITHIN A FEW months, my mother sold Grandmother's villa and sent the money for us to buy a house. With so many refugees pouring in from Cambodia, the price of real estate in Saigon had shot up to the sky. But Chanthu and Chi Nam went out every day searching for houses and eventually found a simple wooden place in Tân Định, a ward of District 1—a busy area in central Saigon.

The house was tucked away on a narrow, working-class street behind a church. Chanthu said it reminded her of our old house in Battambang. I felt that she was overstating the resemblance. It was rickety, tin-roofed, and nearly bare of furniture. My sisters and I shared one bed, and Noh occupied the other one; we stored our clothing in a plain box with no door. Water rose over the floor whenever it rained. Chanthu and Noh ordered a truckload of soil, pulled up the floorboards, and emptied the baskets of soil onto the ground to fill in and elevate the floor. They then replaced the planks

directly onto the soil bed, which meant that mud seeped up between the
floorboards whenever it rained. And the house still flooded during heavy
downpours.

The place was constructed of such poor lumber that sunlight streamed
in through the gaps between boards. I once complained to Chanthu, during
one of my now frequent migraines, that the fingers of light were drilling
into my skull like needles. She stuffed scraps of fabric into the gaps to keep
out the light, a practical approach to problem-solving that was typical of
my resourceful sister.

To me, our diets seemed even more diminished than our accommodations. The days of fish amok were behind us. We ate pumpkin soup, a cheap
staple, until I could not stand the sight of it. Back in Battambang, pumpkin
stuffed with egg, coconut milk, and sugar had been one of my favorite after-
school treats to steal from the kitchen, but the now-accursed gourd had lost
all appeal for me.

I tried not to let my sister see me cry when she served the disgusting
soup. She was doing the best she could for us. And in time, she did manage to improve our menu choices with money earned by sewing clothes for
our neighbors. Her income wasn't substantial, but when the festival season
neared, demand for new outfits soared. I helped her by stitching the hems
by hand. Chanthu said my tiny stitches were perfect. I smiled to myself at
the compliment, my fingertips sore and raw from driving the needle into
the thick hem.

Language was another difficult adjustment for me. Although I had studied the Bible in Vietnamese in Sunday school, I spoke the language poorly,
with a thick accent, and could write very little. So my sister enrolled me in
St. Paul, a Catholic school, where I could continue my studies in French. I
don't know how she scraped together the tuition; I simply accepted this gift,
knowing that it was a burden for her. I rose before first light to walk to class
and did my homework on the kitchen floor after dark so that the lamplight
would not awaken Noh, who had to work in the morning.

I always dreaded the end of the month, when the principal and head priest read aloud a list of students who were late with their fees. My name was always on that list. The shame of it still burns my cheeks whenever I recall it.

I didn't blame Chanthu. I knew there were problems that even she could not solve. Most of all, she couldn't fill the hole that my mother's absence left in our lives. I was used to sleeping beside Mae, and now I had only my sister to comfort me in the night. For months, I cried until I fell asleep.

Chanthu had become a second mother to me, but of course, no one can replace your mother. I longed for Mae, her songs and stories, and her fish sauce and pâté de foie. As the Saigon years scrolled by, and Cambodia's fortunes worsened, I saw that our exile might not be temporary, and I wondered whether I would ever taste those delicacies again.

MY BROTHER NOH could not abide our abject, grimy little house for long. He had almost immediately gotten a job with a French company, and soon he moved to an even better job with a French beverage firm. One day, a little less than a year after our arrival in Saigon, he declared, "I can't live in this house." Noh had gotten a promotion and could now afford to rent something better, so he rented an apartment of his own. In Cambodia, he had been treated like a minor prince; he could not stand living like a pauper.

When he left, I cried and cried; I felt that he had utterly abandoned us, the big brother I admired from afar but never really knew. He was reserved and distant, and for the most part, he had always seemed too busy and important to bend down and chat or play with me. And now, this eldest son, who my father expected to lead the family, could not be relied upon to help us in our time of greatest need.

We didn't see him much. He dropped by once a month or so and brought Chanthu soft drinks and large blocks of ice he'd bought wholesale from his firm for her to resell for a small profit. I was excited for his visits, mostly because he usually gave me a little pocket money.

A few years later, Noh married a doctor named Anh; like us, she had come to Vietnam from Phnom Penh after Lon Nol took power. They got married in 1974 at a Chinese restaurant in Chợ Lớn, Saigon's Chinatown. All I remember about the wedding was delicious food—fried rice with sausage, egg, and lotus seeds.

Hua also left that first year. "I can't live like this," she explained. Much like Noh, after staying in Grandmother's compound and attending school in Phnom Penh, these crowded, reduced circumstances were not to her liking. She left us to join a convent. Sometime after South Vietnam surrendered to the North Vietnamese in 1975, she stayed with us briefly again and worked in a canal-digging brigade. But she was never truly a sister to me. I barely knew her. And a few years later, Yen sponsored her to emigrate to Belgium. We never saw Hua again.

We did see my brother Tung occasionally. He and his young wife, Nary, were living with her family in Vũng Tàu Province, southeast of Saigon. Tung was on his way to visit us one day, a year or two after we arrived in Saigon, when he suddenly felt so ill, he asked the taxi driver to let him out. He went straight back home, and Nary took him to a small provincial hospital.

He had a stomach ulcer, just like Puk, and it was bleeding.

If we had only known what would happen, maybe Chanthu would have pulled me out of school to go and see him. It was all like a grim echo of my father's last days. In this case, his wife's family *wanted* the surgery, but the small hospital didn't have the resources to do the procedure. Instead, his in-laws paid an exorbitant fee for a blood transfusion. It did not help. Tung died of a stomach hemorrhage, the same ailment that felled our father.

He had been my favorite brother: gentle and kind, he never ordered me around like Noh did. And he was handsome—tall like my father, with my mother's straight nose. Chanthu always believed that if Nary's family had taken Tung to a decent hospital in Saigon, the doctors could have saved his life.

• • •

IN THOSE YEARS, after our other siblings were gone, and before Mae made
it to Saigon, Chanthu was my everything—caretaker, teacher, mother. And
she refused to let me give up on my education, no matter what sacrifices she
had to make to keep me in school.

Two years at St. Paul had improved my language skills considerably.
Though classes were taught in French, I learned Vietnamese well. I still
made mistakes, but I'd fallen in love with the novels and poetry of Vietnam,
which has a richer literary tradition than Cambodia. As I read, my spoken
and written vocabulary grew. After fifth grade, I enrolled in the government
school, which cost less, and this took some of the pressure off Chanthu.

I had long dreamed of studying medicine. But by the time I graduated
from high school, the Communists had come to power, and our status had
dropped even lower. I was a half-Khmer Cambodian refugee in Saigon with
little hope of being admitted to a professional school. As I understood it,
most slots were reserved for the ideologically pure young people whose
fathers had worn the correct uniform.

Still, when you consider how most of my generation of "New People"
fared in Pol Pot's Democratic Kampuchea, it feels small and mean to complain. Back in Cambodia, the Khmer Rouge considered city-dwellers like
us "New People" who had been corrupted by education and capitalism;
the "cure" for our corruption was reeducation, forced labor, and often,
execution.

So I was lucky to be out of Cambodia—and to have never been "reedu-
cated" by the instructive blow of a hammer to the skull.

IN SAIGON IN that period, while revolutionaries fought their way south-
ward and we waited for my mother to join us, my fondest food memories are more of food-dreaming than of the actual meals we ate. It was the
dreaming that sustained our minds, if not our bellies.

One of the dishes I learned to crave in Saigon was bún bò Huế, a resplendent, spicy beef and noodle soup from the beautiful old imperial city of
Huế, in central Vietnam. In Battambang, my mother never made it. But it

was a popular and delicious street food in Vietnam, and I loved it from the first time I tried it; my sister had given me some money to splurge on food that day, and I bought a steaming bowl of bún bò Huế.

The next time I asked for bún bò Huế money, Chanthu delivered a lecture instead: "Can you wait? We only eat when we are hungry now," she said. "We don't eat just because we want to." Money was tight, she reminded me. I had to delay my appetite for bún bò Huế until I was ravenous for it. The waiting just made me savor the dish even more—even now, I can still taste the wanting and the waiting.

"We don't eat just because we want to" was an unwelcome policy change in our dining regimen.

Despite the narrowed menu choices for us in Saigon, though, we found ways to make the miserable fare taste more like the richness of our Battambang past. One trick we used again and again was stretching a little bit of pork with a cheaper protein alternative: fresh tofu. The tofu absorbs the flavors of the fatty pork belly, garlic, and soy sauce, and tastes quite substantial. I think of that dish as "tofu in disguise."

On days when we could scrape together the money for decent ingredients, Chanthu had the skills to conjure passable facsimiles of the flavors and scents of Mae's kitchen. Whenever she cooked a familiar dish from home, I watched closely and begged to help.

After about three years in Saigon, Chanthu finally said yes. I was terribly excited: She was preparing broth for a soup, and I was a twelve-year-old pest, shadowing her relentlessly in the kitchen.

"Okay! You can salt the broth," she said. But she neglected to offer any hints about how much salt to add. I was afraid to ask her—I didn't want to look ignorant—so I poured in a giant spoonful.

Usually, Chanthu had a hot temper, but she didn't shout at me about the ruined soup. She laughed actually, right away realizing her error: the instructions had been dangerously unspecific.

After that disaster, Chanthu began to train me more deliberately. Sometimes people would pay her to cook mountains of food for a wedding, and every few months, our priest would offer her a small bonus to prepare a big meal for the church. Those were our best lessons: I would spend entire days helping her, as she explained the complicated steps. For each dish, the shallots or carrots had to be cut into a specific size and shape; morning glories had to be trimmed differently according to what soup or stir-fry they inhabited; limes had to be peeled before squeezing them. Doing things by any other method would ruin the dish; that is what Mae taught my sister, and that is what Chanthu instilled in me. Even now, I feel compelled to cook everything the way my mother and sister did. It's almost an obsession with me. Any way other than my mother's and sister's is the wrong way, and I cannot allow it in my kitchen.

I was proud when I learned to make namya, a golden fish soup with a curry base. We had it all the time in Battambang, and my sister taught me to cook it in Saigon. It's influenced by Thai namya—the dish stole across the border from Thailand to my hometown, and we adapted it to our Khmer palates—but our version is more subtly spiced.

To this day, the smell of fish slow-roasting on charcoal carries me back to Battambang.

Namya Fish Soup with Khmer Noodles (Num Banhchok Samlor Namya)

Because Battambang is near the Thai border, many of my hometown's regional specialties are Thai-influenced. Thai namya is a fish curry served over rice noodles. The curry paste is usually made with chilies, galangal, garlic, lemongrass, shallots, fingerroot (also known as grachai or Chinese ginger), and fermented fish or shrimp paste. My Battambang version is more subtly flavored—I don't use galangal, shrimp paste, or fingerroot. And this a relatively quick curry because you do not make a kroeung. You could even substitute one of the curry pastes labeled "namya" in Asian groceries.

We usually cook a whole fish and then debone it for the soup. But you can save time by using boneless fillets.

Serves 4

Ingredients:

2 pounds flaky white fish, such as tilapia, catfish, or cod (a little less
if using fillets)

½ cup neutral oil

1 tablespoon annatto seeds

2 to 3 medium shallots, minced (about 7 tablespoons)

20 cloves garlic, minced (about 7 tablespoons)

1 (½-inch) turmeric root, grated or minced (or ½ teaspoon
powder)

1 (14- to 16-ounce) package thin rice vermicelli (bún)

3 stalks lemongrass, cut into thirds and bruised

1 bay leaf

2 cups full-fat, unsweetened coconut milk

1 teaspoon sugar

2 cubes Knorr chicken bouillon (optional)

Salt

For serving: Handful of morning glory (7 to 8 stalks; optional);
¼ pound bean sprouts; 4 to 6 sprigs mint or Thai basil; dried red
chili flakes

Grill whole fish or fillets over a charcoal fire until exterior is golden
brown and fish is cooked through. (Or, in a skillet, sauté in ½ cup
neutral oil over medium heat, until skin is golden and crisp.) Let
fish cool, then debone. Cut fish into 1-inch pieces.

In a skillet, heat ½ cup oil over medium heat. Drop in annatto
seeds, stirring until oil turns golden red, a minute or so. Remove
and discard seeds. Add shallots and garlic and fry until translucent
and light golden, 3 to 4 minutes, then add turmeric and sauté for
1 minute more. Remove from heat and reserve oil in the skillet.

Cook noodles, drain, rinse with cold water, and set aside.

Meanwhile, in a stockpot, bring 4 cups water to a boil. Add

lemongrass stalks, bay leaf, and ¼ cup of the coconut milk. Dredge fish in the reserved annatto oil and add to pot. Reduce heat and simmer for 20 minutes. Add sugar and chicken bouillon (if using), and season with salt. Turn off heat and cover. If you have time, let soup sit for 1 to 2 hours to allow flavors to meld.

When ready to serve, return soup to a boil, then add remaining coconut milk and fried garlic, shallots, and turmeric. Do not cover. Remove from heat and let soup cool for 10 minutes. Remove lemongrass and bay leaf. Serve soup warm.

While you wait, cut the toughest part of the stalk from the morning glory (if using) and remove any wilted leaves. Parboil morning glory quickly in salted water, then chop into 1-inch pieces. Blanch bean sprouts in the cooking water.

Arrange rice noodles in large bowls, pour the soupy namya over them, and top with morning glory, bean sprouts, fresh herbs, and chili flakes.

———

CHANTHU'S LESSONS WERE the beginning of my transition from soft, useless girl to stubborn survivor. She was teaching me the skills I would need to fend for myself in a world that had no charity to spare for poor, motherless girls. And she was also preparing me to resurrect Mae's kitchen, one day in the far, far future.

But for now, we were stuck in wartime Saigon, with the North Vietnamese closing in. *This* was our refuge. After Vietnam, where do you run? We had fled one war and soon we would find ourselves in another.

In Saigon, we lived in the eye of a storm. The city was full of South Vietnamese and American soldiers. We watched ghost images of battles on TV and heard the rumble of distant bombs at night. But even in the city, which had mostly been spared, there were solemn reminders: Funerals of our neighbors' sons. Families dressed in the white cotton robes and pointed hoods of mourning. Wooden caskets loaded onto American military trucks. Pregnant widows. Cemeteries full of soldiers. Missing classmates, who never came home.

Catholic Saigon was a kind of brother or sisterhood. After the country was divided into North and South in 1954, thousands of Northern Catholics fled south of the seventeenth parallel for fear of repression by the new North Vietnamese government. Churches were everywhere in Saigon then, as common a sight as pagodas in Cambodia. So whenever our priest announced the funeral of a fellow Catholic, we went to the grieving family's home after mass to pray. Before 1975, those funerals were an almost daily occurrence.

The war was coming for Saigon, too. And we had nowhere else to go.

MANY OF MY Western friends find it strange that my family would escape *to* wartime Vietnam, the conflict that Americans know as the Vietnam War and many Vietnamese people call the American War, which claimed more than 58,000 American and an estimated 3 million Vietnamese lives.

But what we fled *from* was far worse than what we fled *to*.

And so I was spared the cataclysm that began on April 17, 1975, when the Khmer Rouge overran Phnom Penh and restarted time. Do you know what happened in Cambodia that April day, and the four years that followed?

Instead of my telling you the inconceivable statistics, let's do a mental exercise:

Close your eyes. Imagine you are home having breakfast on a hot and sunny Thursday. The radio crackles with news of the army's surrender. You're cautiously hopeful: The rumble of battle has gone quiet. The civil war is over! The victors are marching into the city.

You carry an armful of white pillowcases into the street and wave them at the trucks full of sun-beaten country boys, boys with guns and hard faces, boys wearing the checked krama scarves of rice farmers. At first, there's an atmosphere of jubilation: Laughter. Relief. A collective exhalation of held breaths.

Your children search your face to determine whether they should be excited or afraid. You don't know the answer.

By afternoon, the mood darkens: The country boys fire into the air and shout into their bullhorns: Pack your things. The American bombers are incoming! You must leave the city, for your safety. No cars. You'll leave on foot with whatever you can carry.

You won't need much, they tell you. You'll be back in a few days.

You consider asking one of the young soldiers a question, challenging him, demanding an explanation. And then, you see one of the youngsters crack your neighbor's skull with the butt of a rifle. Your neighbor drops to the sidewalk and does not get up. Further down the street, you notice more prone figures, crumpled in pools of blood.

You pack your things and walk out of the city with your family. You ask no questions. A sea of humanity is on the move: children, grandparents on cyclos, the sick and wounded in wheeled hospital beds.

Nightfall. You've walked all day. The air refuses to cool. Your children are crying. "We are having a picnic!" you smile, hoping to comfort them. But this is a terrifying picnic—with the entire population of your city, thousands of neighbors who stop along the roadside twenty kilometers out in every direction, illuminating the night sky with their thousands of cooking fires. See the sparks spiraling up and up until they merge with the stars, an eerie and beautiful sight.

You cling to a fierce optimism. Everything will be back to normal soon. This is the maximum level of eager denial you will achieve for the next several years. Within a few weeks, you will grasp that this move is not temporary. Within a few months, you will be certain that civilization itself *is* temporary.

You are herded to a village and placed into a horrific sort of summer camp. You and your family erect a bamboo hut for shelter and spend long days digging irrigation canals, or planting and harvesting, under the menacing, watchful eyes of those armed country boys. Amid a sea of rice, you are starving. If you steal an ear of corn for your family, you will be executed. You may also be executed for no reason at all. Or perhaps you will die of cholera or malaria, or be drafted to fight. Death comes easily, and by a wide variety of means.

Zoom out and forward in time; hover above your old street a year later. It is a white-hot day with no promise of rain. The city is deserted; cars and motos rust where they were abandoned that April day. At night, there is only darkness. During the day, only dust. Even the mosquitoes are hungry; there is nothing for them to eat.

The city belongs to the rats. There is no one left there to catch and eat them. Try not to think about what they might be feasting upon.

Except: There's some kind of activity in town, at a school near your neighborhood. Learning of a different sort seems to be happening here. A little closer now, you hear screams.

This is no longer an education center; it is a *re*education center.

The difference is vast. The tools of pedagogy in these former classrooms are not books and chalkboards; they are manacles and knives, pickaxes, and even scorpions. Imagine the most ignorant, sociopathic bully from your school days. Now imagine him in charge of this ex-schoolyard, armed with an ideological excuse to hate you, and the authority to "teach" by whatever means he enjoys most.

More than 12,000 students will "study" at the S-21 interrogation center in the coming years; fewer than twenty will live to recall what they learned there: The survivors learn to confess to invented crimes. The rest confess, too, but it doesn't save them. They graduate into mass graves.

One day, years from now, you return home. Your city does not function. There are no schools, hospitals, banks, churches, restaurants, or pagodas. Someone has erased the monks, doctors, priests, teachers, chefs, and poets, too.

Even the krama-clad philosophers are gone, chased into the jungle by Vietnamese troops. Their departure is the only silver lining.

One of every four human beings you know is dead.

Now open your eyes and do this one final exercise: Go outside and look at the people walking down your street. Use your thumb to cover up one of them for every four you see. They no longer exist. Now go inside and look at your family.

Year Zero. Angkar.

That was the Cambodia of my adolescence.

IN SAIGON, WE knew none of this. The news from home had gone dark, and we worried about the sudden nothingness. And then in 1975, the first survivors began to appear. Later, they would become a flood.

We could not believe the stories they carried with them. Every day, they spoke of more and more impossible things. Things told in low voices, as if the teller was afraid of being overheard. Things that could not happen in the world we had known.

It was as if a very quick nightmare had washed over our lives.

No one knew the whole story. They could only tell us what they had seen close up, and nobody knew what happened to anyone else. Each story of escape echoed the one before: People moved from one village to the next, shepherded to one way station after another. The lucky ones found themselves near the Vietnam border, where there was at least a possibility of escape, secretly and by night. Many who tried to cross were saved by Vietnamese soldiers.

But the tales of horror and loss were singular, individual, original. A nun said she had walked across a sugarcane field flooded with blood. My cousin John told us that he and his father had caught two rats in the streets of Phnom Penh and had cooked up a rat and rice stew. It was my uncle's last meal—he ate the rat-meat stew and died later that night. Perhaps he decided that a life of eating rats was no life at all and eased himself out of the world, before the rat-eating season became the no-eating season.

Before we left Battambang, we had heard of the Khmer Rouge, of

course. My older siblings had a few schoolmates who quit school to join
the revolution. But we couldn't imagine students becoming killers, and
we had no real idea who the Khmer Rouge were or what they were capable of.

MY MOTHER FINALLY made it to us in 1975, several months after Phnom
Penh fell to Pol Pot's advance. I had not seen her for five years.

I came home from school one day to find my sister speaking to a visitor,
but in a much louder voice than usual. I leaned against the doorframe to listen. A second later, I saw that the visitor was my mother. I screamed "Mae!"
and collapsed into her lap. But the smile she returned to me was forlorn, her
face marked by deep creases that hadn't been there before.

In a somber tone, she told my sister about the day Pol Pot's cadres
marched in: Soldiers in black pajamas appeared in her neighborhood,
shouting "GO! GO! GO!" There was no time to pack. The whole city was
suddenly crowded with people—moving, moving, moving, all in one direction, a human river.

More and more people joined the river. They walked for days. Whenever
a soldier ordered a group to one place or another, the group went silently. If
anyone asked why, a soldier might answer with a hammer to the forehead.
Most people found that answer sufficient and asked no further questions.

My mother and my brother Phuong made their way toward the
Vietnamese border during the day and stopped after dark. One night, a
soldier came and asked all the boys and men to follow him. My brother
could not refuse. To this day, I still don't know how my mother made it out
alive, and it never crossed my mind to ask her.

With my brother lost in the black hole of Angkar, Mae could not celebrate her escape, or her reunion with the rest of her family. I was crestfallen
and regretted my show of joy. It seemed heartless to feel relief in the face
of her anguish.

We didn't know where the Khmer Rouge had taken him. But we held
on to the hope that Phuong would soon find his way to us, too.

NOW THAT MY mother was back, I slept beside her like I had as a small girl, pulling at her earlobe. This was not the laughing, youthful Mae I remembered. She looked much older, and her flesh hung loose and dry from the weight she had lost. She spoke very little and rarely smiled. But she still kissed my forehead when she thought I was asleep.

My mother began visiting the Cambodian refugee settlements in Long Khánh Province, to offer sugar and cigarettes to the refugees and ask for news of loved ones. Some nights she came home sick with diarrhea and vomiting. Chanthu told me that Mae was "allergic to the new environment." But I believe that the horrors Mae witnessed—both firsthand and as a sympathetic ear—had infected her like a virus. Many refugees would stop by to visit us; my mother always offered food or tobacco, or simply listened and bore witness. And then, when they had told us their harrowing stories and departed, she would cry herself sick.

One day, the postman from our old neighborhood in Battambang came by. Once vigorous, he had become a withered old man. We asked him about his son, the boy who had menaced our neighborhood during Lon Nol's pogroms.

"Where is Bee?" we asked.

Like the other refugees, he told his story in a low monotone, his face blank. The postman and his son had been moving down the Tonlé Sap by riverboat. One night, a group of Khmer Rouge soldiers rounded everyone up on the riverbank and told them to turn back and start heading north. Bee asked the soldiers if he and his small group could continue south instead. Their answer was an axe to his head.

As I began to hear those awful tales, I knew in my heart that my brother Phuong was dead. Angkar had swallowed him.

Once Angkar had someone, it was unlikely to let them go.

But my mother could not give up believing that Phuong would appear. I suspect that she blamed herself for his fate. She had asked him to stay with her in Phnom Penh, and in the end, she could not protect him.

Whenever we visited Cambodian refugees, my mother asked if anyone had heard news of Phuong. When her investigations and prayers failed to conjure him, she turned, once again, to the stars: She began visiting fortune tellers, searching for the Correct Answer to a single question.

"I went to see another fortune teller," she would say, every few weeks. "He's very famous." And then, after a pause: "Your brother's still alive."

I could not share my mother's optimism, or her faith in empty sorcery. But hope, together with despair, can make you believe in anything. One day, after years of fortune teller wishful-thinking magic, I lost patience. I was sick of Mae enriching every astrological scammer in Saigon who gave her the answer she wanted.

"If he were alive, he would have found us by now!" I said, the words exploding out of me. She turned her face away. I have never forgiven myself for that instant of heartless impatience.

At the time, I could not bring myself to believe in the impossible, fortune tellers, or star signs. But soon enough, I would become much more open to this kind of magic. Soon enough, I would learn that an inverse relationship exists between these two elements: the ferocity of wild, magical hopes; and a reasonable expectation that those hopes have any chance of coming true.

6. With a Side of Cassava

The rice grain suffers under the blow of the pestle.
But admire its whiteness once the order is over.
So it is with men and the world we live in.
To be a man one must suffer the blows of misfortune.
—Hồ Chí Minh

UNLIKE MY OWN gradual toughening, Saigon's transition from a bustling capitalist city to monochrome austerity was accomplished with breathtaking swiftness.

In April of 1975, while my mother was escaping from the Communists of Angkar, the North Vietnamese reached Saigon. The streets came alive with a hectic brew of panic and jubilation. The hours of tense waiting had dissolved into an explosion of relief, as tinny victory tunes emanated from loudspeakers. One woman rushed up and down the street chanting, "Our brothers are coming! Come out to greet them!"

The whole city seemed to be running. On our quiet side street, neighbors rushed toward a busy main road, shouting, "The Hồ Chí Minh troops are here!" in excited voices. I followed them.

A column of tanks and military trucks crawled by on the wide street. All of Saigon, it seemed, had emerged to welcome them, cheering and tossing flowers to the soldiers in baggy green uniforms. The soldiers laughed and fired their weapons into the sky, a sound like fireworks. Everyone waved small paper flags—red over blue with a yellow star. I wondered how everyone had gotten those flags and why my family did not have one.

All over the city were signs of the panicked withdrawal of American troops, diplomats, and other personnel. Along the streets, tables appeared, cluttered with foreign goods for sale: military shoes, chocolate, packets of dehydrated food, and jars of something green that I didn't recognize. (I'd never seen olives before.) Apparently, people had broken into the American Post Exchange and stripped the shelves bare.

Soon we heard that the North Vietnamese had arrived at the president's residence. Later, at home, I watched a tank break through the gate on TV. I was shocked by the television images: evacuees swarming onto helicopters and dangling off the edges, the helicopters thrumming offshore toward big ships; thousands more attempting to scale the walls of those ships from tiny boats, then slipping off into the sea. Anyone who had been allied with the South Vietnamese or American governments was desperate to escape, by any means.

In a flash, South Vietnam as we knew it had ceased to exist.

That evening, I stood in the street watching the shouting and waving until well after sunset. Cheers and gunfire rose from the dark city like sparks from a vast, crackling fire. The electricity was out in our district, and perhaps citywide. Faces from the crowd lit up eerily, illuminated by army truck headlights.

The atmosphere was festive and oddly thrilling. I didn't quite grasp why the citizens of Saigon seemed so elated. Maybe they were celebrating a long-hoped-for peace, or were simply mad with relief that the city had been spared a bloodletting; the heavy fighting had stopped just short of the city's outskirts. Or perhaps the cheers were largely a performance for the benefit of the occupying forces. Either way, I stood watching from behind an electric pole, apart from the excitement. I did not feel that I belonged to Saigon. And for the fourteen years I lived there, this never changed.

I HEADED BACK to my neighborhood. With no electricity, our street was dark and still, like a sleeping black snake. Our house hummed with visitors discussing the incredible events of the day by the warm light of gas lamps. From all over the city came the pop of gunshots, a familiar sound to the war-weary citizens of Saigon. And then we heard a small noise, like someone tossing a stone onto our tin roof.

I was standing right in front of Chanthu. She cried out from a sharp pain in her breast, and blood quickly soaked her shirt. I didn't understand what was happening, and neither did Chanthu. One of our guests shouted that we needed to take her to the hospital immediately.

I entered a dreamlike state. The disorder of the day had momentarily thrilled me, a bewildered teenage refugee in a giant, newly overthrown city; I hadn't lost enough things yet to view such scenes with more cynicism and fear. And then, as darkness overtook the city, I had sensibly taken myself to safety.

Only to find that safety was a mirage.

Since our arrival in Vietnam, Chanthu had been my stand-in mother, positioning herself between me and the worst of the world. She *was* my family. Radio silence still enveloped Cambodia. My mother hadn't yet made it to Saigon. Tung was dead. Noh was too selfish to help us. Hua was barely a part of our family.

And now a bullet shower might end the life of my hard-as-diamond sister who protected me.

After the men rushed my sister to the hospital, I waited for hours in the dark house. I felt no fear of the soldiers; my terror fixed itself on Chanthu: What would happen to her? And if she didn't come home, what would happen to me? We had no idea, then, when—or whether—Mae would arrive. I felt terribly alone.

Chanthu and the quick-thinking man returned a few hours later. At the hospital, where patients crowded the corridors and overflowed onto balconies, harried doctors had waved her away, saying that her injury wasn't life-threatening: The bullet had struck her breast and missed her bones and organs. "Your wound can wait," they told her. She returned to the hospital ten days later to have the bullet removed.

This was the peace we had been promised. A celebratory bullet had descended from the sky—and into my sister. But she was alive, thank goodness.

THE RIOTOUS ATMOSPHERE of April 30 died down, and the new government began to reshape the city in its own image. Loudspeakers blared slogans and military music. A curfew was set at 10 p.m., after which no noise was allowed, including the playing of radios. Policemen patrolled our neighborhood at night, listening for outlawed wireless broadcasts. BBC and Voice of America, which had kept us glued to our radio throughout the war, were now forbidden. At 6 p.m., when the BBC program in Vietnamese came on, my sister turned the radio down to a whisper and pressed her ear to the box.

In the streets there were soldiers everywhere, shouting words we had never heard before, a strange ideological vocabulary we did not understand. They came door to door to notify us that each family was to send a representative to local meetings, where they would be informed of the regime's new rules. My sister attended the Party meetings in our district, held in a churchyard. The assemblies always started and ended with refrains of "Viva Uncle *Hô*! Viva the Communist Party!" She quickly learned to repeat the mantras with the requisite enthusiasm.

That was only the beginning of our new schedule of nonvoluntary celebratory activities.

Schools had closed after the fall of Saigon and did not reopen for several months. That July, I started the ninth grade at Lê Quý Đôn, the oldest high school in Saigon, built by the French in the 1870s. The new government now administered the school. We were to call our new principal Mr. Party Chief.

On the first day of class, every Saigon secondary-school student was informed that we were to attend a political rally. On the day of the rally, thousands of us students marched toward a football field in the northwestern part of the city, many kilometers from Lê Quý Đôn. The long line of students grew like an endless snake as more joined our procession. As the sun climbed toward white-hot midday, some students collapsed onto the dusty road. Ambulances stopped to treat the heat-exhausted teenagers, but our teachers urged us forward. The silent stares of families followed us as we trudged past rows upon rows of small wooden houses. Some scooped water from big clay jars and held the metal cups out to us. We broke from the line and gulped down the water, then rushed to catch up with our classmates. I had never walked so far in one day.

After about five hours, we arrived and arranged ourselves before a stage, where soldiers in green uniforms made speeches and led us in chants of "Viva Hồ Chí Minh!" I have no idea how many times I repeated that phrase over the next few years.

In the evenings, we were required to attend community meetings and "self-confessions," where we learned the jargon of this strange new world. No one used the real words for things; we spoke in euphemisms and slogans. At one meeting, a group leader told us about a young man who hanged himself. "He sacrificed his life," she declared. This was exactly how the new regime described soldiers who had died in battle. The language of war pervaded this new peace. The Communists asked us for sacrifices, as if we were soldiers going to fight. If we suffered, we were told to "turn our pain into strength."

The young man in the group leader's story had turned his pain into death instead. It occurred to me that "strength" was a clever euphemism for death. The dead were stronger than us all; they could endure anything.

There were many who exulted in this lofty new lexicon with the purity of absolute faith. I could see it in the eyes of the true-believer girl who ran through the neighborhood every day, calling us to come outside for the morning exercises. But for me, all those impassioned mantras were incomprehensible echoes in an empty room.

"LABOR IS TRIUMPH" was another slogan that the new regime repeated endlessly. "You must labor with all your energy." All day the loudspeaker intoned: *Be strong. Fight the enemy. Build the country.* Daydreaming about a different life was weakness, and weakness was forbidden.

Everyone was expected to contribute muscle and sweat to the government's plan to rebuild the country. Only one kind of labor counted: heavy physical work, such as growing rice, grinding rock, or cutting roads into a mountainside.

In the summer after my tenth-grade year, as part of a new national policy of "labor contribution," we students spent ten days working with soldiers and "Frontline Youth" volunteers to help build dams and irrigation systems in the countryside. The soldiers and frontliners received an extra ration, along with some clothes, shoes, and money. The students were considered a weaker class and we received no extras.

My labor contribution was to help build irrigation canals and raised beds for planting pineapples in Củ Chi, home of the famous network of tunnels used by North Vietnamese fighters during the war to travel and move supplies covertly from their bases to the outskirts of the city.

By this time Mae was with us in Saigon. I had never spent the night away from our place before, and Mae worried that I would have to work very hard without getting enough to eat. She packed preserved foods to send with me: pork belly with shrimp paste, fried with lemongrass and garlic. I cradled that jar of home like a treasure.

She also gave me most of the rice we had left for that month. I was grateful to Mae for sending the pure rice and preserved meats once I saw the food they had for us in Củ Chi. A small group of women volunteers cooked huge pots of rice mixed with wheat for the hundreds of workers. The burned gruel was worse than tasteless. The women were loud and mean and had the authority to decide how much porridge each person received.

When they realized I'd brought my own rice, they made me empty it into the communal pot. I watched regretfully as the pure white rice sank into the gray mush. Mae had sacrificed her own rations for me, and now they were wasted.

We slept in two rows of thirty bamboo beds in a long, open-air bamboo hut with a thatched roof and earthen floor. My two classmates and I were the only girls in a group of burly male workers, country boys with hardened backs and sunburned faces who had never been to school. They glared at us with contempt and called us "white-skinned" and "weak."

When I arrived at the irrigation canal, a loud man put a long, knife-sharp shovel into my hands. I had never used a shovel before. The tool intimidated me, but the loud man intimidated me more.

I hopped into the trench, which was nearly as deep as I was tall. Muddy water reached halfway up my calves. I plunged the huge shovel into the mud and struggled to pry the sticky clay free from the water's suction. I managed to fill the shovel with mud, but it was too heavy for me to fling up to the sides of the ditch.

"Useless student!" shouted a man who was around twenty years old. "Go sit over there, and I'll weave you a crown of grass! You can wear it like a queen." He was shirtless and muscular, with a sunburned chest smeared with mud.

A few minutes later, he called out to a friend of his, "Have you made that girl a grass crown yet?" Just then, a load of wet clay came free from his shovel and flew toward my head. Black lightning shot across my vision, and my ears throbbed. I sat very still and tried to hide my tears from the man. But I heard him ask, more quietly this time, "Is she crying?"

"You'd cry too if you got hit by a clod that big," said another man.

The loud, grass-crown man approached me. "I didn't mean to do that," he muttered, looking past me. "I didn't see you." After that, he left me alone.

In the evening after work, the students gathered by the shelter to listen to a boy who played the guitar skillfully. He strummed as I sang my mother's favorite old ballad, "The Smile of the Mountain Girl."

The chief of the shelter materialized out of the darkness. "Do you miss the 'rotten regime'?" he demanded, referring to the fallen government of South Vietnam. "Is that why you can't stop singing their songs?" We fell silent and stared at the ground until the chief went away.

I had stepped on a thorn early in the week, and by the fourth day of soaking in mud, the cut had become infected. I reported it to the chief. He stared at my swollen cut, then told me to swallow my pain and get back to work. And then he told the cooks that there was one patient who needed a special meal that night.

By then, I could barely walk on the infected foot, so a cook brought dinner to me in bed. "This is enough for you," she said, pouring me a thin soup of water with a bit of wheat in it. "You didn't work, so you don't need much." My classmates saved some of their dinner—the thicker bobor (rice porridge) with much more rice in it—to share with me.

By the next morning, the wound was red-hot and angry looking. "Brother, I tried to swallow my pain," I told the chief. "But I need to see a doctor." He looked outraged but gave in after I promised him that I would return as soon as my foot had healed. I limped two kilometers to the bus station and took a bus home.

A doctor treated my infection with antibiotics and sterile dressing, and I went back to the camp to finish my rotation. The bitter, sunburned youth who had loosed the mud clod no longer shouted at me; he saw my bandaged foot and found work for me that didn't require standing in mud. His hatred for me, it seemed, had cooled a few degrees.

AFTER THE CANAL-BUILDING camp, we returned to school to learn how to use an AK-47. We practiced taking it apart and reassembling it, then our instructors demonstrated the different firing positions: on foot, from a squat, and on our bellies. I was lousy at shooting, but at least I wasn't likely to be drafted. So many of the boys I knew at school went into the army. Later, in 1978, they would be sent to Cambodia to overthrow the Khmer Rouge and occupy the country. Many never came back.

In Saigon, the air was full of fear. We had to be careful with our words; if you dared to speak of South Vietnam or America, you would be shouted down or shushed. Even singing had become dangerous. The new regime outlawed the old songs Mae used to sing as she swung me in the hammock. The government called them "rotten music" or "gold songs" and said they would corrupt us and make us weak. To replace the songs they silenced, the regime's loudspeakers offered a daily repertoire of news reports and martial ballads. The nhạc đỏ—"red music"—focused on themes of skull-crushing and blood flow, and of soldiers saying goodbye to their mothers and dying happily on the battlefield for a better way of life. The news reports echoed these themes.

I've forgotten most of the songs and slogans from the loudspeakers and political meetings, but the literature lessons I remember well. At school, we memorized verses by the revolutionary poet Tố Hữu. His poems were about socialism and sabotage, victory and blood, just like the lyrics of the nhạc đỏ. But Tố Hữu wrote about these things in such romantic words, we believed them. When he described a soldier's death as nothing more than a tired farmer's well-earned sleep after the rice harvest was done, Tố Hữu made us feel that dying was as peaceful as drifting off to sleep. That we, too, might be content to let go of life for the good of our fellow citizens. How we students cried whenever we recited that poem! We were easily seduced by tales of love and sacrifice, so long as they were composed of beautiful phrases.

The Party's next big venture was the eradication of capitalism. Capitalists, they explained, were enemies of the people. Nguy—the Communists' epithet for South Vietnamese sympathizers—were traitors and puppets. Former South Vietnamese army officers were considered nguy of the worst kind. Several of my friends' fathers were sent to reha-bilitation camps, where malaria and malnutrition were quiet but effective executioners. The officers' families were expected to keep them fed. My best friend in high school, Kim Hoa, had eaten well during the war, thanks to her father's salary as a chief of police. Now the family saved scraps and every few months delivered leftover cured fish and dried pork to the forest rehabilitation camp where her father was imprisoned, an effort that only deepened their poverty.

Business owners also fared poorly under the new regime. They woke to late-night visits from police, who chased the capitalists from their homes and kept anything of value for themselves. Not even the dead were exempt from being evicted. The government declared the storied old French cemetery in central Saigon "corrupt," bulldozed its grandiose monuments, and exhumed the remains of the ex-elites who rested there.

Chanthu and I weren't sure which category applied to us: "nguy" or "the people." We certainly weren't rich capitalists, and we hoped that our minuscule sewing enterprise did not qualify as a bloodsucking activity. People had far less money to spend on new clothes after 1975, but my mother and sister still took in occasional embroidery work, and I would help as well. Fortunately, tiny businesses like Chanthu's weren't usually targeted.

I worked extra hard on my embroidery projects near Christmas, when we'd save the money for a proper Christmas feast: usually, beef stew and pâté. This stew was the only dish that included the now-hated pumpkin that I still enjoyed. In my mother's beef stew recipe, the pumpkin gives the dish a subtle sweetness.

Sometimes, we'd save our earnings for a sumptuous indulgence: bún bò Huế—the mighty soup of spicy beef and pork broth, enlivened with lemongrass, brimming with fat rice noodles, sliced pâté, beef, and pork, and piled high with basil, scallions, morning glory, and banana flower. Eating it made us feel like pampered monarchs. It was expensive, so we'd buy one bowl to share right before curfew and supplement the rich soup with leftover rice to fill our stomachs before bedtime.

I would never have sat still for so long over the tedious stitchery if not for the promise of bún bò Huế. Once, Chanthu woke at 1 a.m. to find me hunched over my needlework and shouted at me for staying up so late on a school night. For a taste of bún bò Huế, I would forego sleep or stab my fingers bloody. *That* was the kind of sacrifice I was willing to make.

I learned to make bún bò Huế from three sisters from Huế who sang with us in the church choir. I sometimes helped them cook meals for the group. Their father had been a general in the South Vietnamese army. After the war, the government took their stately old house and sent their father to reeducation camp. Now they lived in a small, dark house stained with smoke from the cooking fire.

The sisters taught me to make a perfect, clear broth, light on fish sauce but very spicy. They always seemed so cheerful, despite their diminished circumstances. And their bún bò Huế was the best I've ever had.

——————

Spicy Beef Noodle Soup in the Style of Huế (Bún bò Huế)

This dish from Central Vietnam is as popular as phở, but bolder and spicier. You can adapt the proteins, herbs, and toppings to your preferences; the real magic is in building the layers of flavor in the stock and the chili-infused aromatics. Add a portion of the lemongrass-chili condiment to the stock according to your heat preferences, and set aside the rest so people can spice up their own bowls.
Serves 6 to 8

Ingredients:
For the stock:
4 pounds beef bones, such as oxtail, neck, marrowbone, and/or knuckle, cut into 2-inch pieces
2 pounds pork hock, leg, or neck bone, cut into 2-inch pieces
1 pound beef, such as flank or shank
1 pound pork, such as loin (optional)
1 tomato
1 yellow onion, quartered
8 to 12 stalks lemongrass, cut into thirds and bruised

For the soup:

⅓ cup neutral oil

2 teaspoons annatto seeds

4 large shallots, minced

3 to 4 cloves garlic, minced

2 stalks lemongrass, finely minced

2 tablespoons dried red chili flakes (or reconstituted dried chili)

2 teaspoons shrimp paste

3 tablespoons sugar

2 tablespoons fish sauce

½ teaspoon salt (or more to taste)

1 to 2 (14- to 16-ounce) packages round, thicker rice noodles (bún), approximately the thickness of spaghetti (you can usually find packages labeled "bún bò Huế")

For serving: Chả lụa, thinly sliced (optional; see "Notes on Ingredients, Techniques, and Supplies"); cilantro sprigs; Thai basil sprigs; scallions, thinly sliced; bean sprouts; lime wedges; red cabbage, shredded (optional); yellow onion, thinly sliced; Thai red chilies or jalapeños, thinly sliced; banana flower (optional; see "Notes on Ingredients, Techniques, and Supplies" for prep tips)

Prepare the stock: In a large stockpot, quickly parboil bones and hock, then rinse the solids and scrub the pot. (This makes a clearer broth.)

Return bones and hock to stockpot, then add beef, pork, tomato, onion, and lemongrass stalks. Refill pot with cold water (about 5 quarts) to cover the solids, bring to a boil, then reduce heat to a gentle simmer. Skim foam from the surface. Periodically check beef and pork for doneness; pork may be done in a half hour or less, whereas larger, tougher beef cuts could require 1 to 3 hours.

When cuts are tender and cooked through, remove them, cover, and refrigerate. Continue simmering bones, vegetables, and lemongrass for 2 to 3 hours more, then remove the solids, set aside oxtail/pork hocks, and strain stock through a fine-mesh sieve.

Make the soup: While the stock is simmering, heat oil in a medium skillet over medium heat and sauté annatto seeds until oil turns golden red, about a minute. Remove seeds, then sauté shallots, garlic, lemongrass, chili flakes, and shrimp paste until shallots and garlic soften, 2 to 3 minutes. Add sugar, fish sauce, and salt, and stir until a loose paste forms and begins to smell tantalizing. Transfer ¼ to ½ of the paste into the stock and simmer for a half hour more. Reserve remaining paste to serve as a condiment.

Meanwhile, cook noodles. Drain, rinse with cold water, and set aside.

Taste the soup and adjust fish sauce, salt, and sugar. You'll know it's right when your cheeks flush with spice-heat and pleasure.

To serve, slice beef (and pork, if using) thinly against the grain. Pick meat from the oxtail and pork from the hock (or whatever you used to make the stock). Divide cooked noodles among the bowls, add sliced beef and pulled pork (and chả lụa, if using), then pour hot stock over everything. Artfully arrange vegetables, herbs, and limes on a platter for guests to add to their bowls. Serve with ramekins of remaining lemongrass-chili condiment.

———

ANOTHER CAPITALISM-ERASING TASK of the new regime was abolishing the old currency. We had to bring all of our cash to a district office and trade our South Vietnamese đồng for liberation đồng—at an exchange rate that decimated our savings. What little we had was now worth a fraction of its previous value.

Not to worry! our comrades assured us. The new regime would henceforth be taking control of staples like rice, meat, fish, and sugar. Each family would receive a ration book that entitled us to price-controlled monthly supplies from the communal store.

And with that transition, our menu options declined even more dramatically.

We were to follow the Party slogan: "Work with all your vigor and collect what you need." My sister commented that the communist ideal sounded like the Catholic notion of Heaven: work together and share, and you will not want for anything. I couldn't detect any sarcasm in her commentary, but I found the new policy difficult to accept. Maybe it was the soft little Battambang girl in me, the one who'd had all the new clothes and treats she wanted. But it seemed to me that a discrepancy existed between the ideal and its implementation. The equation seemed weighted toward vigorous work and light on the what-you-need side.

I quickly deduced that this new rationing math wasn't as simple as the slogan implied; the rules were in constant flux. Initially, we were to receive nine kilos of rice per month. That sounded reasonable to us. But the next month, we were only alloted three kilos of rice. "Three kilos of potato equals one kilo of rice," we were told, and so we received two of our three kilos of rice in the form of six kilos of potatoes.

We did not agree with the formula, 1 kg rice = 3 kg potato. According to our own theorem, rice was not a variable that could be halved or thirded or replaced with inferior starches. Rice was food itself to us, whereas potatoes were an occasional snack or a poor man's food—plus, I hated them.

Some staples are more equal than others.

Soon, the math became even more baffling. The following month, the authorities declared triumphantly, "Now you will receive not merely rice and potato, but also cassava!" As if by deducting rice and adding cassava, we had been granted a wealth of options, instead of being deprived of the one thing we actually wanted.

The month after that, it was announced that the potato ration would again decrease—initially an exciting prospect, as we had consumed quite enough potato. But the Party replaced the potato deficit with a stone-hard, whole-wheat bread, made from bad Soviet flour and fortified with small black insects.

Our meat and fish rations were often only theoretical. We were promised five hundred grams of pork or one kilo of fat per family each month. Sometimes we actually received these items. The quantity of fish we could get our hands on depended on how much the communal store had on any given day. There was no beef included in this ration—no explanation given.

Everything we received was recorded in the ration book my sister kept for our family. Losing that book was not an option; we had to produce it at the distribution center every month in order to receive our allotments. The challenge was figuring out which distribution center was the correct one on any given date. The district chiefs notified us by sending an officer around the district with a bullhorn. "It's time for *riiiiiice*!" the announcer would call out. "It's time for *fiiiish*!" Once we heard the officer's cries, no matter the time of day or night, everyone raced to the center for a prime spot in the queue. As the youngest in our family, it was my job to listen for the announcement and run to the supply queues.

More often than not, the center had run out of food by the time I reached the front of the queue. In those cases, there was no choice but to trudge home and wait for the next announcement.

Most of Saigon lived in a state of sleepless vigilance, ready to run at any moment. It reminded me of the story of Jesus in the garden of Gethsemane, asking his disciples to stay awake with him in his last hours. I liked the idea of Jesus there with me, urging me to alertness. And I wondered if my sister's analogy could possibly be right: If Heaven were anything like this utopia, would I spend Eternity chasing after rations?

THIS NEW SAIGON was tasteless and colorless, devoid of the flavors I craved. Every month we received whatever combination of potatoes, cassava, rice, bug-bread, whole wheat grains, and substandard noodles the Party deemed edible. We sliced the cassava and dried it, then mixed everything together in one pot and choked down the gray, horrible mash. Eating it made us feel that we had devolved from human beings to pigs, forced to swallow slop from a trough. We had no idea what to do with the grains of wheat, which were difficult to chew, so we just threw them in with the rest.

I wish I could provide a recipe here for some culinary magic that could transform cassava-rice-noodle-potato mash into a palatable meal. The best we could manage was to boil the mash with a stock made from a chicken's neck or head. I can only advise you to apply your best techniques, then garnish your bowl of mash with plenty of scallions, sliced elegantly on the diagonal—simple, but chic. A culinary euphemism for obscuring bitter truths.

SAIGON WAS PLUNGED into a new sort of food insecurity, in which even rice had been transformed into a luxury. We only permitted ourselves meals of pure rice when we were ill and could not keep down the usual gruel. I rarely threw up the utopian rations, because I didn't fill my stomach with them in the first place. I ate less and less, and my body shrank accordingly. Truth is, I was thrilled with my new, wasp-slim waist—if not with my new diet.

People became obsessed with hunting for decent food. The government allowed a limited number of independent stands, small stores, and coffee shops to operate. At those markets, we could find extra vegetables (usually eggplant); small and foul-smelling fish; sugar, salt, and MSG; and less desirable chicken parts, like the feet, bones, and heads. I ate so many chicken feet and necks after 1975 that I actually came to love those cuts—there's something satisfying about sucking the meat from a bone. I see it as a metaphor for my Year of the Buffalo birthright. Anything I wanted, I had to fight for it, like stripping the meager flesh from a chicken neck. The hard work sweetens the reward.

Fish had also become a rare commodity. Big, fresh fish had ceased to be available in Saigon. Occasionally, we could find good-sized sea fish in the market, cut into thin strips, but it was old, soft, and foul-smelling, like prahok. Decent small fish were available at the Party market five kilometers away. But instead of walking that far, we bought it from our neighbor, who left at 3 a.m. to buy her family's ration, then sold it in our little street market at a small profit. That fish smelled very strong after languishing for so many hours in the sun, with no ice to keep it fresh.

Shrimp and prawns were even more difficult to come by. Anyone caught selling a shrimp or prawn larger than a person's finger would go to jail, or so we were warned. If you wanted a taste of contraband protein, vendors would smuggle the meat inside their trouser leg and arrange a covert meeting for the transaction.

Market police wearing red armbands patrolled constantly, wielding their whistles like weapons. A fog of confusion surrounded the laws about which kinds of commerce were illegal and which were permissible. And even when selling was legal, vendors were taxed heavily. People whispered that every year, the government doubled that tax. If vendors failed to pay on time, a police officer would close the store and confiscate their inventory.

Certain varieties of commerce had become a dangerous political act.

THROUGH IT ALL, I was gradually turning my pain into strength. "With strength, we can make gravel into rice," the Party said. I had seen this with my own eyes: A soft, useless little girl from Battambang was becoming someone else, someone useful.

I absorbed a lot in those Party meetings and during my brief work as an inept canal digger at the pineapple plantation. I learned not to show weakness. I learned to avoid trouble with the sunburned boys who despised us, and to understand them better. When they called us weak students and wondered why we were still in school as teenagers, we knew what they were really asking: *Why are you allowed to study while I must work and fight?*

They sometimes misused their authority over us, shouting and sneering. But it was useful to remember that for all their lives, they'd had so little, and I'd had everything. I *was* weak, and they had always had to be so strong.

I was sure the boy who bullied me in the irrigation canal didn't go to the doctor if he had a cut on his foot. His mother hadn't packed preserved pork for him in a jar. And he certainly did not cry over lost pâté de foie. He had never expected such richness from life in the first place and was less inclined to feel disappointed by how little of it was delivered. What right did I have to such sumptuous flavors in the first place? And who was I to complain about drab rations that, at least, filled an empty belly? It was, in the most literal sense possible, "what you need."

The Communists had transformed Saigon and narrowed our choices. But they were right about one thing: Pain could become power. I saw that alchemy at work in how our troubles had changed Chanthu, how she seemed able to handle anything, even a bullet to the chest.

I watched. I kept quiet. I sang the new songs, memorized the poems, and followed the new rules, no matter how arbitrary.

The rules for ration queues include (but are not limited to) the following:

1. Do not lose your ration book. Ever.
2. Be ready to run to the distribution point at a moment's notice.
3. Learn to wait.
4. While waiting, adopt an inscrutable facial expression.
5. Do not display impatience with the slowness of the queue.
6. Do not display hunger symptoms, visibly or audibly.
7. Do not question the logic of the ration queue. There is none.

8. Do not question the decision of the authority figure at the front of the ration queue, even if it means you return home without any rice.
9. Do not question the Party's definition of *need*.
10. Do not question Party mathematics.
11. Locate the internal organ that controls righteous indignation and kill it dead.

These rules are subject to change with no notice. Be prepared to change your plans accordingly.

7. Silken Rebellion Fish Fry

Hunger helps you eat even food that has gone bad.
—Vietnamese proverb

FOLLOWING THE NEW rules was essential to preserving the body. But small acts of internal resistance were essential to preserving the mind.

The high-flown rhetoric flowed ceaselessly, booming from loudspeakers and the mouths of our teachers, in political meetings, and from revolutionary songs and posters. The empty phrases ate into our sanity; the artless art dulled our senses.

It didn't take long to realize that the recipe for building theoretical utopias was not to my taste. It was a simple process of (mostly) subtraction: remove choices. Deduct harmless indulgences, personal expression, and culinary creativity. Add a pinch of patriotic slogans and songs. Garnish with banners and stars.

We were lucky to have our lives at all, of course. But they were not lives of our choosing. We couldn't work for our own happiness because we were expected to sacrifice for the happiness of everyone. It was a beautiful notion. But the reality bore little resemblance to the triumphant images of smiling workers and prosperous farmers.

Working for everyone felt like working for no one. It was like tossing your mother's fragrant white rice into a pot of dishwatery porridge—an equality of uniform drabness.

We had no thought of resistance in any practical sense. For us, resisting simply meant staving off despair—by finding solace in the small pleasures we were supposed to renounce. And by surviving. But occasionally, it meant minuscule acts of insubordination, which served no purpose except to safeguard a private mental refuge that felt almost like freedom.

Here is my recipe for quiet defiance under an authoritarian regime:

Recipe: Silken Rebellion

Find the pockets of freedom available to you. Exploit loopholes. Play the role of a defeated subject when necessary. Remain undefeated in the important ways, wherever possible.

Work with all your vigor, but don't expect to receive what you need. Definitions of *need* may prove wildly variable under certain regimes. Be vigilant about the shifting definitions of other previously familiar words, such as *loyalty* and *independence*. Don't let propagandists or revolutionary poets corrupt your vocabulary.

Determine what you need and find a way to get it for yourself. It will not necessarily be supplied to you, no matter how earnest the promises.

Maintaining internal resistance is a tricky undertaking. I learned the techniques from my mother. Her mastery of strategic disobedience—disguised as moonlight-dutifulness—showed me how the task might be accomplished. I absorbed her stories about defying the dictatorship of her mother-in-law. And the culinary uprisings she mounted in her Saigon kitchen showed me that we did not have to surrender to dreary-gray blandness.

Southeast Asian women have long been well placed to gain mountains of expertise in soft, silken power. We have no muscle to flex, so we learn to exert our influence in the way of flowers: Charm and guile can accomplish a great deal. Raised in a strict Asian tradition, I had few opportunities to exercise my talent for insubordination. I was taught to keep silent and do as I was told without complaint. But like a mouse greedy for kitchen scraps, I could sniff out the tiniest cracks to wriggle through and perpetrate some small act of defiance. Minor criminality, or at least thought crime, was a life raft for a small refugee girl with mutiny in her heart.

Free will is a muscle. It requires exercise.

Generally, my little insurgencies were so inconsequential as to be absurd—like, say, the improper handling of garlic as a purely symbolic act of sabotage.

I had been summoned to a district Party office to help cook for some large celebration honoring our soldier-liberators. Each household had to supply a pair of hands. My sister's hands were busy, so Chanthu and Mae sent mine. This was not a request we could ignore. Openly disobeying any Party order, no matter how small, could bring a barrage of sanctimony upon our heads: "You are a traitor, a follower of the South," the refrain would go. Already, we were treated like sinners because we had lived under the South Vietnamese regime.

We were especially wary in the presence of low-level functionaries who ran the local offices or volunteered for collective missions like celebratory food preparation or announcing the morning exercises. Often, these types were zealots, the kinds of unspectacular sycophants who would have been ignored by respectable people in ordinary times, but were suddenly elevated to minor positions of power. Their faces glowed with faith and unearned self-importance. Who knew when they might make it their mission to root out quiet apostates and denounce them?

Worse yet, you could never tell what variety of partisan you were dealing with: the true believer or the canny cynic with a malevolent agenda. Both were dangerous and unpredictable.

The unhinged diehard at the food-prep collective was a woman from my neighborhood whom I usually took pains to avoid. That day, she gave me a five-kilo basket of garlic and ordered me to start peeling cloves for a giant feast of pork curry. As I worked, she chattered inanely about the neighborhood soldiers, praising their essential proletarian righteousness. "He is so *lovely*!" she declared of one soldier after another, until I was ready to stuff her mouth with unpeeled garlic cloves.

She took a short break from her laudation of soldiery to correct my garlic-peeling methodology. "Here, use the knife to smash and break the garlic," she instructed ostentatiously. "You can peel it much faster this way." I didn't answer her. But I quietly peeled each clove of garlic my own way, one by one, as slowly as humanly possible. At 5 p.m., I told her I had to go home and cook for my mother. I had served my half-day, so she had to let me go, even though most of the garlic remained unpeeled.

Ignoring her instructions was a delicious pleasure.

Even at home, I had quiet ways of rebelling—and getting what I wanted. You might also call it manipulation. If Mae lost her patience and chastised me, I never talked back; I simply made myself disappear. For hours, or even days, I would avoid eye contact and speak not a word. At mealtimes, I would practice looking aggrieved and eat only a few bites of rice.

This strategy never failed. The following day, my mother would always bribe me back to life by splurging on banh sung, an exquisite street-food salad comprised of fat rice noodles rolled by hand and served with thin threads of pork, fried spring rolls, crunchy fresh vegetables, and two delicious sour-sweet sauces.

Banh sung was Mae's way of making peace. Whenever her anger flared, I always knew I would be having that dish the next day. The portions were small and the price was high because each noodle took so long for the vendor to shape by hand.

KIM HOA WAS my frequent partner-in-crime. She and I shared everything. If one of us managed to procure a treat—a colorfully wrapped candy, a guava, or a green mango dipped in chili salt—we would bite it in two and each take half. Some afternoons we used the breakfast money Chanthu gave me to buy movie tickets. We saw propaganda films from Poland, the

USSR, and East Germany, but others were superb films about music, art, or love. One of our favorites was *Le Petit Poucet*, a French fairy tale about a poor boy whose starving parents abandon him and his siblings in the forest during a famine. Little Poucet is small but smart, a tiny survivor. When hungry birds devour his bread-crumb trail and foil his plan to escape the forest, he formulates a new plan: outsmarting a murderous ogre to save his brothers and stealing the monster's magic boots to make a fortune for himself.

Hoa and I enjoyed the story of the luckless boy who turned disaster into triumph using his wits. We enjoyed each other, too; it was an easy and immediate affinity. Like me, Hoa had grown up in an educated family, with plenty to eat. But the fall of Saigon had carried her family's fortunes down with it.

She was talented at Vietnamese traditional dancing—graceful in her flowing áo dài, as she held a candle in each hand, bending so far backward her head touched the floor. We didn't have to share our secrets to understand each other. I preferred to laugh with her and keep my sorrows to myself. We walked to school in the morning, cooking up plots against our classmates or holding heated debates about religion. She came from a Buddhist family, but she didn't believe in Buddha—or any religion, for that matter. She was an incorrigible rebel, the most irreverent person I've ever known. If you told her she would go to hell if she stamped on a picture of Jesus, she would do it right then and there.

She feared nothing: not divine authority, not the minor Party functionaries who ruled over our lives and our studies. The more earnestly a teacher or principal declared his ideological purity, the more Hoa hungered to mock him. She laughed like crazy anytime someone extolled the greatness of our ally in the Caribbean: *Cu* was a slang term for "penis," and *ba* meant "father," so the phrase "Viva Cuba" absolutely slayed her.

Anyone could end up on the wrong side of a Kim Hoa practical joke, even an authority figure. Teachers received extra rations, and our high school math instructor had brought his cabbage head to class and had it out on his desk. He was not popular with the students. He enjoyed humiliating us in front of our peers, and we did not respect him. So when he left the room, Hoa shouted, "Hide it, hide it!" We stashed it in a classmate's desk drawer.

The math teacher became sweaty and short of breath as he ran up and down the stairs, searching for his vegetable. Eventually, we took pity on him and returned the cabbage. He turned red and shouted, "Eat it yourselves! Just eat it, all of you!" We felt guilty about the joke—rations were precious. But we still called him Mr. Cabbage for the rest of the year.

Hoa always dragged me into the middle of trouble, but I was a willing fellow traveler. I worshipped her brazenness. Every day, she passed me notes during class. One day, instead of a note, I received a packet of sticky rice with one bite left for me. Hoa had stolen it from the head of the class, a bearlike girl named Nhu who sat in the front row. As the rice moved toward me in the back row, everyone took a bite and passed it back. Nhu didn't speak to us for several weeks after that.

Hoa and I could make a game of anything. We competed to see who could scribble in a notebook the fastest; consequently, our notes were illegible. But a friend of mine named Tuấn offered to rescue our scrawled class notes. He knew I was awful at drawing the maps we had to memorize, so he offered to copy my messy but thorough history notes into a more presentable form if he could share them with our classmates; in return, he would draw maps for me.

Tuấn always had a scheme. He was a year ahead of me, the smartest boy in his class. Soon, we began exchanging secret smiles.

"He only looks at you," people teased, but I said I had no idea what they were talking about. Then Tuấn and I started leaving letters, or small gifts of fruit, in each other's desk drawers. He always wore crisp white shirts and jeans and a big, honest smile.

Tuấn didn't finish high school. He was drafted at eighteen, but for some reason, he didn't have to fight the Khmer Rouge in Cambodia, like most of the boys did. Instead, he was stationed at army headquarters in Tây Ninh, near the Cambodian border. He visited me when he was on leave. He was courteous and attentive to my mother and sister, so they loved him. "This boy is nice and polite," Mae said. "You can talk to him." And then he and I would go to the veranda to chat.

I REMEMBER THE day Hoa earned her nickname. She had made me a bookmark from the leaf of a Bodhi tree, usually grown on pagoda grounds. She soaked the leaf in rice rinse water until only the vein was left, then dyed it a bright color. Hoa forgot she'd given me the leaf, so when I opened the book to my bookmark, she dove for it and cried, "That's mine!"

We were in class when she shouted it out and our teacher was delivering a lecture about Cambodian prehistory: "Ancient Cambodia was formed from two countries: Chiêm Thành and Sonla," he droned. In Vietnamese, *đất nước* means "country"—or literally, "soil and water," but he used the shortened version: *nước* ("water"). Hoa suddenly realized the teacher had stopped lecturing and was staring right at her. "Stand up!" he commanded. "Tell me what nước formed the old Cambodia?" After a long silence, he began mocking her, shifting to the word's alternate meaning: "What kind of nước? Fresh water or seawater?" he sneered.

"Nước cam!" she said. Orange juice. The class exploded with laughter. "Hoa nước cam" was her nickname from that day forward. The history instructor's face turned deep red as he struggled not to laugh with us. He soon gave up on reestablishing order and walked out of the classroom.

Orange Juice Hoa and I always found each other after school, joking our way through the afternoon tasks the chief teacher of our class assigned us—usually, opening and closing the gate for students coming and going.

Sometimes we'd pool our change to buy ice cream. Our favorite was kem chuối, a flattened frozen banana shot through with strands of coconut flesh, roasted peanut, and sometimes avocado. It is delicious and refreshing on a hot day (and easy to make).

I spent three years of high school sharing snacks, laughter, and

everything else with Kim Hoa. Those were some of my happiest times in
Saigon.

━━━━━━

Banana Ice Pops (Kem chuối)

These frozen banana treats are a popular street snack in Vietnam. Ice
pops made with smashed bananas, shredded coconut, and crushed
peanuts are delicious on their own, but a coating of sweetened coconut
cream makes them even more decadent. You could even press in a thin
slice of perfectly ripe avocado.

Ingredients:
1 (13.5-ounce) can coconut cream
2 tablespoons palm, cane, or light brown sugar
½ teaspoon salt
1 tablespoon cornstarch (or a slurry of 1 tablespoon tapioca starch
and ¼ cup water)
8 very ripe lady finger bananas (or 4 regular ripe bananas cut in
half)
½ cup shredded coconut, toasted
½ cup unsalted roasted peanuts, crushed

Special equipment:
Parchment paper
Plastic wrap (or resealable plastic bags)
8 ice pop sticks

In a medium saucepan, bring coconut cream, sugar, salt, and
cornstarch to a simmer over medium heat. Cook, stirring, until
mixture thickens slightly, about 5 minutes.

Peel bananas, then place between sheets of parchment paper.
Using a cutting board, flatten bananas to about ¼ to ½ inch thick.

Transfer each banana to plastic wrap, spoon 1 to 2 tablespoons of coconut cream over the banana, and press ½ tablespoon toasted coconut and ½ tablespoon crushed peanuts into that side. Turn banana over and repeat on the other side. Push an ice pop stick lengthwise into each banana, seal tightly in plastic wrap (or small, resealable plastic bags), and freeze for at least 4 hours.

AFTER GRADUATION, I rarely saw Kim Hoa. She got married soon after high school and invited me to the wedding. I had no money for a gift, so I didn't attend. She had been important to me. But there were so many losses to grieve in those days, the part of me that missed her seemed to dissolve in all the other heartaches.

Without my brilliant bad-idea friend, I turned to more solitary guilty pleasures. One thing the Communists hadn't taken away was the bookshops. They were everywhere, and I loved to linger there after school and page through stories of romance, adventure, and sacrifice. I was hungry for escape, and those stories offered tastes of a sweeter life. If I skipped breakfast, I'd sometimes have enough money to rent the latest Vietnamese novel.

Years later, when the regime started to relax the postwar austerity measures and open up a bit, I read a novel about a soldier from the North who falls in love with a girl from the South. "Love is weakness," the Party tells them, and forces her to leave her lover's jungle camp. While hiking in the rain to her own camp, she slips into a stream and drowns. The book hints that her fall is no accident, that someone has killed her because her pregnancy has been discovered.

Grief shatters the young solder's faith. Suddenly, he imagines himself as a horse with a bundle of green grass dangling in front of him. No matter how long he walks, he will never taste the grass.

The promised utopia would forever remain just out of reach.

I was amazed. Throughout my years in postwar Saigon—we never got used to calling it Hồ Chí Minh City—I thought the soldiers from the North had never doubted their cause. On both sides of that divide, it seemed, there was little room for uncertainty.

But slowly, we discovered that we had all believed tall tales and myths about people from the other side of the seventeenth parallel. The soldiers from the North expected to find us Southerners living in darkness, in the thrall of devils. A Northern school friend told me his father had lied to him: they were shocked when they marched into Saigon and found tall buildings, bustling streets, and civilization proceeding as normal.

Even before the wars, there had long been a cultural divide between North and South. The stereotypical Northerner was rigid and formal, while Southerners were seen as friendly, but uncultured. In the South, we called Northerners "morning glories," while their nickname for us was "bean sprouts." These nicknames were more than just reflections of the regions' most popular vegetables; they were mild slurs, not intended kindly.

Even the cuisines are different. Southern dishes tend toward the oily and fried. Southern hủ tiếu broths are made from pork knee and topped with pork belly and garlic, whereas in the North, broth for phở is a simple stock of beef bones and meat, with less fat and topped with onions. Northerners eat boiled vegetables dipped in fish sauce, while Southerners like their vegetables fried. Compare also Southerners' beloved sizzling crepe dish, bánh xèo, to its restrained Northern cousin: bánh cuốn, a dish made from delicate fermented rice sheets, steamed and filled with chopped meat and mushrooms, topped with boiled bean sprouts and a few slivers of fresh herbs.

Culinary differences aside, the civil war had made the cultural and ideological divisions between North and South ever starker: We were told that the North Vietnamese were brainwashed savages who cared nothing for human life, willing to sacrifice themselves, their families, and their lovers for the ideology of their Party.

Of course, that was all nonsense—we'd been fed wartime propaganda just like they had. And as that novel about the Northern soldier reminded me, we were all, on both sides, equally human and capable of heartbreak.

THE REGIME RELAXED the strict rules of rationing a bit during Tết, the Lunar New Year and the biggest holiday of the year in Vietnam—an acknowledgment, perhaps, of human needs beyond basic sustenance. For Tết, we were allowed to have a few extras—specifically, ingredients for bánh chưng and bánh dầy, square "earth cakes" and round "sky cakes" traditionally prepared for New Year celebrations. In the South, we made bánh tét, a similar glutinous rice cake in a cylindrical shape. It's made with mung bean, sticky rice, and pork (or sometimes a bit of dry, salty fish), then boiled and wrapped elaborately in a banana leaf.

The Vietnamese tell a folk tale about how earth and sky cakes came to be. Long ago, a king proclaimed that his sons should each prepare a dish to bring to the palace, to honor their ancestors for the New Year. One of the princes, unlike his brothers, had chosen a humble country life, far from the pomp of the palace. This prince, named Liêu, lacked the means to prepare a fancy gourmet dish.

That night, he dreamed of his mother. She assured him that he didn't need exotic ingredients or fancy techniques to prepare an exquisite dish. If he cooked something with love and sincerity, it would be worthy of anyone, including his regal father. Liêu asked the dream-mother for a little more detail, or possibly a recipe, but she declined to go into specifics. Instead, she gestured cryptically toward the surrounding rice fields, one eyebrow cocked meaningfully: *Hint, hint!*

By morning, Liêu had grasped what the apparition had been trying to say: *Make rice, young man.* What better way to respect the ancestors than to prepare a dish that even the poorest farmer could make? Such a dish would celebrate both the past and the land itself.

Liêu molded bean paste and sweet rice into squares (to represent the earth) and circles (to pay homage to the sky) and wrapped them in green leaves. Everything had come from the fields on his own land; nothing was wasted.

Those simple cakes pleased his father far more than the exquisite delicacies his brothers had traveled far and wide to procure: a delicate sea fish with chili and lotus; wild boar and ferns from distant mountains. Liêu had proven his wisdom and humility, so the king passed on the realm to him.

As king, Liêu taught his people to prepare the earth and sky cakes every year at Tết to place in the household altar, as an offering to those who came before.

Of course, there are various iterations of this fable, involving fairies and wizened old men offering culinary tips. But this one is my favorite. I prefer the dream-mother to all the other folk-tale messengers. These days, I wish my own mother would turn up at night to advise me on recipes. If she did, I would ask her the secret to her bánh tét. The cake was so big, it had to boil for twelve hours. She used a half-kilo of glutinous rice, then mixed in grated coconut and added pork fat to the middle instead of the traditional pork belly.

How I wish I could have her cake again! After working on it all night, we would unwrap the first one and eat it hot, the sweet-savory coconut and pork-fat flavors filling our whole bodies with rapture.

Decades later, I made the cakes for my children. I was missing Mae and wishing my children, Clara and Johan, had their grandmother. The cakes took all day to wrap and all night to boil, but it was cheerful work. I lay in a hammock by the cookpot for twelve hours, stoking the fire every hour or so. It reminded me of long days by the charcoal fire with Chanthu and Mae. But the spell was broken when I tasted the cake: It did not taste like my mother's.

Home is an unstable phantom. It can dissolve at the slightest unfamiliar flavor.

FOR A FEW days every year, the New Year cakes distracted us from our hungry longings. Any such break from our drab culinary routine was welcome. Sometimes we would discover an impossible artifact, a treasure from the past. Saigon markets were a strange lottery. Usually, you found the same bland nothing, but on occasion, something marvelous would appear.

One day, my sister found a piece of trei ngeat Angkor, a large fish left to cure for two days, then salted and dried in the sun. The very best trei ngeat hailed from the Tonlé Sap, the great Cambodian lake not far from Battambang. Back home we'd often had a big dried fish hanging high up in the kitchen; my sister would cut off a sliver and grill it over charcoal.

When Chanthu came home smiling one day with this salty piece of pre-war Battambang in her bag, we were delighted beyond all reason.

Anything could set off a discussion about food, or our memories of food: a growling stomach, the aroma of fresh soup in the market. And whenever we started talking, I asked questions and listened closely. I observed, remembered, and repeated whatever my mother and sister said about the old recipes. And I always did my best to copy their techniques in the kitchen.

One of my favorite make-do dishes from these lean years was my mother's lemongrass fried fish. Mae concocted a simple potion of diced garlic, lemongrass, chili, and salt—all ingredients even a poor refugee could obtain—and cast a spell upon the old, putrid fish we would buy from our neighbor in the market. The salt toughened the soft flesh a bit, and the fragrant lemongrass hid the odor of too-old fish.

Chopping the lemongrass was always my job. You have to cut off the root and the ends of the stalk, then remove the tough outer layers to get to the softer inner part. Slice the stalk in half, lengthwise; with the flat side down, it's easier to cut. You'll want to pound the inner stalk a bit and dice it very fine; this will flood your kitchen with a powerful aroma of bright citrus.

I still fry Mae's lemongrass-chili fish almost every week. I love the assault of chili and too-much salt, to remind me of how, in Saigon, we mastered the art of culinary disguise. For us, restoring flavor to the tasteless, gray palate of our lives felt like a tiny act of rebellion.

If you ever find yourself in a resource-poor environment, I recommend the magical properties of garlic, chili, and lemongrass. They taste almost like prosperity, or at least make you forget, for a moment, what you're missing.

As a bonus: the strong flavors linger in your mouth for hours, making you think you just ate moments ago.

The lemongrass-fried fish lives on in the altar of my mind, a simple and exquisite homage to Mae, who taught me the art of rebelling as quietly as a whisper of silk.

Silken Rebellion Fish Fry
(*or* How to Make Unfresh Fish Taste Rather Delicious)

This is an excellent training dish for a teenage refugee girl who is learning to cook. It is also useful for turning spoiled girls into useful household members, and for transforming spoiled fish into a palatable meal. Finally, it's a powerful weapon in the arsenal of any resourceful cook faced with a poverty of resources, because of its cheap ingredients and big flavors. (Note: This treatment also works well to enliven plain tofu.)
Serves 4

Ingredients:
2 pounds old fish
Too much salt
6 to 8 stalks lemongrass (white part only), minced
8 to 10 cloves garlic, minced
At least 4 Thai red chilies, minced
1 cup neutral oil

Buy the least rotten fish you can find in the communal store or from your neighbor in the market. Grind down a knife edge as sharp as you can get it—the better to chop the tough lemongrass stalks into fine granules. In a bowl, let fish sit for 1 to 2 hours in too much salt, chopped lemongrass, garlic, and a vast quantity of chili. Overdoing it on the salt and chili will make your eyes water and imbue the old fish with a taste of forgetfulness—the idea is for you to forget that this is a very bad fish, indeed. You want to taste salt and chili, not bad fish.

In a medium skillet, heat oil over high heat. Turn the heat down and fry fish slowly, until golden and crisp. Eat it with jasmine rice. If a bad-fish memory reasserts itself, season with more salt and chili as needed.

8. Chanthu's Tofu Venture

The fining pot is for silver, and the furnace for gold:
but the Lord trieth the hearts.
—Proverbs 17:3

THE LITTLE ROUND box was stored in a chest under the bed. It was a handsome old French box that had once held some delicacy—cakes or cookies, maybe. The lid was decorated with gold trim and a red rose. As a preteen, I loved the box and would sometimes pull it out to admire it. There was nowhere in our Saigon house to keep it locked up, although its contents would determine our futures.

Every time I slid it out from its hiding place, the box seemed a little bit lighter. Over the years in Vietnam, our family's small cache of gold necklaces and earrings—the box's treasured contents—gradually disappeared, until one day, I removed the box from its hiding place to find it empty. I didn't understand at the time that my mother was selling the pieces of gold for food.

The one piece of jewelry we had left, as far as I knew, was a gold necklace that Chanthu wore under her shirt. It was her only inheritance. One day, she came home from the market with her shirt torn at the neck and the necklace gone. She and my mother shared furious whispers, and Chanthu wept over her washing chores.

I didn't dare to ask what had happened. In that time and place, a young girl had no right to demand explanations. So I learned to be a detective, to discern truth from partial information. Even today, I can see clues in people's faces and assemble their stories from what I perceive.

That necklace was our last piece of gold.

FORTUNATELY, WE STILL had Chanthu, my golden sister—our family's living treasure even in the worst of times. She never seemed defeated by our worsening circumstances. She always came up with some new idea for making money, with the energy to spare for implementing it.

When I was in my second year of high school, Chanthu asked our neighbor to teach her to make fresh tofu. With her newfound skill, my sister started a small side business making tofu to sell at the suburban market.

Her hard work kept hunger a few steps further from our door. With the extra money she made, we could afford fresh river fish every so often. Or a bit of pork on the black market, bought on the sly and slipped under a pant leg—and later, into a delicious soup.

Sometimes we would share a decadent breakfast of hủ tiếu—better known as kuy teav to us Khmer-speaking transplants, who were hungry for something reminiscent of home. Even for me, the former kuy teav hater, scarcity and nostalgia had redeemed the dish, which I now slurped down happily whenever we could get it.

Mae and Chanthu got up at midnight to start making the tofu, so it would be perfectly fresh at 6 a.m. when they offered it for sale. Our neighbors made a much larger quantity of the tofu than we did, but they cooked it with coal from the northern mines. The coal was cheaper fuel than wood, but it burned too hot and infused the tofu with an acrid, smoky flavor. (Usually, I loved anything cooked over a charcoal fire, but this harsh coal-smoke taste was too powerful for the delicate tofu.)

Because we made a smaller quantity, we cooked our tofu over a wood fire. It came out softer and more delicious compared to the coal-cooked version. This made Chanthu's tofu popular.

I rose at 4 a.m. to help for a few hours before I left for school, so Mae could rest before it was time to go to market. Making tofu is tricky because you have to be quick. The process is a bit like making cheese: Chanthu soaked soybeans for eight hours, then rinsed them until the water was clear. She ground the beans and emptied them into a large sack before squeezing the whole enterprise to extract the soy milk.

My sister carefully brought the milk to a boil, then removed it from the fire before the rolling boil got going (to keep the milk from spilling over). She stirred the liquid coagulant gently into the hot milk and covered it for a minute or two, then repeated this process until white curds appeared. She separated the curds from the liquid and poured them into a mold.

She and I rushed to pour the heavy jugs of steaming soy milk into the molds as quickly as possible. If the milk was too cool, the tofu didn't stick together properly. Only hot milk came out of the pressing as smooth, silky tofu. Last, we pressed the tofu and strained it, cut it into blocks, and packed it into baskets to carry to market.

The atmosphere in the kitchen during this process was often charged. Chanthu's shouting taught me to work much faster. Even today, I can move very quickly in the kitchen, steeled by that early pressure. And handling the hot tofu leatherized my fingertips permanently. My children are amazed that I can pick up something steaming hot from the stove without burning myself.

"Mom, your hands are made of iron!" they exclaim.

Of course, we ate lots of tofu in those days. Tofu by itself doesn't taste like much, but with a little effort, it can be quite delicious. We had two favorite tofu dishes: a simple soup with chive flower, flecked with bits of pork or shrimp for flavor; and a green curry with lots of fresh vegetables.

Green Curry with Tofu

This is a sister dish of Thai green curry and of samlor kako, a one-pot Khmer soup with vegetables, coconut milk, toasted rice, shrimp paste, and green kroeung. Though I've suggested kabocha, long beans, and

eggplant, you can use whatever vegetables you'd like. The lime leaves and
green part of the lemongrass give this kroeung its color.
Serves 6

For the curry:
7 tablespoons kroeung (see below)
½ to 1 cup neutral oil
1 (12- to 14-ounce) package firm tofu, drained and pressed for
30 minutes
1 to 2 (13.5-ounce) cans full-fat, unsweetened coconut milk
2 teaspoons salt (plus more to taste)
6 to 8 Asian eggplants (small and green), quartered, or 2 long
purple eggplants, cut crosswise into 1-inch slices
½ kabocha squash (or 2 sweet potatoes), peeled and cut into
½-inch cubes
½ pound Asian long beans or green beans, cut into 2-inch pieces
1 large onion, halved and sliced lengthwise into 1-inch pieces

For the kroeung:
5 stalks lemongrass (the green part), thinly sliced
5 slices galangal
6 makrut lime leaves, thinly sliced
6 cloves garlic, smashed
3 shallots, roughly chopped

Prepare the kroeung: Using a mortar and pestle, pound
lemongrass, galangal, lime leaves, garlic, and shallots to a fine paste
(or grind in a food processor). Begin with tougher ingredients,
then add softer ones. (Freeze any extra kroeung.)

Make the curry: In a large skillet, fry whole block of tofu over
medium heat in enough oil to reach halfway up the tofu. Cook

until all sides turn light golden and a bit crisp, about 6 to
8 minutes per side. Remove tofu, let cool, and cut into 1-inch
cubes. In a bowl, place tofu in 2 tablespoons of the kroeung,
6 tablespoons of the coconut milk, and 1 teaspoon of salt.
Marinate for 1 hour, stirring occasionally.

Soak eggplant in water with 1 teaspoon salt for 2 minutes and
rinse. (If you omit this step, the green curry will turn brown.)

In a large pot, heat 2 tablespoons oil over medium heat. Add
2 tablespoons kroeung, then sauté kabocha squash until it browns
slightly but is not cooked through, about 8 to 10 minutes. If
necessary, cook in batches to avoid crowding the pot. Remove
kabocha and set aside.

In the same pot, heat 2 tablespoons oil over medium heat. Add
2 tablespoons kroeung and fry until mixture turns yellow-gold,
around 3 minutes. Add marinated tofu. When the mixture starts
to bubble, reduce heat to low, cover, and simmer for 15 minutes.

Add rinsed eggplant to pot with simmering tofu. Sauté for
10 minutes, then add squash and long beans and simmer for 2 to
3 minutes. Add onion and remaining coconut milk. Bring to a
boil, stir in remaining kroeung, cover, and reduce heat to low. Add
more coconut milk if needed—the curry should be soupy rather
than pasty. Simmer for 10 minutes to let flavors meld. Season with
salt. Serve curry with jasmine rice or rice vermicelli (bún).

———

IN VIETNAM AT the time—unlike in Cambodia—many Buddhists practiced chay ky, a scheduled vegetarian diet to be followed for a few days of
the lunar month. On those days, business was good—everyone bought our
tofu. That meant Mae was able to afford her favorite treat: a large (and ille-
gally obtained) freshwater shrimp that she sautéed in garlic and salt. She
always offered to share it with us, but we knew it was her favorite, and very

expensive. So Chanthu and I always came up with an excuse to refuse it: "I don't want to get fat," I'd say. I loved watching Mae savor the shrimp even more than I would have enjoyed eating it.

When the tofu business was going well, my sister used some of the earnings to buy cloth and make a new shirt for herself and for Mae, who missed the elegant new clothes she'd bought so often in Battambang. My mother hardly went out except to go to the market, but she still insisted that I iron a fresh change of clothing for her each day. I joked that the police might arrest her if she wore the same outfit from the day before.

When it wasn't a food treat, my own preferred indulgence was shoes. We were a little less hungry and poor when my sister was selling the tofu—at the very least, we had plenty of tofu to eat. Chanthu paid me a little to help her with the business, and she often gave me a few đồng for breakfast.

I skipped the morning meal and saved my money so that every few weeks, I could buy a new pair of stylish guốc—wooden platform clogs with an elevated heel. The clogs were so lightweight and comfortable, I could run through puddles in them. Each pair had a different style and color of strap attached.

I didn't care much for cosmetics or clothes—our school uniform was loose black trousers and a white button-down shirt, and my two worn, shabby sets were all I needed. But I got lots of compliments on my sandals.

Over the two or three years that Chanthu ran the tofu business, I probably collected forty or fifty pairs. Many days, I came home faint with hunger from missing breakfast, but like any teenage girl, I congratulated myself for staying thin—and I loved showing off my fetching new guốc.

My mother shouted at me for spending money on a collection of useless clogs: "I should use those as firewood!" But the money was mine, and I could spend it as I pleased. Besides, the shoes were very cheap, and they made me feel glamorous and rich, even as I ran to join the ration queues.

WE RARELY SAW my brother Noh after the war. In communist Saigon, his status plummeted. His new position at the transportation ministry sounded impressive but paid a pitiful salary. His wife, Anh, found work at a busy medical clinic outside of the city in Đồng Nai Province, and he rode forty kilometers every weekend on a beat-up bicycle to visit her and their children there. She supported them, and I think the shame of not being the breadwinner sat heavily on him.

The fall of Saigon had brought my eldest brother crashing down to earth. The reverence Noh received all his life suddenly bought him nothing at all. His diminished status seemed to shrink him to a sliver of his once-proud self. I had once both feared and admired him; now it pained me to see him so reduced.

He still came by to eat dinner with us occasionally, but he rarely spoke or laughed, and he no longer brought us money. I sensed that accepting financial support from his wife was a dishonor he could not bear. And then one night at dinner, there was one final mortification. Chanthu asked him about his rice ration—would it be possible for him to contribute his own portion for the meal? We had only enough for the three of us. His answer was silence.

After that, Noh stopped coming to dinner.

My brother's birthright accustomed him to prestige, the kind of gilded good fortune that's of no use during times of upheaval. The pampering he received had turned him into the wrong kind of man for the era that overtook him. I ached for him and his quiet anguish. Chanthu had been too harsh on him, I felt, and I even forgave him for the unkind things he had said when he'd moved out of our house. I wish we had found a way to reassure him that in times of narrow fortune, we all contribute according to our gifts—a bitter lesson I learned from the Communists.

It turned out that Chanthu's gifts were better suited to our desperate era. She may have been considered "cloth" in the social order of my childhood. But in the chaos of war, revolution, and regime change, she became a virtuoso survivor. My sister was expected, from childhood, to work harder than anyone, with no expectation of reward. As it happened, those were the rules of our brave new world in Vietnam.

IN RETROSPECT, IT seems inevitable that an illness of the belly would end my brother's short life. We had no idea he was sick until Mr. Quang, an engineer who worked with Noh, came to tell us that my brother was at Bình Dân, a hospital for officials of high rank. Mae went to the hospital immediately, but it was already too late. Noh had died of untreated peritonitis.

When Chanthu went to his home afterward, she found a house with nothing in it but a dining table, two chairs, and a small bottle of aspirin. The books he had brought from Phnom Penh were gone. Even his prized Omega watch was missing. My father had once taken it from his own wrist to give to his beloved son, simply because Noh had said that he liked it.

We understood that my brother must have sold everything. Mr. Quang offered another clue: Noh had sometimes played cards with some colleagues at work. I remembered Puk's stern warning to me when I'd played kla klok as a girl. What would he have said to his eldest son, gambling away what little money he had?

We didn't judge Noh. We just felt so very sorry. Staring around that skeleton-bare apartment, my sister cursed herself for asking him to contribute his own rice to the meal.

Anh was as shocked and inconsolable as we were. She wept for days—like Chanthu, tormented with guilt that she had failed to help him. She had been so busy seeing to her own patients, she hadn't realized her own husband was critically ill.

I sensed that Anh and Noh's relationship had become quite strained. She didn't see him much, and she would sometimes give their son a little cash to pass on to his father. I could scarcely imagine how much that must have shamed him. At his funeral, Anh told us she had offered to buy him a Vespa, to speed his forty-kilometer weekend journeys, but he refused, saying he couldn't afford the gas. She had also saved enough money to buy the house that Noh rented; he had died before she could keep that promise.

Anh declared that we could at least give Noh the best casket to be had in Saigon. We asked some men from our church to select a beautiful coffin with the money we'd collected. Instead, they came back with a shoddy box of thin wood. They must have assumed that this was the best casket imaginable for a poor family like ours.

Anh nearly fainted when she saw it. We'd denied him rice and medical care, she cried. And now we had botched his final resting place.

By then it was too late to buy a different casket, even if we could have afforded it: An old superstition held that if you bought two caskets, you would end up having two funerals.

Of course, my brother wouldn't have cared about the quality of his casket. He hadn't cared about anything for years, it seemed; he hadn't cared enough to share his pain with his family, and he apparently preferred to die alone rather than to ask for help.

In the end, our superstitions did not stave off a second tragedy. Soon enough, we would be in the market for another pauper's casket.

ONLY ONCE A year, during Lunar New Year, Chanthu played mahjong and would wager a very small amount of money. She believed that the outcome of the game foretold the success of her business ventures in the coming year.

In 1982 my sister visited Mae's cousin in Cu Chi for the New Year. The next day, she came home wild with elation: She had never won that much in her whole life! Chanthu was so excited about her auspicious mahjong winnings that she went to see a fortune teller, to confirm that the game had forecast correctly.

Chanthu was born in the Year of the Dragon, which supposedly conferred a strong character and good business sense (although it was said that a Dragon-born female would have a hard time finding a husband, as her unfeminine power might intimidate suitors). My sister's life so far had borne out this prophecy. The fortune teller added that the year 1982 would "bring the dragon up to the clouds."

This saying—"The dragon meets clouds"—implies a wonderful event, an excellent opportunity, or simply good luck. In Chinese and Vietnamese

astrology, dragons symbolize strength and good fortune, so Chanthu inter-
preted the fortune teller's words to mean that our luck was about to change.

Chanthu, Mae, and I were overjoyed. We had a good feeling that the
worst of our hardship was over. For the holiday, my sister gave me a generous ang pau, a red envelope of money given on holidays and special occasions. I dreamed of a new pair of custom-made shoes and all the bún bò
Huế I could eat.

Instead, I used the money to play mahjong with my friends, hoping to
duplicate my sister's good luck. I still believed in my Year of the Buffalo
fortune: that nothing I wanted would ever come easily to me, but only after
years of hard work. And sure enough, I lost the money—no fancy new shoes
for me. But I wasn't terribly upset about it. I trusted Chanthu and felt sure
the coming year would be the best one we'd had since leaving home.

ON THE THIRD day of the New Year, I woke at 4 a.m. as usual, but
Chanthu had not gotten up to make tofu. For several mornings after that,
she complained of a pain in her stomach. Minh, a friend from church,
worked as a nurse at Bình Dân Hospital, where Noh had been treated; she
told the hospital Chanthu was her own sister and got her admitted. Because
it was chiefly a hospital for high-ranking party officials, Bình Dân was free,
had posh, air-conditioned rooms, and offered better care than most of the
other medical centers.

Every day for six weeks, my mother cooked meals for Chanthu and carried them by cyclo to Bình Dân, far from our house in District 1. My sister's
stomach hurt so much that she could only manage a few sips of soup. None
of the treatments did anything to lessen her pain.

Chanthu shared a room with a woman whose ulcer had been treated
successfully with surgery a week earlier. She was gradually able to consume liquid, then porridge. Now the patient was sitting up and eating fat
bowls of rice, practically without discomfort. We felt encouraged by this,
and Minh got Chanthu moved up on the waiting list for the same surgery.
Minh reassured my mother that she would look after my sister during the

two remaining weeks before the surgery, as Chanthu wouldn't be able to eat Mae's deliveries anyway.

Mae and I headed home to resume the tofu business on our own. Now Mae had twice as much work to do, without any break between midnight and market time. We hired a woman from the neighborhood to fill in so Mae would have time to visit the hospital.

Chanthu made it through the day of the procedure safely. After a week, she still wasn't strong enough to get out of bed, but she asked Mae for food; the doctor said we could give her anything she wanted. She asked for fried crab and mắm kho, a Vietnamese fermented fish dish similar to prahok. We had always believed that a person with a fresh wound should not eat seafood because it could cause scarring. But my sister, with a deep surgical cut to the belly, would have nothing but fish and shellfish.

Chanthu still did not seem as vigorous as her rice-eating roommate had a week after the same surgery, but her cravings reassured us. I was immensely relieved that she was recovering nicely and out of danger. Mae was overjoyed, and was delighted to splurge on the lavish seafood meals.

Two weeks later, the hospital notified us that Chanthu could return home. While Mae went to fetch Chanthu, a group from our church arrived to welcome my sister home. One of the young men had brought a bunch of white lilies. I glared at him and the bouquet; I hated that flower. Since Puk's funeral, the white lily had signified death for me.

Mae came through the door with Chanthu, followed closely by Minh. The room went silent, and every eye turned to them. Minh burst into tears. The hospital had sent her to inform us that when the surgeons opened my sister's belly, they found not an ulcer but a malignant tumor. The doctors could do nothing for her. Chanthu knew it, too. But in our culture then, it was common to keep secrets like this. We rarely talked openly, even within the family.

Chanthu had kept the grave news from us for as long as possible. She had asked my mother to bring all those strange seafood dishes to lull us into believing that she was getting well.

Mae and I realized that we had never actually seen her eating any of the food we had brought. Minh explained that the minute Mae left the hospital after her visits, Chanthu gave all her food away to the staff. She asked Minh to keep her secret, and thus keep our mother's hope alive, for as long as possible. My sister couldn't bear to see Mae grieving again, so soon after losing her eldest son.

To make matters worse, Chanthu's surgical wound had become infected, so we took her to a neighborhood doctor who specialized in Japanese remedies. He prescribed five differently colored beans, roasted over charcoal, and gave her a boiled ginger tincture to swab the oozing wound. Anything she ate caused her extreme pain, and she needed nutrition. So we boiled longan berries and gave her the slightly sweetened water to drink, hoping that a natural sugar source would be easier on her stomach. But even that sent her into spasms of agony.

Nothing helped. My sister died three months after she left the hospital. At her funeral, everyone wept; the priest praised her sacrifice, saying "Chanthu lived her life for others. Today we send a lily to God in Heaven." In Khmer, the name *Chanthu* means "lily."

I DID NOT see Mae cry at the service, or anytime afterward. Her sorrow was so profound that it seemed to silence her entirely—my mother's tears and words simply stopped flowing. She had wept for more than a decade already—for her husband, her sons, her old life, and our lost, ruined world. Some days, she leaned her forehead against the wall, as if her head was too heavy to carry. For weeks on end, she hardly spoke at all, and she never smiled or laughed anymore.

Another light had left her eyes—it seemed that, with each child lost, a flame in her was extinguished. She and I were the only family either of us had left, practically speaking. Phuong was alive only in Mae's heart; I was certain we would never see him again. Yen was in Belgium with the rest of her convent. She was extremely devout and had never shown much interest in staying in contact with our family. Hua was also in Europe and out of our lives.

After Chanthu died, we tried to keep up the tofu business for a while, but our sales kept declining, and the rising tax levied by the Party ate more and more into our profits. Mae was around sixty by then and was often unwell; she tired easily and could not summon the strength to wake up so early to make tofu with me, then finish the cleanup when I went to market. And then one morning, a tall, young tax policeman in a red armband made his rounds to all the market stalls. "Next quarter, the tax will double," he said mechanically, his face empty.

The market seemed to float for a moment, suspended in silence. And then the robotic official was gone, and the vendors exhaled their shock.

"What are we going to do?" said a woman selling noodles. "I make so little as it is!"

After that, Mae urged me to give up the tofu business. She swallowed her pride and wrote to Yen, who began to send us money—a few hundred dollars every few months, enough to keep us from starving. Yen also offered to sponsor my mother and me as refugees in Belgium, but Mae refused to go. "What would I do in Belgium?" she said. She would be a nobody there, my mother explained. No one would know her. No one would visit her.

I didn't go, either. I couldn't bear to leave my mother alone, after everything she had already lost. Besides, I hardly knew Yen. I had only seen her a couple of times a year in my early childhood, when we would visit Phnom Penh from Battambang. She was a blurred face in my memory, a distant unknown who had played almost no part in my life.

Looking back, I wonder whether starting a new life across the globe required more energy and will than Mae could summon. The inconceivable cascade of losses we'd suffered had robbed her of even the ability to express grief. She seemed resigned to a life of worsening tragedies. One night, she told me a story: Many years ago, a taxi driver in Cambodia told her that her children would all be intelligent and educated, but she would bury them before she died. Then she had ignored the dark prophecies of taxi drivers, but now our plummeting fortunes had fueled her strange faith in fortune tellers and omens.

Mae could no longer weep, but her tears transformed into stories to tell her young daughter. It was just Mae and me now. I had very little left to lose. But in some ways, I had everything to lose.

9. Mae's Memory Lunches

If a father dies, the children eat rice with fish.
If a mother dies, the children sleep on a leaf.
—Khmer proverb

MY RECOLLECTIONS OF our last year in Saigon are mostly wrapped in darkness. Sometimes, the blackout was literal: the city's electrical grid was unreliable, and so we lived many nights by the light of kerosene lamps. But a metaphysical gloom also seeped into our hearts. Exhaustion. Hunger. Resignation.

In my memory's fragmentary reel, even the daylight hours play back as faded and dreary. We could see no future for ourselves, Mae and I. But we had each other.

I had graduated from high school with few prospects. Mae and I were getting by on the money Yen sent, but this was not a sustainable plan. The only career option I knew of, for a zero-status, half-Khmer refugee like me, was teaching. There were two- or four-year teacher-training college programs and even three-month courses to train primary teachers for assignments in remote parts of the Mekong Delta, thanks to a national literacy campaign.

Teaching paid poorly. But the postwar years were very austere. Vietnam's economy was still reeling from war, rapid restructuring, and embargoes.

Poverty was so rampant, and jobs so hard to come by, that many young people whose families couldn't support them enrolled in the training so they wouldn't be a burden to their parents.

When I asked Mae for permission to attend the teaching college, she showed me an article in the youth newspaper: "A Writer + A Reporter + A Teacher = A Poor Person," it read. It was a sardonic commentary on the economic realities we faced, and a rather surprising thing to have written in a newspaper then.

"If you can eat nothing but rice and salt for the rest of your life, go ahead," Mae said, as I digested this information. "But why work hard to be a poor teacher, when you can stay home and be poor here with me?"

"But what will happen to me when you're gone?" I asked her.

"You can worry about that later," she said.

IN OUR FINAL year together, after we lost Chanthu, my mother and I lived in a bubble of shared denial—she seemed to want to cushion me from the relentless hardness of our Saigon life, and I suppose I played along. Sometimes I blame her for not forcing me to be more realistic about what lay ahead. Other times, I see that she tried, and I did not always listen.

I also know how painful it is to admit to your babies—and to yourself—how difficult their futures are likely to be. In my work now, I see poor families teaching their children to fight from a very young age: The noodle soup vendor shows her daughter how to eke out a living from the streets using only a cookpot. The farmer's sons plant beside him in the paddies when they are still small enough to stand in his shadow.

It's a tragic practicality, but I understand it. For many years, I was so afraid of making my own daughter soft, I did not hug her. I did not tell Clara I loved her. I have been very tough on my children to ensure that they will never be as vulnerable as I was.

Mae could also be tough, in her way. She had come from poverty and remade herself as the ideal middle-class wife for 1960s Battambang: an elegant beauty and a brilliant cook, seamstress, and hostess. She had out-witted her mother-in-law and set herself free. She had taken care of my father, as a good wife was expected to. But she could also raise her voice when she disagreed with him, a rare act of defiance for a woman of that era. Those skills meant little in this drab new world of self-denial and fer-vid slogans, where a person's best efforts were poured into a gray collective pot.

We both grasped that I needed to take some kind of decisive action, but *which* action to take? In that devastated country, with its stagnant economy and inscrutable new rules, the options for getting ahead through self-reliance had drastically narrowed. That's why so many people felt they had no futures there, and fled abroad in those years.

I did not question Mae for staying. I trusted her completely. To me, she was infallible, like a god. So I allowed myself in some ways to remain a child, and to believe that somehow, together, we would be okay.

OF ONE THING, Mae was sure: A proper girl should know how to sew. In the old order she knew best, a woman could make a decent living as a seam-stress. Chanthu had done just that back home in Battambang, and also in Saigon before the city fell. So Mae urged me to enroll in a sewing class.

I had little patience for sewing—really, for anything that involved sit-ting still. At the machine, a minute felt like an hour. I returned home and told Mae that I might kill the sewing machine before I managed to absorb any of the training. But my "yes" had made her happy, so I told her that I would finish the course.

It was a promise I did not keep. I lost interest in the class and stopped attending. Mae said little about it. Not long after that, Thai, a friend of mine from the church choir, got a group together to sew Vietnamese army shirts and trousers. The stitchery was very basic: I used Chanthu's machine to sew the straight seams needed for cuffs and collars. And I found that working with my new friends was more fun than the drudgery of a boring sewing course. It was a job of sorts, even though it didn't pay much—just enough to go out for coffee or see a film. But it was an excuse to get out of the house and distract myself from my anxiety about the future.

Every day, I came home during the midday break to have lunch with my mother. She had begun preparing extravagant lunches, dishes we usually only cooked when we were hired to make a wedding or holiday feast, which we still were sometimes. The sumptuous fare usually appeared right after Yen's money came in the mail—and then, for the rest of the month, the quality of our meals diminished.

I was surprised to see my mother spending money on such elaborate meals. It worried me, but I would never openly question her. I accepted her explanation: her frequent sinus colds and diarrhea had exhausted her; the good food would settle her stomach and make her stronger.

Whenever she found a dish that made her feel a little bit better, Mae made it again and again. She resurrected several recipes I hadn't tasted in years: her marvelous fish amok, and a fried fish dish whose name I can't recall, served with raw tomato, cucumber, and a dipping sauce of lime juice and fish sauce. Sometimes I came home to find the place smelling of deep-fried shrimp. By then it had become much too dangerous to buy or sell the big contraband shrimp she loved so much. So she made do with smaller shrimp—or at least, the heads. These shrimp heads took many days to make their way to us in Saigon, so they smelled rather unfresh. Whenever I cleaned them, the stench filled my nostrils and made my head ache. But Mae loved to suck the rich orange "cream" from the shrimp's head after it had absorbed the salt from the cooking water. This was possibly my very least favorite dish, but it made me smile to see my mother enjoy it so.

She made another dish with those shrimp that I loved, however, marinating the stinking heads in heaps of garlic, shallots, salt, and black pepper, wrapping them in rice paper, and deep-frying them.

I make this dish today, only with delicious, nonstinking shrimp. It's a popular favorite with my guests (and a complicated memory-lunch for me).

——————

Mae's Memory-Lunch of Wrapped Fried Shrimp

Make at least three of these per diner. It is impossible to prepare too many. The dipping sauce is similar to the Vietnamese nước chấm. We call it teuk trei pa'em, which means "sweet fish sauce."
Serves 8

Ingredients:
24 large shrimp
3 cloves garlic, minced
1 large shallot, minced
Pinch of salt
6 turns of the pepper grinder
1 package (16 cm) rice paper wrappers
½ cup neutral oil
1 head leaf lettuce (optional)
1 cucumber, sliced (optional)

For the teuk trei pa'em dipping sauce:
2 tablespoons sugar (or to taste)
3 to 4 tablespoons rice vinegar
3 to 4 tablespoons fish sauce
2 large cloves garlic, minced
1 Thai red chili, diced

Peel, devein, rinse, and dry the shrimp. (Leave the tails.) In a bowl, combine shrimp with garlic, shallot, salt, and pepper and let sit for 30 minutes and up to an hour.

Meanwhile, prepare the teuk trei pa'em dipping sauce: In a small bowl, stir sugar and vinegar into ½ cup warm water until dissolved. Add fish sauce. Adjust vinegar, fish sauce, and sugar to taste. Stir in garlic and chili, cover, and refrigerate. (If you add garlic last, it floats on the surface and looks nicer.)

Line a baking sheet with parchment paper. Cut rice paper wrappers into half-moons. Working over a flat, clean surface, brush water onto the rough side of the wrapper with your fingers, and let sit until the wrappers are soft enough to fold (but not too sticky), 1 to 2 minutes. Wrap each shrimp tightly in the rice paper, with the tail sticking out as a handle, then place on prepared baking sheet (*not* touching—wrappers will stick together). Store in a cool, dry place for at least 30 minutes before frying.

In a large skillet, heat a half-inch of oil over medium-high heat until it shimmers but is not smoking. (If oil is too hot, wraps may burn before the shrimp cooks through.) Carefully place shrimp into the hot oil—it will pop menacingly at first. Don't crowd the skillet, as wrappers can stick together and tear when pulled apart. Fry wrapped shrimp until cooked through and crisp, about 2 minutes on each side.

Serve immediately on a platter with lettuce and sliced cucumbers (if using) alongside teuk trei pa'em dipping sauce.

———

THE DISH MAE seemed to crave most often in those months was a small crab, traditionally fried with a special kind of green peppercorn. When we couldn't find the peppercorn, Mae fried the crabs with garlic, shallots, and scallions instead. We rarely had it because it was both difficult to obtain *and* expensive once you did.

But I recall one stretch of weeks when we had that crab almost every day. After five days, I couldn't eat it anymore; I just ate rice and listened to Mae. In my memory, those lunches lasted for hours, Mae languidly savoring the garlicky fried crab, with a faraway look in her eyes, as she shared her memories from before I was born.

It was during those indulgent midday meals that my mother told the story of her life: her parents' poverty and pride, her mother-in-law's imperiousness, her plot to liberate herself from the old woman's tyranny. Those memory-lunches were a rare glimmer of sunlight for me during that dark time, and they remain so in my recollections. I loved hearing these stories as many times as Mae would tell them.

"Don't ever be a helpless housewife like me," she blurted out one day after she'd finished telling a story about her marriage. "You don't want my life. Get a job and take care of yourself."

I was astonished. I had always thought my parents must have wanted me to get married and support my husband—to reflect his sunlight, like a moon. Why else would they name me Chantha, "the light of the moon"? Maybe my mother's prewar life hadn't been as fulfilling as I'd assumed. I searched my memory for clues. What hidden regrets had I failed to see?

After that day, she repeated her prescription many times—usually after lunch, as I was about to head back to our little sewing syndicate. In some distant way, I knew she was right. But still, I depended on her. And we both depended on Yen's regular envelopes.

We were a mess of contradictions, Mae and I, taking solace in each other's company instead of planning for the future.

ONE DAY I came home for lunch to find Mae looking weak and pale, wracked by vomiting and diarrhea. Her food sat untouched. She sent me to fetch some Chinese medicine, but I ran to a clinic instead and asked the doctor to come. After a brief examination, he told me to take my mother to a hospital immediately. I was still in touch with my former sister-in-law, Anh; she advised me to bring Mae to the provincial hospital where she worked.

After three days, she brought my mother back to our house in Saigon and told me Mae most likely had intestinal cancer.

My memory of the following month is a blurred reel of worsening revelations, flickering across a screen at triple speed. We transferred Mae to a cancer hospital, and they performed emergency surgery soon after she was admitted. On one of my visits, a nurse pulled me aside. "I've never seen a patient leave this place alive," she whispered: a warning.

I believed, and I did not believe. I worried, and I did not worry. I teetered between denial and dread, like a buffalo swept by rapids toward the roar of falling water.

I gazed at my mother's worn face. "Go home," she insisted. She told me not to be afraid, that I should keep working at my sewing and visit her when I could. I obeyed her and turned up at my machine the next morning, but I was worse than useless. I spent all morning removing the collar and sewing it back on, only to do the whole thing over again. I failed to finish even one shirt.

After several hours of this, Thai, the sewing-group organizer whose machine faced mine, stood up and clapped his hands. "Enough!" he cried. "You have removed the collar ten times. You have no soul in you today. Let's go and get a coffee."

He was right; my soul was hovering over Mae in her hospital room, hoping that Anh's diagnosis was wrong. I wasn't ready to lose my mother. *Maybe when I'm forty,* I thought. *But not now. Not yet.*

Anh had paid a nurse, Chi Vân ("Big-Sister Van"), to look after my mother at the hospital. But in the evenings after sewing, I went to visit Mae myself and then straight home to sleep. My mother rarely left me alone late at night, knowing how terrified I was of sleeping alone in the dark.

Now I was lonely and scared, and needing a bit of lightness and laughter. So one night at the hospital I asked Mae if I could go out with Tuấn, the boy I'd liked in high school. He made good money working for the army as an accountant at a base near the Cambodian border. Whenever he came to Saigon on leave, he was flush with cash and would take me out to a posh café. Usually, I manufactured an alibi for these dates, but this time I simply asked for permission.

To my amazement, Mae said yes.

Her voice sounded weak and small. But otherwise, she seemed to be recovering. To me, the only unusual thing about the night was that she'd agreed to let me accompany a boy into the city on my own.

It was a beautiful, perfect evening—a taste of freedom in the company of a handsome young friend. And I enjoyed it all the more because I had permission. I hadn't had to sneak around behind Mae's back, so I was guilt-free and lighthearted.

Late that night, after my date, a voice roused me from sleep. It was Chi Vân. When I opened the door, a taxi driver brought my mother into the house and lay her body on the bed.

"She died," said Chi Vân.

I could not understand the words. I stared at my mother's face, waiting for her eyes to open and her lips to say something. Instead, Chi Vân spoke. "She still loves you no matter what," she said. "And she is very worried for you."

This made no sense. How could Mae love me or worry for me if she was dead?

A screamed word *NOOOoooo* filled the night sky. I have no idea whether the sound came from my lungs or only existed inside my skull. I ran outside and jumped on my bike. My whole body shook as I pedaled, struggling against a flat tire that flapped against the pavement.

Inhuman sound after inhuman sound blared from my mouth, but my eyes produced no tears.

I dropped the bike at Thai's house, burst in, and told him, breathlessly, that my mother was gone. Together, we ran the many blocks to my house, and I reoccupied the same spot where I'd been thirty minutes before, when the taxi driver brought in a lifeless body that was supposedly my mother's. The dead woman's visage resembled my mother's sleeping face, except that it wore a mask of deep sadness.

Thai held my arm tightly while I stood there shaking, as Chi Vân cleaned and dressed my mother's body. It was all a terrible mistake. At any moment, Mae would wake up and tell me so. But the dreadful silence held, unbroken.

WE HAVE A saying in Khmer: "If a father dies, the children eat rice with fish. If a mother dies, the children sleep on a leaf." It means that when you lose your mother, you lose everything. She is the roof over your head and the rice in your bowl. She is your strength.

I was not a child when my mother died, but she was the only thing keeping me from a life in the streets, and my reason for continuing to live. And what had she left me? No tangible inheritance, only a trove of recipes that would surely prove useless to a girl with no money to procure the ingredients.

In my despair, I blamed her for keeping me too soft, for failing to prepare me for how hard our world had become. Maybe my kitchen education, and all those delicious memories, weren't a strength at all. Maybe it was a weakness to begin life with every luxury, only to lose it all, one splendid thing at a time.

Maybe it was unfair to hold Mae responsible, but I was mad with grief and fear; but more than anything, I cursed myself—for depending so completely on her and Chanthu. Now I was double-motherless, losing two mothers only a year apart from one another, and I was in very deep trouble.

AS THE FUNERAL approached, I moved through the preparations like a person in a trance. I notified church people and sent a telegram to my sister Yen, who was now in France. Tuấn spent his own money to buy the coffin, an extravagant gesture that had people asking me, "Why don't you marry him? He obviously loves you." But with my mother gone, I cared nothing about friendships or the idea of getting married. The only future I could imagine was death. I had dark fantasies about falling beneath the wheels of a truck.

My church friends gathered around me at the funeral. By then, I had found my tears. For two hours during the service, I wept and sang hymns with wild fervor. At one point, Tuấn told me that my crazed singing was scaring him. I ignored him and sang even louder, exhausting myself with tears and songs. I wanted everyone to leave me alone. But going home to the empty house was even worse. The darkness that invaded that place after we buried Mae was dense and cloying, drenched with the sickly-sweet aromas of flowers and incense. The smell of death.

I lay awake in terror, unable to shake the image of my mother drowning in muddy water. After the new regime took over in 1975, many old cemeteries had been cleared and the remains beneath them exhumed. Mae had said that she did not want to be burned or buried in water. I needed to find a resting place worthy of her.

We found a plot for her in a cemetery thirty kilometers outside of Saigon. It was on low ground; you hit water at around three feet down. Normally, the workers would at least drain the water from the grave. But on the day of her burial, they just pushed the casket underwater and poured the soil on top. I was mad with grief at the thought of her body floating and turning in the black water.

THREE DAYS LATER, I received a letter from France with a black band on the corner of the page. It was from my sister Yen. "I've done my duty as a daughter," the letter said. While she felt sorry that I was on my own in the world at such a young age, she explained that she could not continue to support me now that our mother was gone. I felt betrayed and utterly alone.

I had no idea what to do next; Mae was not there to tell me. But something she'd said, half in jest, once floated into my head: "I could fill a fifty-kilo rice sack with your shoes and use them as fuel for cooking fires for a very long time!"

She was right: Those shiny wooden clogs filled the rice bag to the top. I didn't need stylish new shoes anymore. I could use them to fuel a cooking fire and save the money I would have spent on wood. I didn't have much to cook, anyway—just rice. For "flavor," I poured on a bit of cheap fish sauce from the state store. My mother never would have bought the disgusting sauce, a brownish liquid with salt and MSG. It didn't taste like fish at all.

One night a neighbor came by to check on me. I was eating rice on the floor of the empty house. She frowned at the smell of the fake fish sauce. "Before, whenever I smelled good food, I knew it was from your house," she said. I didn't answer her.

The shoe-fuel lasted for a month. Every night, I lit a few shoes and cooked a small pot of rice over the fire. I felt nothing, not even hunger. I wanted nothing, except to forget everything and disappear. I was consumed with thoughts of death. But suicide was a sin—I knew this. So I pushed away those dark dreams and willed myself to forget.

Recipe: Rice Bowl of Forgetting

Ingredients:
1 cup rice
2 cups water
1 50-kilo rice sack
Clay pot for cooking rice
A large variety of cheap wooden clogs
Fake fish sauce from the state store

Fill a large rice sack with the dozens of pairs of stupid clogs you bought to make yourself feel less poor. These will serve as excellent firewood, per your mother's suggestion. You'll have only rice for dinner from now on, to stretch out what little savings you have left. Season the rice with the very bad cheap fish sauce from the state store, the one that tastes like salt and MSG and unlike fish.

It doesn't matter what it tastes like. You cannot permit yourself any more indulgences. The delicious Thai fish sauce your mother always bought, one of her few splurges, is no longer for you.

Combine water and rice in the clay pot, bring to a boil over the fire, then simmer. Feel free to overcook the rice. Burn it even, black and crunchy around the edges. All the better, to forget the delicious things that came before. Forgetting will dull the ache of craving what no longer exists.

Now is the time of forgetting. Burn the shoes, burn the rice. Burn away the spoiled-girl softness.

Your rage makes the embers flare up, red and shimmering. A soft, young girl with nothing at all will not survive the Saigon streets for long. You are not ready for this.

10. A Failed Sugar Smuggler

If you travel with Buddha, wear a saffron robe.
If you roam with spirits, wear paper clothes.
—Vietnamese proverb

I WOVE THROUGH the bustle of a narrow Saigon street, navigating a crush of people carrying parcels, bicycles and motos edging by handlebar to handlebar. It was a chaotic working-class neighborhood near a pagoda, but the address I'd been given was for a tiny house that looked well tended. I approached an iron gate and knocked, looking over my shoulder, terrified that I'd come to the wrong place.

The gate creaked open, revealing half a face. "Who sent you here?" the face whispered. When I spoke the name of the person who had referred me, the door swung open to admit me to the fortune teller's lair.

I had never been to a fortune teller before, and I couldn't believe I was visiting one now. Although many Vietnamese traditionally consulted soothsayers or astrologers when making major decisions, such superstitions were forbidden under the Communists. "Backward thinking," as they called it, was deemed immoral, and fortune tellers were banned after the war. My mother and sister had taken a risk in seeking them out, which is why this fortune teller wouldn't open the door for just anyone. I had to be introduced by a person he trusted. It was a spy's game of code words and secret knocks.

It was improbable that I had ended up here. But my world had torn loose and tumbled into a vacuum of blackness. I was in free fall, alone in the world, with no skills or income. I had less than a hundred dollars to my name. There were days when I could barely buy myself a handful of morning glory to stir-fry. For months, I had eaten nothing but rice and fish sauce. All that stood between me and life on the streets were a few sellable goods: a bicycle, some clothes, Chanthu's sewing machine, and the house, with its meager contents.

I cursed the memory of the empty gold box. At such a moment, when my faith lay dying, gold was a thing I could believe in.

But there was no gold to be had. Unlike the mean grandmother, my mother and sister had placed their faith in God (as well as the occasional fortune teller), in each other, and in their own kitchen magic—but never in gold. We had let our treasure slip away too easily, had spent it on shoes and fabric and bún bò Huế dinners. In Saigon, even as we spiraled into destitution, we indulged our "bourgeois" cravings, and we shared what we had with our poorer neighbors.

Too often we had taken minivacations from poverty, to pretend for a moment that we were still safe in Battambang.

Where did all that careless pretending leave me now?

Passing through the gate, I entered a tiny apartment stacked with books and sat down at a plastic table. The fortune teller's wife asked for my birth time and date, then folded open her Chinese book of stars. She bent over a scrap of paper, working her mysterious celestial math, while the fortune teller disappeared to finish some washing.

She traced a circle in the middle of the page and drew lines radiating out, like a sun. The circle contained my stars. The lines represented lives: one line was my own life; others stood for my parents, siblings, children, and future husband.

When she finished her "fate calculations," the fortune teller returned, settled at the table beside me, and began reading my stars. I held my breath.

A proper fortune teller must be both a mathematician and an artist. This one was a high school math teacher. But he was also a master of his art: a performer, a storyteller, and an astute observer. I never knew his real name.

I hoped he would reveal some secret that might harden me for the struggles ahead, but he offered no such clues. Instead, a film of my childhood flickered before my eyes as he studied my stars and began to speak. "Your father was a mechanic," he said. "The eldest child in your family is a girl."

A good star-reader always begins with a reckoning of the past, to prove his skills and win trust.

"You are the youngest in your family," the fortune teller added.

How could he have known these things about me, Puk, and Chanthu? As he spoke, my thoughts followed his voice back into my childhood: The smell of oil and smoke on my father's clothes. My contempt for our stingy grandmother. My devotion to Mae and Chanthu, and how they cared so little for money or power—what Jesus called "mammon." My mother and sister had always loved people, not gold.

That's what I learned from my mother and sister: to share and to love. I wish I had learned a little more about making a living and surviving on my own.

How DID I end up at this fortune teller's house? In the time since Mae had left me, I'd been trying to figure out how to take my life into my own hands. Questions of belief aside, I needed a plan. A survival strategy. In the absence of any good ideas, I had the less good idea to try my hand at smuggling. My neighbor's tenant told me that coconuts and white sugar—plentiful in Bến Tre Province, where coconuts grew and sugar was produced—would sell well on the black market in Saigon, where both were scarce. She was planning to give the venture a try, so I asked to go along. Neither of us had any idea what we were doing.

I was nervous: What if I had no talent for smuggling, and I lost the last of my mother's money? What if I ended up begging in the street? And if the Bến Tre police caught me, this entrepreneurial spirit might cost me more than money. The rules about what constituted "smuggling" seemed very vague to me. But I felt I should diversify my investments and risks, so I accepted a second opportunity from an old high-school friend. He planned to slip into Cambodia, buy cheap Thai-manufactured clothing, and sell it for a profit in Vietnam. All I had to do was invest in his scheme; he would take care of the rest.

I sold my bicycle to raise the capital for these covert enterprises. But I was anxious, which is why I had used some of the bicycle money to arrange the appointment with the fortune teller. I needed to know whether my future held any light at all—or only the forever-darkness of the black hole where I had fallen. And in a more practical sense, I hoped for assurance that my investments would bear fruit.

I looked at the fortune teller now. His next words echoed my mother's lunchtime warnings about self-reliance. He had finished with my past and was examining the stars and planets descending from my birthday skies, looking for my future there. In the stars, he found a husband for me. My future husband's sky contained a sun.

"It's a supreme sign," the diviner said. "He is capital. He can make very good money. But you can never be his dependent. You will have to take care of yourself."

I wanted to laugh. What's the point, I thought. I marry a millionaire and still have to be on my own?

But the order of things had changed forever. Our traditions were in ruins, for good or ill. The ideal of *Chbab Srey* femininity was extinct; moonlight-deference counted for nothing under a Turn-Your-Pain-into-Strength regime. No one could protect you; it was everyone for herself.

Still, it was hard to imagine a future that contained both a husband and an independent Chantha. I had never seen a family operate like that. I couldn't fathom how it would work.

And besides, how on earth would I get there from here? I'd depended too much on my mother, and now I was helpless.

"Do you have any questions?" the fortune teller asked, after he had finished his astonishing lessons about my past and future.

My words spilled out, unplanned: "Will I be poor my whole life?" In Vietnamese, the idiom was, "Will I be 'white hands'?" But I wasn't thinking of my whole life. I was thinking of now, and of what would happen with my risky ventures. Secretly, I was asking, *If I use my last dollar to become a black marketeer, what will become of me?*

The fortune teller did not answer that unspoken question. You'd think he would have known what it was. Instead, he told me something so wildly improbable that I laughed and laughed and laughed.

"You are good at cooking and sewing," the fortune teller said. "That will carry you."

And then: "When you are older, you will be very famous. Many people will know you. You will build your name and make your living by talking."

I could believe that perhaps, one day, I might work as a cook. Sewing seemed a bit more doubtful, given that I was a sewing-school dropout. But becoming well known for my words? That was an impossible future.

Of course, I should have had more faith in impossible futures. After all, we'd already endured a series of them, each more unimaginable and unforeseen than the last.

The fortune teller continued. "You are poor now, but when you are thirty-three years old, you will really be 'white hands.' You will have nothing," he said.

That I could believe.

"But when you are thirty-seven, you will build yourself a small house high above the ground, on a big piece of land."

Many years later, I would remember the fortune teller's words and realize that they had all been true. At the time, though, I laughed and forgot his prediction. Because soon afterward, everything I feared came to pass.

MY CAREER AS a black-market sugar operative was terrifying and brief. I bought five coconuts and five kilos of sugar at the local market, and we carried our purchases onto a ferry. Suddenly, everyone started running; the Bến Tre police had boarded the ferry and were checking everyone's

goods. I gave one kilo of my sugar to a woman carrying a bamboo basket full of empty cans and bottles for recycling, hoping the police would
assume that small amount was for personal use, not for reselling. But the
officer grabbed the sack of sugar right away. "Please," she pleaded. "It's just
a kilo."

"If you are so poor," said the policeman, "how can you afford to eat
white sugar?" And he carried the sack away.

Maybe I don't look as poor as that woman, I reassured myself, clutching a
shoulder bag containing the other four kilos of sugar and five coconuts I'd
bought with the other half of my bicycle money.

The policeman took away my sugar with barely a glance at me. It was
agony, seeing my future disappear into the officer's hands. At least he left
me the coconuts.

And the friend whose clothes-smuggling operation I financed? I never
saw him again. What a fool I had been to trust him without question. So
much for my investments.

Smuggler's Sticky Rice with Coconut and Sugar

*This simple, sweet treat of glutinous rice, coconut milk, and palm sugar
is inspired by the elusive ingredients of my failed smuggling enterprise.
I hope these elements will be far safer and easier for you to obtain.*

*As an alternative, you can serve rice warm in bowls with sweetened
coconut milk spooned over and sliced mango on top.*

Serves 6 or more

Ingredients:
2½ cups glutinous or "sweet" rice
2 (13.5-ounce) cans full-fat, unsweetened coconut milk
½ teaspoon salt
½ cup palm sugar (see "Notes on Ingredients, Techniques, and
Supplies")

Optional toppings:
½ cup shredded coconut, toasted
¼ cup toasted sesame seeds
Fresh fruit (such as mango)
1 bunch mint

Place rice in a large bowl and cover with hot water by 2 to 3 inches. Soak rice for 2 to 24 hours, then drain. Transfer rice to a bamboo or metal steamer lined with parchment paper (or a rice cooker with a "sweet rice" setting). Cover and steam until tender and chewy, 20 to 30 minutes.

Meanwhile, in a small saucepan, heat coconut milk over low heat. Stir in salt and sugar until both dissolve.

Transfer cooked rice to a large bowl. Stir in sweetened coconut milk and let cool for 10 minutes to allow flavors to meld. Spread rice over a baking sheet lined with parchment, sprinkle with shredded coconut and sesame seeds (if using), and let cool for at least an hour. Cut into squares, top each with a mint sprig or slice of fruit, and serve at room temperature.

———

I BEGAN EMPTYING the house of anything I could sell, including most of my clothes. I kept a couple of black outfits. What did I need colors for? The hues of mourning suited me fine.

After that, I sold Chanthu's sewing machine, the most valuable item I had left besides the house. My next-door neighbor and close friend Ngọc suggested I buy us dinner with the proceeds. I figured, why not? I was sure she would do the same for me. By then, Ngọc and her mother, Thim Que, were two of the few people I could still trust. They watched me sell my belongings, one by one, and offered small loans to help me get by.

I was grateful to them, because a terrible truth was dawning on me:

Now that I had nearly nothing, my relationships were shifting in ways I had not foreseen. Two aunts I had been sure would help me after Mae's death initially let me move in with them, just outside the city, and help launch a tofu business. But they had no more use for me once I taught their daughters to make tofu. Even relatives wanted nothing to do with a poor orphan. I went back to Saigon, feeling betrayed.

The next casualty was Tuấn. After my mother died, he had left the army and become a customs and tax officer. Even though he wasn't the one who'd confiscated my sugar, I despised his uniform and what it represented. I had seen his kind destroy so many small businesses—and with them, the lives of the very workingmen the revolution had sought to elevate.

"I hate them," I told Tuấn one day, "and now you are one of them." He stayed very quiet.

Tuấn's position could have been useful to me, but I couldn't play at love to maneuver an advantage for myself. You didn't collect friendships like treasures in a box, to cash in at a later date. And I didn't like the feeling of owing him something.

Of course, that is the foolish philosophy of a person who has everything. A person with nothing must learn a new game.

I was slow to learn. Mae's values were sticky and would not let me go.

BACK IN SAIGON after being kicked out by my aunts, I ran into Nga, a girl I vaguely recognized from the neighborhood. She came from a different sort of family than mine. She was loud and brash and quick to pick a fight. In Vietnam, she was the mistress of a married man and had a daughter by a previous boyfriend. If Mae were alive, she would have forbidden me to befriend Nga.

What counted for me now was that Nga was strong in the ways I wasn't. I admired her ferocity and thought she might be a streetwise accomplice in some new business, even though we had few skills and very little capital.

We opened a small café on the ground floor of an apartment; the café had a welcoming and airy feel, with the front screened and open to the street. It was small: just four low tables and two stools at each table. I still had some of the money my neighbor Thim Que had loaned me. Nga and I pooled our cash to pay for the first three months' rent and basic supplies: coffee, milk, alcohol, and simple snacks like peanuts and pickles.

We called it a café, but really, it was a bar. Right away, we were busy with regulars—mostly men who were twice our age or more. They rarely ordered coffee. Every night, they filled the tables, drank beer or liquor, and struck up conversations with us. It seemed that Nga and I were part of the draw.

WHEN THIM QUE found out I was doing business with Nga, she became furious and demanded that I settle my debt with her immediately. Thim Que made it clear that she didn't trust me anymore, now that I was associating with a person like Nga. She strung barbed wire between our houses, and her daughter, my friend Ngọc, started avoiding me, too.

After I sold my bicycle, Ngọc had let me borrow hers whenever I needed one. Now, eyes averted, she informed me that her mother would no longer let her lend it to me. One day I overheard mother and daughter arguing. "If you lend her that bike, she'll just sell it," said the mother.

"Mom! That's not true!" Ngọc cried.

I didn't have the money to pay Thim Que back yet. I was nearly out of cash again, and nearly out of friends. I told Thim Que that the only thing I had left to sell was my house. Right away, she offered to buy the house and deduct the money I owed her.

After her deduction, there was very little left. It didn't take me long to grasp that she'd coveted the house all along. Those loans had been her way of gaining enough leverage to compel me to sell it to her.

I moved in with Nga, her parents, and the two younger brothers. Her married paramour stayed with us two or three nights a week. Nga and her mother yelled at everyone constantly. The men of the household were like shadows thrown by the women's fire: The louder Nga and her mother shouted, the more the boys and their father dimmed. The father, a chauffeur, spent most of his time after work sitting in a corner, giving everyone the side of his eye. Nga's female cousins dropped by often and were noisy and argumentative like Nga and her mother. One worked at a massage parlor, and another, at a nightclub. Someone's hideous boyfriend frequently drifted in and menaced the house. It was never clear what this nasty-looking old married man had to offer Nga's slim and pretty cousin. Not to mention that the women in the family seemed to be doing most of the actual moneymaking.

NGA PROVED TO be exactly the right sort of person to run a bar. She was beautiful and wore sexy outfits and thick makeup. She could chat people up or demand payment without drawing a second breath. Nga would sit down to flirt and laugh with the patrons, while I preferred to stay in motion, pouring drinks and stopping at each table briefly to make a joke. We reached the break-even mark after a month or two. Things were going fairly well; our cadre of regulars arrived early and stayed late.

I was starting to believe I could become a new kind of person, someone who worked in a bar and talked to strange men every night. It wasn't the life I would have chosen, but the luxury of choosing was behind me. Nga was rough and coarse, but she was savvy in the ways of survival. Having nowhere else to go, I depended on her completely.

And then one night, one of the patrons started asking me lots of questions. He was a karate-do trainer with ropy muscles and bruised hands. Nearly twice my age, he dressed neatly and spoke in a gentle voice.

I didn't like talking about my previous life. To me, revealing my sadness to strangers meant lowering myself in their eyes. My disclosures were a gift they had not earned. But my reticence only made the customers more curious. They said I looked sad and spoke a different language than Nga. What they were really saying was, Why is someone like you working in a bar?

I resisted their interrogations by answering in proverbs and slogans. When the karate-do teacher asked me where I came from and how I ended up there, I told him, "With monks, I wear a robe. With ghosts, I wear paper clothes."

"Ah! A clever girl. That's why you're so different from Nga."

One night he asked me to dinner. I didn't think of it as a date. I considered him an older-brother figure. He was polite and respectful throughout the evening. And then, as he dropped me off at the bar after dinner, he asked if I'd like for him to to buy me some nice clothes. "You look so sad in black."

Without thinking, I said I would like that.

And then he promised to buy me something nice to wear—if I went home with him that night.

I had no idea what to say. First my friend's mother had assumed I was a bike thief, and now this man expected me to sleep with him in exchange for a few outfits! This was the first time a customer had proposed such an arrangement to me, but I feared it would not be the last.

I said no in as jovial a tone as I could manage, so he wouldn't get angry and leave the bar. For the rest of the evening, I smiled and nodded absently as he chattered, even though I wanted to dissolve into the darkness. I knew we couldn't afford to lose any customers. But after that night, Nga could tell something was off with him—and with me. And I could tell she wasn't happy about it.

Nga was my last resort. I couldn't afford to be ejected from the bar *and* her parents' house. But I also worried that if I stayed, I'd come to the same impasse again.

Deep down, I felt that I was not like Nga. But who was I to judge her, when she was feeding herself the best way she knew how? She hadn't cast aside the pretensions of respectability—she'd never had the luxury of possessing them in the first place. This was part of her strength.

Now I was faced with the terrifying question: What strength could *I* draw from? Was my own sense of propriety too heavy a weight for a poor girl to carry?

I had to decide who I was and what I was willing to do to survive.

Recipe: How to Change Cloth into Diamond

Ingredients:
1 pampered little girl
2 communist revolutions
2 civil wars
1 genocide

Take a well-fed nine-year-old with a big family and a fancy French-Catholic-school education. Fold in 2 revolutions, 2 civil wars, and 1 wholesale extermination. Separate her from home, country, and a reliable source of food.

Slowly subtract small luxuries, life savings, and family members, until all are gone. Shave down childhood dreams for approximately two decades, until only subsistence remains.

11. Khmer Noodles, Battambang Style

Ah, so happily we live,
We who have no attachments.
We shall feast on joy,
As do the Radiant Gods.
—*The Dhammapada*

I ALWAYS SMILED when a certain friend of Nga's stopped in for a drink. Chan wasn't like the other customers. He was younger and maintained a tidy appearance. Right away, I noticed his warm smile and his long, graceful fingers.

Chan lived in Nga's neighborhood, and I could tell she was a little bit intimidated by him. Witty and smart, he had the easy assurance of a university student—except that, despite his intelligence and curiosity, he had almost no chance to be admitted to a university. Slots at universities or medical schools were for the families of soldiers—and for a tiny sliver of the most elite, brilliant students in the city who could pass the entrance exams.

Whenever Chan sat down at one of our tables and ordered coffee, I felt more like myself. With his sense of humor and big charm, he made the bar roar with laughter. I found myself pausing at his table for longer spells. We talked about music and books. He understood my jokes. Soon, I was sharing things about my life with him that I had never told any other patron.

We were a lot alike, both orphans from educated backgrounds who had fallen a long way. Partial-Khmers, driven from Cambodia under Lon Nol because our families were composed of the wrong ethnic ingredients. Chan was half Chinese—another ethnic minority targeted by Lon Nol—so his mother fled with him and his older sister in 1970, when Chan was a boy. They took refuge in Chợ Lớn—Saigon's Chinatown—where their mother ran a thriving business. She died before Chan came into my life, and when I met him, he was staying with his aunt, whose husband had left her. He described their little family as "two sad people living together."

Here in Vietnam, we were both sinners from the losing South, with no powerful connections or career prospects. We had even gone to the same high school. Chan graduated from Lê Quý Đôn a year before I did. Most of all, we were both alone and adrift, with nothing to keep us in Saigon. At odd moments, we recognized ourselves in each other: "You read that label in perfect French!" he once exclaimed, when we ducked into a pharmacy to buy medicine. And I heard echoes of my own dark thoughts when he confessed that he could see no future for himself in Vietnam.

We soon became friends. Maybe just a little bit more than friends, but not exactly in a romantic sense. It was a partnership of sorts, an unspoken understanding between two people in an equal amount of trouble. With no one left to trust, we decided to trust one another.

After a month or so of sharing jokes and confidences in the bar, he invited me to a concert. By 1984, the government had begun to loosen its grip on some aspects of life, so the "rotten" music from before 1975 was no longer prohibited. That night we lost ourselves in the old sentimental ballads that my mother used to sing.

Nga didn't like it when I went out with Chan. "Don't make yourself look so cheap," she said after one of my outings with him. "He's looking down on you." Maybe she was jealous or saw him as a threat. Or maybe she sensed that we were keeping an important secret from her: our shared dream of fleeing Saigon. We fantasized about how we might accomplish it.

"Why don't we just . . . *go*?" he said one day. "Us two?"

For fourteen years, my Saigon life had seemed like a dark tunnel with no end. Now Chan had illuminated an exit. Suddenly, what had long been a farfetched shadow-thought, dormant in the recesses of my mind, blinked into life: America. France. Australia. Anywhere but here.

Anywhere except Cambodia, that is. The Vietnamese army had invaded Cambodia at the end of 1978, ousted the Khmer Rouge, and set up a new regime; but the occupation had not brought peace—the Khmer Rouge still controlled large swaths of forest, and the fighting raged on.

We missed home, but home as we knew it no longer existed. Home had been plowed under and seeded with mass graves. We longed to sow ourselves into a new home—ideally, somewhere not afflicted by autocratic rule or guerrilla warfare. We would have to strike out, like explorers, to find a new place to belong.

Before I met Chan, I could not have imagined such a scheme. But having him as a co-conspirator gave me twice the courage to face an uncertain adventure. We had an equal measure of nothing to lose. He had ideas and strategies, and a stubborn prudence focused on the future.

I had a few special skills, too, as it turned out. I knew how to ask strategic questions and listen for things left unsaid. I had cast aside my attachments and learned to let the past go without looking back. I had mastered how to watch and wait. But to find out that I was also capable of action? This was as much a surprise to me as anything has ever been. It turned out, with Chan by my side, I could draw in breath and step off a precipice, into the unknown.

AFTER WE FIRST spoke our idea out loud, Chan and I talked of nothing but escape. At the bar, we pretended everything was normal, so Nga would suspect nothing. After closing, we met in the park near the Notre-Dame Cathedral, where we could conspire freely and no one would look at us twice.

Running from Vietnam was no simple matter. First, it was illegal to leave the country without official permission, so we could not discuss our plans with just anyone. You had to meet the right person, someone who knew how things were done but wouldn't report you to the police.

I turned to a loose network of people from our old church. Most of our fellow Catholics lived in a similar limbo, with little to hope for in Saigon, except the possibility of a new life someplace else. Everyone talked about leaving or whispered about the ones who'd already gone. If a neighbor went missing, news would trickle through the network: "He's in Australia," they said. "He's in Guam."

Most of the people we knew of who'd left had taken to the South China Sea in small boats and aimed for the big refugee camps in Hong Kong, the Philippines, or Thailand. That's how the phrase "boat people" was born. A million or more fled that way between 1975 and the early 1990s. No one knows how many died at sea—possibly in the hundreds of thousands. And those who reached the camps often endured horrible things along the way: starvation, illness, and terrible thirst; storms and searing heat; raids by pirates who robbed, raped, kidnapped, and murdered refugees at will.

Sometimes there was no news at all. A couple of years before, what was left of Chan's extended family had scraped together enough money to fund his sister's escape. They never heard from her again and presumed she had been lost at sea. My high school friend Kim Hoa joined the boat people, but she was luckier. She made it to the camps, and then all the way to America.

I'd mostly lost touch with Kim Hoa after we graduated, and she got married. When Mae died, I distanced myself even further from all my old friends, who I now considered above my station. I was ashamed of how far I had sunk and could not bear the thought of them pitying me. But I missed laughing with Orange Juice Hoa.

She had sent a letter to Nhu, the head girl from our high school class, who had brought it by my house to read. Kim Hoa wrote that she and her husband, Khoa, had been adrift at sea for ten days without food or water.

"Anh Khoa did not make any poo, since he had not eaten anything to make poo from," she wrote, funny as always, even when describing a brush with death. She told Nhu to ask her friends to write to her in America, but

Nhu suddenly became very guarded and refused to show me the envelope. "Bring the letter to me," said Nhu. "I will send it."

By then, when so many of us were casting about for escape routes, friends and relatives in America, France, or Canada had become assets to hoard. Nobody wanted to share the addresses of contacts who had made it to the West. Perhaps the refugee-relative in America could become a lifeline, but there was always a threat that it could be stretched too far. If too many people asked the émigré for help, no one would get anything—or so the thinking went.

"Forget it," I told her. I would not beg her for Kim Hoa's address. I didn't want her to think that all I wanted from Kim Hoa was her help, so I never brought Nhu a letter to send along. I never heard from Orange Juice Hoa again. I hope she found a joyful life in America. Wherever she is, I am sure she is surrounded by laughter.

BESIDES BEING DANGEROUS, fleeing Vietnam by boat was ruinously expensive. You had to find a group and pool a great pile of money for a boat, something halfway decent that stood a chance of staying afloat across a vast expanse of open ocean.

I sold Chan's bike and a few other things of his to raise some cash, but we had nowhere near enough to pay for our share in a seaworthy craft. Meanwhile, I was considering another strategy: exiting Vietnam over land to the west and making our way across Cambodia, to the refugee camps in Thailand. And from there, to what I imagined to be Heaven—some free society in the glittering West.

Crossing into Cambodia would be the easy part. Cambodia had effectively become a Vietnamese satellite, occupied by the Vietnamese military, so we were free to go there—buses crossed the border every day.

The problem was crossing the western parts of the country and making it to Thailand. Skirmishes, banditry, and millions of land mines had made the countryside treacherous, especially in the borderlands near Thailand, where the Khmer Rouge holdouts still held power. And of course, Cambodia had only just started counting back up from Year Zero. Civilization had not, shall we say, fully resumed—or so we heard.

Still, we weren't sure how much dysfunction—or even violence—to expect. Noh had told us a story of going to Cambodia once with his job at the Ministry of Transportation. Soon after they crossed the border, someone emerged from the forest and pointed a rocket launcher at their vehicle. They turned their car around, and Noh never asked for any more road-building projects in Cambodia.

But I had also heard that thousands of Vietnamese had fled *to* Cambodia, to squat on uninhabited land and eke out meager livings as street vendors. We could not fathom what war-ravaged Cambodia might have to offer the ambitious migrant, besides ample opportunity to become hungry or dead. I imagined the place as an End-of-the-World theme park for the very brave—or the very desperate. Maybe the Vietnamese pioneers figured they had nothing to lose.

We had little to lose, ourselves. I made my case to Chan. We both spoke Khmer and Vietnamese, so we could ask most anyone we met for help along the way. It would be dangerous, but we simply didn't have the means to cross the South China Sea.

He agreed to the plan. We were going "home," if only for a few months, until we could make it through to somewhere better.

WHEN I TOLD Nga I was leaving, she flew at me, shouting, slapping, and biting. If Chan hadn't stopped her, she might have done some damage. I walked away from the bar and never looked back.

I also stopped by my old house again, to see it one last time. Thim Que had reinforced the structure with brick, so much so that I barely recognized it. I didn't see Ngọc, but her mother was there, looking unhappy to see me. I told her about splitting with Nga, and how she had attacked me when I informed her I was quitting the bar.

"You made your choice," Thim Que said. "That's what you get."

Even after so many years of neighborly compassion, I could never be rehabilitated in her eyes for taking up with Nga. In her view, I'd cast aside my mother's decency and fallen into disgrace. I pitied Thim Que. She still feared the Worst that Can Happen; whereas for me, the Worst *had* happened, so that particular fear was gone—and left me with a strange sort of freedom.

I said goodbye to my home of fourteen years, which had never been a real home at all. We had always considered it a waypoint. Leaving it behind made me feel almost weightless.

One day, not long before we left, I saw Tuấn. His family had opened a stand for selling chè thập cẩm—a sweet dessert of fruit cocktail, beans, coconut milk, and shaved ice. Chan and I happened to pass by the stand in the street. "Where have you been?" Tuấn asked, his eyes wide. "I went to your house so many times, but you were never there." I was still bitter about his exploitative work as a tax and customs officer, but also ashamed that I had let him spend so much money to buy my mother a coffin—and that I had nothing to give in return. I walked on without a word to him.

The day before we left, Chan and I met at our conspiracy park one last time, then went to a concert at a café. Even the light felt different that afternoon: gilded and sparkling. *Tomorrow*, I told myself, *a new life begins.*

I FOLDED TWO changes of clothes and some cash into a bag, and Chan and I made our way to Tây Ninh, a small city in Vietnam near the Cambodian frontier. There, we climbed onto a bus and headed toward the border. What seemed like every few minutes, we stopped at another checkpoint, where Vietnamese soldiers boarded the bus and swept their eyes over every face. It felt as though they could see into our minds. We were not repatriating; we were running away. They knew it. And at each checkpoint, my stomach roiled until the soldiers had finished their scan and exited the bus.

When we crossed into Cambodia, Chan and I exchanged a glance. A smile had wrapped itself around his face, and I could feel one creeping across my own. It was the first time I'd felt so hopeful since before I lost

Mae. Every minute put more (s)miles between us and our cheerless Saigon lives. And as the distance grew, we felt lighter and freer. We had no idea what would happen next, but we were confident that together, we could sort things out as they came.

But as the bus pushed deeper into Cambodia, we could see that something wasn't quite right about the scenes that scrolled by. The years since Zero (or 1975, depending on your preferred calendar) had altered the countryside in ways I couldn't pinpoint. A fevered sunlight scoured the too-quiet landscape. The villages we passed looked beaten down, with most houses in disrepair and some in states of near collapse. The ordinary buzz of life seemed slowed down or suspended in time, as if the images in our bus windows were part of a Stone Age natural history exhibition.

When the bus stopped in a village, hollow-faced vendors surrounded us and stared into the windows. I bought num ansom, a sticky rice cake usually filled with pork and mung beans, and asked the seller, "Is there coconut in this?" She shook her head without smiling or speaking.

This num ansom was nothing like the street food of my childhood. It not only lacked coconut, it lacked everything—there were no mung beans or meat in it at all. My first bite of Cambodian food since I was a little girl was just plain sticky rice with a few lonesome white beans, wrapped in a palm leaf. It tasted like nothing I remembered.

Slowly, I began to grasp the magnitude of what had changed. Before, even in a very poor settlement, you saw flashes of prosperity: new tile roofs, a splash of bright paint, a few motos zipping around, or at the very least, a freshly thatched roof. Instead, we saw unrelenting privation. There were no motos or bicycles, only a few drowsy oxcarts. Even the rice fields seemed more unkempt and trash-strewn than the pictures in my memory.

I saw no children riding to school or playing in the fields, just a few old people with faces of crumpled paper, solemnly selling meager fare by the road. And a high percentage of the remaining population seemed to be wearing a Vietnamese army uniform.

I didn't know this place at all. I had kept nothing from my past—no photos or artifacts, only memory. And now my home country, as I remembered it, had ceased to exist, too. I truly belonged nowhere. Nothing was mine.

UPON REACHING PHNOM Penh, our first act was searching for dinner. I will never forget my first meal that truly tasted like home, after fourteen years in exile: It was fitting that it should be prahok—our defining (and aromatic) national condiment. We found someone preparing a version very much like my mother's splendid cooked prahok: mixed with kroeung spice paste, minced pork, and young tamarind leaves, all wrapped in a banana leaf and grilled. Although I had never developed a taste for raw prahok as a child, that day the luscious, pungent fish was, for me, the flavor of Cambodia. I closed my eyes and drank in the familiar aromas. A sense of relief and well-being washed over me. Something essential from that lost world had survived, after all.

That feeling lasted as long as my first few bites of prahok.

No matter how hungry I'd thought we were in postwar Saigon, nothing prepared me for what I witnessed in Cambodia in 1984: people living in inconceivable starvation and squalor, with little relief. Which is why, even with the Khmer Rouge out of power, we Cambodians still streamed toward Thailand by the hundreds of thousands. And Thailand reeled from the onslaught.

Phnom Penh was a dark and crippled city. This was no longer the elegant capital that had bewitched me as a little girl, as I zipped around its glittering streets on the front of my brother Noh's moto. The stately old buildings were chipped and faded or crumbling into the street, their courtyards and sidewalks overgrown and buckled. The usual big-city bustle of cars, cyclos, street-cart vendors, and families piled onto motos had stilled to a wary murmur. There were no young girls floating by in elegant dresses, no scrubbed and spoiled children dressed in their finery and dragged toward churches and pagodas, no whisper of music drifting out of windows.

A few saffron-robed monks had somehow survived. In the mornings, they strode in quiet rows, much as before. But most of the resplendent old churches, pagodas, and monasteries were now derelict shells or razed to the ground—the Khmer Rouge had demolished many places of worship. Others they had repurposed as storehouses, meeting halls, prisons, or extermination sites. They had converted the national library and archives into a kitchen, and its walled garden into a pigsty. The books and records had been burned; our written history used as firewood.

The city did not function in any meaningful sense. Electricity was rare, and clean water was nearly unobtainable. Trash and sewage were everywhere. Shops and businesses were shuttered and dark, and many houses sat empty. Except for the very occasional moto (or moto-remork towing a long cart), the only vehicles on the roads were military trucks. Everyone seemed to have the same idea: move into an empty house and find some miserable items to sell in the street. Postwar Phnom Penh was a ramshackle city of squatters, hustlers, and beggars. Of hollowed cheeks and protruding ribs. Even the Vietnamese soldiers looked hungry and haunted.

But the rats and flies thrived.

Chan and I rented a bed in a shabby apartment building where many Vietnamese-speakers lived. It seemed as though the majority of the city's inhabitants were recent Vietnamese émigrés. There was a dark air of mutual suspicion between the old and new Phnom Penh residents. Many Khmers viewed the Vietnamese more as occupiers than saviors. In a sense, they were both.

We didn't fit neatly into any category. The politics of occupation and empire hardly mattered to us at that point. Our idea was to put both Vietnam and Cambodia behind us as quickly as possible. We planned to make our way northwest to Battambang, and from there, to the Thai border crossing at Poipet.

We began asking people how to find transport. Again and again, we heard the same answer: that traveling to Battambang and beyond was extremely dangerous. The Vietnamese army had pushed what remained of the Khmer Rouge westward into the forests near Thailand, where there was still heavy fighting.

Chan and I had no idea what to believe. We were acting blindly on rumors we'd heard in Saigon. But we soon learned that the farther you got from the Thai border, the less accurate those rumors were. Practically everything we had heard in Vietnam was wrong. Now all we knew to do was keep moving, like twigs floating downstream, no turning back.

We climbed into a packed army truck, hoping we'd be safe in a vehicle full of soldiers, and rattled toward Battambang over the worst roads imaginable. I sat beside a friendly Vietnamese soldier who asked us where we were headed. For some reason, we trusted him and told him our plans. "That sounds like a risky adventure," he said. "But at least you have each other. With help, you can do anything." We smiled and agreed that this was true.

In Battambang, I walked with Chan, looking for anything that might ignite a memory. I could not figure out where our house had been. There were a few old colonial buildings that seemed familiar, but my church and school were gone. For that matter, I don't recall seeing any functioning churches, schools, or pagodas at all. Many buildings were crumbling and vacant. Few houses had doors; no one had anything worth stealing, anyway, so why lock up? Most shops and restaurants were closed, too. But the market, at least, was as I remembered—bustling with fish and vegetable vendors in the early morning and quiet by noon.

Our first breakfast in Battambang unleashed a flood of sensory flashbacks: num banhchok—"Khmer noodles"—was one of my favorite street-food treats from the market when I was small. I loved the hand-extruded, lightly fermented rice noodles and the many comforting dishes made with them.

There's a folk tale about a clever Khmer hero named Thun Chey who brought rice noodles to China. According to the legend, people loved the num banhchok he made so much, he was invited to prepare the noodles for the emperor.

The sheer number of steps it takes to transform rice into long, slender noodles is enough to deter most aspiring "Khmer-noodle"-entrepreneurs. Here is a simplified summary:

1. Soak rice in hot water to soften it. (You can mix soaked rice with cooked rice for the next step.)
2. Grind it with a stone mill to make dough.
3. Put dough in a sack and squeeze out excess water.
4. Ferment dough to make a dry, sticky flour.
5. Boil flour to solidify dough.
6. Pound dough with mortar and pestle to make a springy paste.
7. Put dough-paste into a rudimentary extruder: a cylinder with a bottom of perforated metal.
8. Settle onto the end of a long wooden lever to press dough through the extruder and into a pot of boiling water.
9. When noodles rise to the surface, scoop them out.
10. Rinse noodles and drop them into cold water.
11. Lift small fingerfuls of noodles out of the water, squeeze out excess liquid, and fold them in artistic curlicues on a wide, flat basket lined with lotus or banana leaves.
12. Carry noodles to market at first light.
13. Sell them all and return to step 1.

If you are craving num banhchok, watch for sleep-deprived women carrying baskets on their shoulders in the early morning in any Cambodian town. Making them by hand every day requires grit and perseverance, the street vendor's extraordinary work ethic. Every region has its own "Khmer noodles" dish with its own broths, sauces, and toppings. In Battambang that first morning, we had num banhchok teuk samlor Khmer—vermicelli in a soupy fish gravy made with lemongrass and kroeung spice paste, served with herbs, banana blossoms, and raw vegetables, and topped with teuk omrith, a savory-sweet sauce native to Battambang, made with coconut milk, chili, palm sugar, and garlic.

We joined a cluster of satisfied diners squatting on benches the vendor had set up by her stand. I'm convinced that num banhchok cannot be consumed properly while sitting or standing; to get the experience just right, you must squat to eat it. It wouldn't taste right any other way.

That hastily slurped breakfast was one of the best meals of my life. It tasted like home and happiness, like a past I chose to remember as perfect. As a little girl, I had loved the slippery, soupy noodles made fresh every morning. Maybe it was because I wasn't usually allowed to have them; we always had kuy teav instead. But that morning, back in Battambang after fifteen years, no one could have kept me away.

I WAS FAIRLY certain that the district where we ate num banhchok was near where my old church had stood. I walked around the neighborhood, asking if anyone was left who had lived there before the war. "That woman over there," someone said, pointing to a house. "She used to be an orphan in the convent."

She was a round and jolly woman of about fifty, with eyes that closed to slits when she laughed. Her husband was a carpenter. When Angkar—Pol Pot's "organization"—collapsed, they had drifted back to Battambang and moved into an empty house near the convent. I told the couple that my father had an auto shop on Street Number Three.

The husband remembered my father's garage. "Oh yes!" he said. "You were small then. I always saw you in a car in those days."

Chan shot me a look.

"Why didn't you tell me about your rich family?" he asked later.

"I could have told you I was the daughter of Prince Sihanouk," I shrugged. "After meeting me in a bar, would you have believed me?"

Nothing about my appearance now suggested a spoiled little girl who went to French school and rode to church in a Mercedes.

THE BATTAMBANG COUPLE took us in without asking how long we planned to stay. They fed us meals and never once asked for anything in return. That was the Battambang I remembered: kindness as a matter of course.

But the town itself had fared little better than Phnom Penh. The river reeked of sewage; the municipality had no functioning toilets, so everyone used the riverbank to evacuate their bowels. And because the water system hadn't been restored, people used river water for everything. Someone had set up a business pumping river water into trucks and delivering it in oil drums. More than once, I saw feces floating in the water jar at our host's house.

Battambang was bustling with people on their way to Pailin, in the Cardamom Mountains to the south, near the Thai border. Pailin was said to be terribly dangerous, a Khmer Rouge stronghold home to a number of mining encampments—rumors abounded that area was littered with gold, rubies, and other gemstones. Many of the men we met were headed there to work the mines. Chan was seduced by the rumors and decided to try to make a little money as a miner in Pailin. He told me he would be back in a month or two.

While I waited for him in Battambang, I found work at a restaurant, washing dishes in exchange for daily meals and a little cash. And I asked around about crossing into Thailand near Poipet.

Impossible, everyone told me. And deadly.

The borderlands were an impenetrable chaos of fighting among the Khmer Rouge holdouts, the Vietnamese army, and the non-Communist guerrillas of various ideologies and loyalties. The refugee camps on the Cambodian side of the border were not refuges in any sense of the word. Each was controlled either by the non-Communist resistance fighters or by Khmer Rouge soldiers, who used the camps as their bases. They controlled food supplies, the flow of aid, and black-market trade; the helpless refugees were left to languish amid abominable squalor and violence, in a state of near-starvation, and at high risk of being conscripted to fight. At any moment, the camps might be shelled by the Vietnamese army—or even the Thais, whose main concern was keeping the Vietnamese military as far from their border as possible.

The only real refuge lay across the border, in Thailand, in one of the many camps administered by international aid organizations. Thousands of refugees had died attempting to cross. Guerillas, soldiers, land mines, or Thai border guards might kill you before you got anywhere near the refugee camps—or so it was explained to us by everyone we asked.

Chan returned a few weeks later. He had found a few rubies and been paid in gold. But it was a meager harvest—the money he made from selling the gold would not go far. I did my best to hide my disappointment.

I told him what I'd learned about the dangers of crossing the border into Thailand. We abandoned the Poipet plan and formulated a new one.

Chan and I said goodbye to the family that had helped us, and they wished us luck. Those kind, laughing people had taken us in without ceremony, and they bid us farewell in the same way. We knew we would never see them again, which made their gift of shelter and food all the more extraordinary—there was nothing in it for them.

What a stroke of good luck, to be so tenderly cared for by strangers.

Khmer Noodles, Battambang Style
(Num Banhchok Teuk Samlor Khmer)

Like namya, this dish is based on num banhchok—the lightly fermented, handmade "Khmer noodles." But whereas namya is Thai-influenced, this dish is signature Khmer, served in a greenish-gold fish curry. Every region has its own style, and this recipe—with a bonus sauce (teuk omrith)— makes this dish taste like Battambang to me.

You won't find just-made noodles in a grocery, but you can make do with much faster thin vermicelli (bún).

Serves 4

Ingredients:
For the soup:
7 to 8 tablespoons kroeung (see below)
1 pound flaky white fish, such as tilapia, cod, or catfish (whole fish or boneless fillets)
2 tablespoons neutral oil
1 tablespoon prahok, finely chopped (you can substitute 5 small anchovies or 1 tablespoon shrimp paste; optional)
3 tablespoons roughly crushed roasted peanuts
Salt
Pinch of sugar
1 (14- to 16-ounce) package thin rice vermicelli (bún)
1 to 2 (13.5-ounce) cans full-fat, unsweetened coconut milk

For the kroeung:
4 stalks lemongrass, thinly sliced
10 slices galangal
1 (1-inch) turmeric root, grated or minced (or 1 teaspoon powder)
4 inches fingerroot, sliced (optional)
6 makrut lime leaves, thinly sliced
6 to 8 cloves garlic, smashed
2 shallots, roughly chopped

For toppings, any assortment of the following:
Cucumber, cut into 2-inch matchsticks
Bean sprouts
Long beans or green beans, cut into 2-inch pieces
Mint

Thai basil

Banana flower (see "Notes on Ingredients, Techniques, and Supplies" for prep tips)

For optional Battambang-style bonus sauce (teuk omrith):

4 tablespoons coconut oil

2 cloves garlic, minced

1 large shallot, minced

1 teaspoon dried red chili flakes

¼ cup palm sugar (see "Notes on Ingredients, Techniques, and Supplies")

1 (13.5-ounce) can full-fat, unsweetened coconut milk

Pinch of salt

Make the kroeung: Using a mortar and pestle, pound lemongrass, galangal, turmeric, fingerroot (if using), lime leaves, garlic, and shallots to a fine paste (or grind in a food processor). Begin with tougher ingredients, then add softer ones. (Freeze any extra kroeung.)

Prepare the soup: In a large pot, bring 6 cups of water to a boil. Poach fish gently until it flakes easily with a fork, about 15 minutes (depending on thickness). Remove fish and debone; reserve poaching water. In a bowl, lightly crush fish together with 4 tablespoons of the kroeung.

In a small skillet, heat oil over medium heat and lightly fry prahok (or anchovies/shrimp paste, if using) and 2 tablespoons kroeung until kroeung turns yellow and the fermented smell turns into a delicious smell.

Bring 4 cups of the poaching water to a simmer and add fried prahok and kroeung. Reduce heat to low, then add fish, remaining kroeung, and crushed peanuts. Simmer for 15 to 20 minutes. Season with salt and sugar.

Meanwhile, cook noodles, drain, rinse with cold water, and set aside.

Add 1 can of coconut milk (or more, as desired) to soup, stir, and cook over low heat until soup starts bubbling. Remove from heat and let soup cool for 10 minutes (it's traditionally served lukewarm, not hot).

While you wait, make the teuk omrith (if using): In a small saucepan, heat coconut oil over low heat and sauté garlic and shallot until golden, then add chili flakes and fry for another minute or so. Add sugar and coconut milk and bring to a boil, just for a moment. Season with salt. The sauce should be lightly sweet, with a hint of salt.

Serve num banhchok noodles in a large bowl, then ladle soup over them and scatter with toppings of your choice. Drizzle with about 2 tablespoons of teuk omrith, if desired.

12. Kuy Teav Is Eternal

Be thrifty with your rice and look after yourself...
Even if you have so little, you must work hard and
try to find more; you cannot just do nothing.
—*Chbab Proh*, the "Rules for Men"

FROM BATTAMBANG, WE headed south to Koh Kong, a gritty harbor town near the Thai border, at the confluence of a wide estuary and the Gulf of Thailand. The estuary brimmed with hundreds of boats: tiny wooden boats for fishing, fast boats driven by Thai traders bringing goods into Cambodia. It was a smuggler's town: boats of questionable purpose, full of humans with questionable intent.

From Koh Kong, Thailand was so close we could almost taste it. One had only to cross the river delta and a few kilometers of wooded peninsula, and there it was: freedom.

Proximity can be deceptive.

The town and surrounding forests were bristling with soldiers, who patrolled the border and the coast. We'd heard that Thai officials were turning boat people away from their shores and pushing refugees back across the border. In one notorious incident, Thai soldiers had deported tens of thousands of refugees back to Cambodia by force, driving them through the minefields of the Preah Vihear Mountains far to the north, at great human cost.

Thailand did not want any more of us. Hundreds of thousands of Vietnamese, Laotians, and Cambodians had streamed into the country since 1975 and were languishing in camps the size of cities. Many were welcomed by the West, but others were stuck in a limbo of forever waiting. And still, we kept coming—by boat and on foot, braving pirates, guerrillas, and minefields. What choice did we have? What kind of life could we have in devastated Cambodia?

Our plan now was to try to make it to Thailand by boat. The idea of being at sea in some tiny, miserable craft filled me with dread, but our alternatives were closing, one by one.

THE TOWN OF Koh Kong was a lawless jumble of shanties, brothels, and makeshift markets rife with gunfire and teeming with five categories of people:

1. Abject-looking refugees who shared our plan of escaping to the West;
2. Abject-looking laborers there to exploit, sell things or services to, or rob the first category;
3. Black-market traders smuggling goods from Thailand to Cambodia and fresh fish (along with fresh Vietnamese and Cambodian refugees) in the opposite direction;
4. People fishing for their dinner, or pretending to fish when they were actually smuggling goods and refugees;
5. Soldiers and police trying to prevent people in categories 1 to 4 from accomplishing their mission.

We found new friends in a tiny fishing encampment by the river, where a dozen Khmer, Chinese, and Vietnamese families had thrown up rickety bamboo-and-leaf huts. Five of us slept in one hut, and additional guests came and went. Chan joined the men on their nighttime fishing expeditions; they trolled the mangroves for crabs to sell in the market and brought home small fish for me and one of the fishermen's wives to cook for the household. Chan and I pooled the minuscule proceeds of the crab sales to buy rice and cooking ingredients, so we wouldn't have to dip into our small escape fund.

Most days, we only had enough fish to make soups: samlor machu kro-eung (Khmer sour soup) or samlor machu trakuon—tamarind sour soup with lots of morning glory and a spoon of prahok and chili. Sometimes our only protein was prahok; we stretched it into a decent meal with stir-fried eggplant, chopped lemongrass, and Thai basil, with fresh vegetables such as water lilies, cucumber, bean sprouts, and morning glory on the side.

On rainy days, the men fished from the riverbank instead of taking the boat out on the estuary. Other days, Chan fished a small pond in town and brought home bigger freshwater fish. We grilled the big fish on a charcoal fire and served it with a dipping sauce made from crushed green tamarind, fish sauce, garlic, and chili. On days when Chan landed a particularly good fish, we made a special dinner: steamed fish wrapped in bánh tráng (rice paper), served with lettuce, fresh herbs, bean sprouts, rice noodles, and cucumber, and a simplified teuk trei pa'em for dipping.

The fishermen and their families shared our goal of escaping to Thailand. But it was nearly impossible to save much money by selling the meager seafood harvest at a market glutted with the product.

After a few months, we joined forces with three families who owned a small wooden fishing boat, and we waited for a moonless sky. At midnight one very dark night, three couples and two small children packed ourselves, several jugs of water, and a heavy load of fuel into a small long-tail fishing boat—the curved wooden craft common to Southeast Asia that's powered and steered with an auto engine. The border was a half-hour away at most, just across the estuary, but we weren't sure how to get there undetected. If we hugged the shoreline, we might be caught by border control and turned back before we ever reached Thailand.

The open sea frightened us, but the authorities frightened us more. "Go out farther," someone urged the man who steered us, as we passed out of the river's mouth and into the ocean. "We'll be safer."

As we crossed the river, Chan ripped off his military-style jacket and tossed it into the sea. He didn't want to be mistaken in Thailand for a soldier. But also, it was a gesture of relief, as if he were throwing off our old lives. And then we motored straight out into the Gulf of Thailand.

The big water.

A silky blackness enfolded us as we headed out to sea and turned northwest (we hoped) to parallel the coastline. There was little to navigate by. Thick, wet clouds concealed the stars, and we soon lost sight of even the few dots of light flickering along the coast. The darkness consumed us and stole our bearings. The muggy air exhaled inky swells that seemed to be gathering strength. Our little vessel rose and fell, and we huddled in the shallow hull, hoping the wind and current would not carry us too far from shore.

Just before dawn, a storm began—an onslaught of boundless waves and water. The women and children lay under a plastic tarp, still pummeled by rain. Chan and several of the others became violently ill from the intense rocking motion. Daylight came, but the sun did not. Angry gray crests merged with gray slashes of rain. Sea and sky became one.

The men emptied our canisters of fuel into the sea and tossed the engine overboard to lighten the boat. As waves rose over us like skyscrapers, we felt sure that one would crash over the little craft and swallow us in the sea's maw. I heard someone weeping. A quavering voice said, "If I survive, I will shave my head and become a monk." I promised God that if He saved us, I would become a vegetarian for a whole year.

The wind, rain, and waves seemed to lash us for days, although it was probably only an hour or two. By some miracle, the craft stayed upright, surfing the crests like a tiny, dry leaf.

Finally, the downpour slackened to a gentle rain. The men took turns rowing toward shore. I fell asleep curled under the tarp and woke beneath a spent silver sky. A distant shoreline was visible; our spirits rose as it drew nearer. And then I felt the boat hull scrape to a stop on a white, sandy beach.

I have never been so relieved to feel the earth under my feet. Chan and I flashed each other identical smiles that said, We are free.

WE HALF-WALKED, HALF-RAN toward a cluster of tiny houses, where women worked at salting and fermenting shrimp in wide baskets, to make shrimp paste. An old woman stared as we ran to her, unable to say anything she could comprehend. The villagers shrugged and gestured toward some buildings just visible up the coast.

We arrived to find three or four Thai marines slouching on a bench with a monk sitting quietly nearby. We ran to the group, and I addressed the monk. "Can you help us?" I said in breathless French. "We are boat people trying to escape Cambodia." Everyone just stared.

Finally, one of the marines led us to a long shed with sides open to the sea air. Someone brought steaming bowls of beef and vegetables swimming in a flame-red broth. The children started crying after the first bite, and I soon learned why: This was the spiciest food I had ever eaten. Thais use much more chili than Khmers do, and a few sips of soup sent surges of heat out through my nose and tears streaming from my eyes. Obviously, I had given up on my promise of vegetarianism almost immediately. "It's a stupid idea," Chan said, when I told him. As he pointed out, it would be an impossible promise to keep in a refugee camp.

If weeping eyes and burning lips were the price of freedom, we were willing to pay it. I was overjoyed to be alive, warm, and dry, and to be fed anything at all. But for the first day or so, we wondered whether this trial-by-chili was a special torture reserved for refugees who dared to enter Thailand. The baseline level of heat the Thais consumed at every meal was inconceivable to us. Even the fried eggs were reddened with chili. We almost laughed out loud when the men gave us a side dish of chilies—"in case you need more," they grinned.

We soon got used to the heat and even started to like it. After spending a decade in Thailand, I became a true chili believer—now I can't eat a meal without it.

FOR SEVERAL DAYS, the marines let us stay in the open-air shelter and brought us three meals a day. I watched the tall cook preparing breakfasts of porridge and big pots of soup for dinner. Sometimes, I stared out toward the sea, placid against a gray monsoon sky. One afternoon between rain showers, I saw a school of whales playing in the water—a joyful sight.

One morning, the officer who had questioned us gathered us together and walked us eastward toward the forest. This was not the direction we had hoped to be going: back into Cambodia. I eyed the soldiers' weapons with alarm, and Chan and I exchanged a look. *They are going to shoot us*, I thought. Chan's somber expression echoed my fears.

Again, we offered prayers to our respective gods. "We may as well kiss goodbye," I whispered to Chan. But the commanding officer's face did not look like the face of a man about to execute a group of refugees. He probably had no idea why we seemed so anguished.

When we reached the border, the officer pointed across it and gestured for us to walk that way. I don't know why they waited three days to march us back—perhaps they were waiting for the heavy rains to abate.

After a half-day's walk along a desolate forest track, we reached the river. There, across the water, was Cambodia—back where we started, only minus our vessel, our savings, and Chan's green jacket.

THIS TIME WE stayed on a tiny island just across a narrow river from Thailand. There was a small, ramshackle settlement there populated mostly by Khmer soldiers and Thai traders. Warehouses lined the riverfront. In another part of the settlement was a busy brothel area—a jumble of huts with tin roofs and plastic sheeting for the walls. Everything flooded when it rained.

We planned to try another sea escape as soon as we had enough money for another long-tail boat. Next time, we vowed to avoid the Thai marines.

Chan found work as a porter, although as skinny as he was, I imagine he was a rather ineffectual hauler of heavy objects. He didn't make much money, but carrying goods for hustlers, traders, and soldiers gave him a chance to intercept whispers, and hopefully, to make contact with other refugees who might go in with us on a second attempt.

Meanwhile, I looked for steady work that would help fund our exit strategy.

One day, my eyes landed on a food stall in the middle of the brothel area. I drew closer, entranced by the familiar aromas of pork stock, shallots, and fried garlic: kuy teav. My family's favorite breakfast. It was the first time I had tasted it since before my mother died. One thing, at least, had not changed: the pork-and-shrimp broth tasted exactly the way it had when I was five years old, when Mae fed me spoonfuls of it by hand. This still wasn't my top choice of the Great Cambodian Breakfast Soups, but the familiar flavors inundated me with a pleasure-and-pain feeling of *This Is My Mother*.

It was almost like she was standing there, spoon-feeding me an idea. I could run this kuy teav stall. I had never done it before, but I knew all the essentials. How to make a delicious stock. How to fry the garlic to a perfect golden crispness.

I walked up to the kuy teav vendor, a young woman with a toddler at her feet, and asked her if I could work there. She said yes.

From day one, my soup sold well. I made a traditional kuy teav stock from pork bones and pork meat, dried shrimp and squid, carrot, and daikon. The secret to making the broth rich and clear is love and care. The process cannot be rushed. Cook over a low fire with the lid ajar, to keep the liquid from boiling too violently and the meat from separating from the bone and clouding the soup. Simmer the broth slowly and skim the brownish foam (but not the fat) off the surface, until no more foam rises. The finished broth will be completely clear with a thin layer of fat on top.

Kuy teav is usually served with thin, squared-off rice vermicelli noodles and a protein, such as ground pork. These days, some fancier stalls and restaurants offer a huge array of additional choices, such as shrimp, squid, sliced pork, liver, dumplings, or even duck; you can opt for tapioca noodles or egg noodles, or you can even have your kuy teav noodles "dry," with the broth on the side. Eaters customize the soup with their favorite garnishes and sauces. Float a few fried Chinese-style crullers (you char kway) on top like croutons, and you are ready to begin.

I topped my kuy teav noodle soup with sliced scallions, fried garlic, and tang chai—chopped dried cabbage preserved with garlic, salt, and a little star anise. I offered customers lots of side dishes for decorating their soup: freshly ground black pepper, chili sauce, sugar, and chopped fresh chili.

In the afternoons, I used the leftover pork and stock to cook bobor—a soupy rice porridge like congee, usually made with a protein (such as chicken or pork) and whatever additives you can lay hands on: fried garlic, scallions, cilantro, bean sprouts, fish sauce, and plenty of chili. Bobor is a workingman's dish—savory and filling—and made from cheap ingredients like blood or offal or whatever meat is left over from the day before.

Every day, a line of young women stood waiting, before I had even finished the porridge, and I had hardly a moment to rest before it ran out. The chopped pork bobor was a massive hit with the brothel workers. It is the ultimate comfort food, in a place where comfort was very much needed.

So much of Cambodia had changed forever, but bobor will always soothe us—and kuy teav is eternal.

Cambodian Noodle Soup with Pork (Kuy Teav)

I did not learn to make kuy teav at home in Battambang, but it didn't take long to figure out. If you know how to make a rich, clear stock, kuy teav is within your skill set, too. The variations are almost infinite. Serve with a wide variety of toppings, herbs, sauces, and proteins, so eaters can customize their bowls; the quantities don't really matter.

Serves 6 to 8

Ingredients:
2 pounds pork bones, such as ribs or neck bones
1 large daikon, quartered
1 white onion, quartered
1 carrot, cut into 1-inch pieces
½ pound pork (shoulder or tenderloin)
1 teaspoon dried shrimp (or 1 medium-size dried squid), soaked and rinsed (optional)
½ teaspoon salt
½ teaspoon sugar
2 cubes Knorr chicken bouillon (optional)
1 (14- to 16-ounce) package flat rice vermicelli (you can usually find packages labeled "Hủ tiếu"; flat egg noodles, tapioca noodles, or bún can also be used)
Additional proteins of your choice, such as: shrimp, ground pork belly, sliced beef, or basically anything you can imagine (poach quickly using a spider skimmer in the simmering stock)
For toppings, any assortment of the following: 2 heads garlic, minced then fried in neutral oil over medium heat until golden and crisp; 1 bunch cilantro;1 bunch scallions, thinly sliced; 1 bunch Thai basil and/or mint; ¼ pound bean sprouts; fish sauce; Golden Mountain Seasoning Sauce (or your favorite soy sauce); lime wedges; Thai red chilies, sliced; chili sauce/chili oil; freshly ground black pepper

In a large stockpot, quickly parboil pork bones, rinse them, and scrub the pot. (This step makes a clearer broth.) Return bones to stockpot, then add daikon, onion, and carrot. Refill pot with cold water (about 5 quarts) and cover. Bring to a gentle boil, uncover, and reduce heat to low; skim foam from the surface. Add pork and simmer until tender, about 20 minutes, then remove it and slice it thinly against the grain. Set aside. Add dried shrimp or squid to

stock and continue to simmer over low heat, uncovered, for 2 to
3 hours.

Remove solids and strain the stock through a fine-mesh sieve.
Add salt and sugar (and chicken bouillon, if using).

Cook noodles, rinse with cold water, and drain. Divide noodles
among deep soup bowls. Arrange sliced pork (or other proteins)
on top, then ladle the hot stock over everything. Top with all the
good things you like best.

————

THE OWNER OF the stand was happy to let me manage everything. She
stopped by twice a day to check on me, then headed off to play cards. Her
family was part of the thriving local sex trade. Her younger sister owned a
brothel, and her mother and sister-in-law worked in one. We lived in a temporary structure in the middle of the brothel area, a compound of rickety
wood structures that exuded impermanence. Small cells with bamboo beds
sheathed in plastic were arranged around common areas thronged with girls
lounging on low chairs, smoking cigarettes, and shouting to one another.
Plastic sheeting separated a lounge area from cells barely large enough for
the pairs to complete their business—usually very quickly.

The brothels never slept. A procession of policemen, soldiers, Vietnamese
porters, and Thai traders came through every night and disappeared into
the cells. The women didn't seem to sleep much either. When they weren't
with customers, they drank, smoked marijuana, played cards, and shrieked
with laughter. I rarely saw them sober. Most were really just girls, many of
them sixteen or younger. At first, I couldn't understand how these lovely
young creatures could have chosen such a life. Why hadn't they gotten
married?

I laugh now at the innocence of that question. I suppose I was con-
gratulating myself about my own choice, back in Saigon, to say no to the
man who offered me a new outfit in exchange for sex. For an instant, I had
imagined the realities of such a life, how easy it could be to say yes. But

something in me would not allow myself to do it—the voices of my mother and sister, perhaps. The voices of the nuns and priests who taught me in Catholic school. Or my own pride.

At least, that's the story I told myself then.

It would be many years before I fully understood that, unlike these Koh Kong girls, I had the freedom to say no. Because I had not (as I imagined) fallen as low as one can fall into poverty and desperation. Years later, when I worked with Doctors Without Borders (Médecins Sans Frontières, or MSF), I would learn a great deal about poverty and freedom, desperation and "choices." In my hospice work with Cambodian sex workers dying of AIDS, I would be humbled by the unimaginable strength and suffering I witnessed. I would rethink the definition of pride.

But even in those first weeks cooking amid the Koh Kong brothels, I saw that freedom of choice exists on a continuum of duress. A girl does not have to be kidnapped and chained to see no other destination for herself than a brothel. An outsider may not understand the pressures she faces, but to her, they are everything.

For the beautiful young girls of Koh Kong, there was little chance of salvation by marriage. The men from their home villages were dead or destitute, and in no position to support families. Some of the girls had been brought there by their mothers to become the family breadwinner, as if the daughters were property to trade.

I sometimes slept in an earthen-floor hut just outside the main brothel structure, where some of the girls who worked during the day rented sleeping huts at night. This was also where the girls came to weep in private between clients, drinks, and card games. Once, I heard a girl, in such pain she could barely walk after some cruel drunk was finished with her, crying out for her mother. And then, the mother's voice, shushing to calm her. "I know, baby," the mother murmured. But what she did *not* say was: "You don't have to do this anymore. Let's go home." The girl was tiny, no older than fifteen, with long hair and long eyelashes.

I saw it many times: mothers who took their daughters to the brothels to earn money in order to start a business back in their home villages, where no one knew what they were up to in Koh Kong. Most of the motherless ones cared nothing of plans. They spent their money on alcohol or gambled it away. They burned their lives down and rarely spoke of the future. I thought of my own teen years, when Kim Hoa and I spent our days conspiring to hide the teacher's cabbage or saving our money to buy tickets to the zoo. I had withstood losses: my mother and Chanthu; my sense of safety; a delicious and pampered childhood; my hopes for a rich future. I'd felt despair and considered suicide.

But I had chosen to escape Saigon. Such a choice was within my power. What say did these girls have over their fates?

I might have condemned the vicious brothel owners and their brutish clientele, but I could not condemn the brothel girls. They didn't share their private sorrows with me. When I served them meals, they only joked or chatted about nothing. But when they drew near, I could smell them. They could not clean themselves properly; the bathing area was a muddy earthen corner where they poured murky water from a jar over themselves. Even this indignity, they bore without complaint. They were very strong and very brave.

The mothers were harder to forgive. But I had to acknowledge that they had lived their entire lives in a depth of poverty I could not fathom, even in my reduced state. The money they earned by selling their daughters could change their families' lives. If I had no hope and nothing to sell for food, maybe I would do the same—how could I know for sure? Still, my empathy for the mothers melted away whenever I witnessed one of the brothel patrons treating a girl like an animal. I remember one drunken Khmer soldier laughing as he dragged a girl into a stall and made a brutal performance of throwing her around in every position, while the vile company of men in the common area peeked between the slats. I was heartsick and outraged, and there was nothing I could do to stop such things from happening.

SOME NIGHTS, THE kuy teav stall owner let Chan and me sleep at her house, but lying on the rutted bamboo floor all night left me feeling bruised and beaten. It hardly mattered; there was little time for sleep, anyway. I got up at 4 a.m. to start the pork broth and was rarely finished much before 11 p.m. After a few weeks, I told Chan that I was exhausted. My body ached; I couldn't work at that pace much longer.

He urged me to stick with the job a little longer. And as he kept reminding me, keeping us fed, *plus* saving enough money to smuggle ourselves to Thailand by sea again, was going to demand all our effort and strength.

I had by some miracle found a reserve of water-buffalo industriousness within myself. What I lacked was Chan's good-humored endurance. He pressed ahead without lingering on his doubts, as if he could see decades into our future, whereas there were nights when I could barely see myself rising from the bamboo floor the next morning. The grueling workdays were eating away at the hope I'd felt as we had crossed into Cambodia a few months earlier.

Like Mae and Chanthu, I had long weathered setbacks with religious resignation: "It's God's will," I told myself. I had heard my mother say it so many times—whenever we met with yet another shattering loss. I must have repeated it too often in Koh Kong, because one day, Chan had heard it enough. "If you just keep calling God's name, how will you find a boat?" he pointed out. "If you don't go and ask for a job, how will you find food?"

My anger bubbled over. "God can hear you. He will put you in hell," I spat. But later, I saw that Chan was right. Maybe "God's will" thinking can help us accept a terrible truth that we cannot understand. Maybe certain happy futures can only be born of some dire present. But God's will is not a reason to give in to despair.

Nor is astrological fatalism. For too long, I'd believed in Mae and Chanthu's warnings about my inauspicious Buffalo birth. I had surrendered my own will to the inevitability of stars and planets.

Chan once told me something that changed how I felt about star fate, too. He pointed out that I may have been born in the Year of the Buffalo, but I was also born in the hour of the tiger. "This is one of the Four Pillars of Destiny," he smiled.

According to Chinese astrology, the Four Pillars that determine your character and fate are the year, month, day, and hour of your birth. What Chan had said was true. I was born during the tiger's hours, between 3 a.m. and 5 a.m., the time before dawn when she stalks her prey.

My buffalo birth year had made me hard-working and self-reliant, or so the zodiac said. But the tiger-ascendant sign adds another layer of traits: courage, passion, ambition. "Anyone born to the tiger hour can become a king," Chan told me. That's when I started to believe that I might have some power over my future after all.

Sometimes, magic works, whether you believe in it or not.

There's a Khmer proverb about belief and fate: "Kru teay mday tha." It means, "What your teacher (kru) and your mother (mday) foretell about you will probably come true."

I've always wondered: Does that saying mean that your teacher and your mother know you best, and can guess where your character will lead you? Or does it mean that because you trust them, you'll tend to fulfill their prophecies?

And by the way, the word *kru* can also mean "fortune teller." Already, some of my fortune teller's more unlikely forecasts were coming true: "Cooking or sewing will carry you," he had said. I thought about that as I cooked kuy teav and bobor amid the bustle of the brothel district. This wasn't the kind of "carrying" I'd imagined that day in the fortune teller's apartment. But I had to admit: Here I was, turning to my mother's kitchen lessons to keep us afloat.

IT WOULD BE years before I learned to convert my faith in God and stars into a belief in myself. Instead, in Koh Kong and for the decade to come, I trusted in Chan. He was strong-minded and clever, and he never let despair take hold. Whenever my resolve collapsed, he knew what to say to prop it up again. Sometimes, a kind word or a joke worked. Other times, I needed a sharper prod. Pointed truth-telling—edged with sarcasm—was his specialty. And once my indignation cooled, I could feel his point sinking in and altering my perspective.

Chan changed my thinking about stars and agency, which gave me the strength to struggle against circumstances that seemed preordained. I felt lucky to have found the perfect partner for this period in my life, a time of so much struggle and disappointment. I don't know how I would have survived Koh Kong, or everything that happened in the years that followed, without his steadiness.

AFTER TWO MONTHS, the kuy teav and bobor I sold at the stand had become neighborhood staples. And so, when I finally told myself that I could not sustain the long workdays with so little sleep, I was able to find another job right away.

And that is how I began cooking for the owner of a brothel.

This was, in many ways, an upgrade from the kuy teav stand. It paid about the same but required much less work. I only had to cook for five to ten people twice a day—no more eighteen-hour days on my feet. And the brothel itself was outside the thronged sex-trade district of squalid shanties. It was in a Khmer-style wood house on stilts, with rough wooden floors and five private stalls with doors. It was cleaner and did not flood. Chan and I slept in a real bed in the kitchen.

The brothel owner was a cheerful woman in her thirties, with curly hair and long red nails. I never heard her shout at the girls like the other owners did. But the improved accommodations did not change the truth of that horrific industry. Night after night, I saw young girls shaking with sobs after disappearing with drunk men twice their age; hours later, they would be drunk themselves and laughing like lunatics. Sometimes, I looked at those girls and vowed, *No daughter of mine will ever live like this.* I swore to myself in Koh Kong that I would not bring children into such ugliness and squalor. I would bear them once I had lifted myself out of this hell, or I would not bear them at all.

I waited a very long time to have my own daughter. She graduated from a university in America and a graduate school in London, and she can take care of herself quite well. I feel lucky for her, and lucky for myself. She is smart and strong, and she has choices so innumerable, they are beyond my imagination.

I was not a perfect mother. But I focused all my energy on keeping my family out of the life I saw in the brothel district of Koh Kong. And I found a calling in helping other families stay out of that life as well.

SPENDING MY DAYS inside that brothel focused my mind: *I must work hard to get out of here and be sure I never return.* One late morning when I was cooking lunch, one of the men—a Thai trader—staggered in and pointed to me. The brothel owner shook her head. "She's not available," she said. "Choose another one."

I was shaken but still reasonably sure that she would say "no" to anyone who requested my services in a nonculinary capacity. The owner liked me. I was more valuable to her for my cooking than my sex. As she saw it, the girls were an infinitely renewable resource. But a good cook was hard to find.

Still, it was a risk I did not want to take any longer. And it was nearly unbearable to witness the nightly torment of innocents and be powerless to help them. The only kindness I could offer the young women was to feed them something delicious and special. I made them simple Khmer dishes like the ones I imagined they might have had back home: fried fish, a cha of stir-fried vegetables with fish or sautéed meat, a samlor proher with whatever vegetables I could find, or grilled prahok. It was a small way for me to show the girls I cared for them, in that tragic place with so little to hope for.

WE HEARD THAT the owner of a small medical clinic was looking for an assistant, someone to cook for her and clean the clinic—which was really just a room in her house. I went to see her and got the job immediately.

I was happy to leave the brothel. "What a pity!" the owner said when I told her. "Can't you stay?"

I could not.

My new boss was a trained midwife in her fifties who received mostly Thai patients. The only payment she offered us was room and board. We slept on the clinic floor, and she paid for food and allowed us to eat the meals I prepared. She went on and on about how much she loved my cooking: This grilled pork is so tasty! This soup is very nice! And so on.

I was to wake up at five every morning and begin my chores: preparing breakfast and sluicing down the floor and table. If I hadn't moved by the time she exited her bedroom, the owner slammed the door to wake me. But I earned her respect the day I read a drug label out loud to her and told her what the drug was for. Her face swiveled toward me. "You seem educated," she said with surprise.

After that, she started taking me with her on house calls. One night, we went to a tiny wooden house where a young woman was in labor. The delivery went well, and my boss showed me how to cut and dress the umbilical cord and repair the mother's episiotomy.

When we returned to remove the stitches, the mother burst into tears and told us her story. She had met the Thai father at a bar in Phnom Penh where she worked. He had already tired of her, she said. Now he was threatening to leave her and take their son back to Thailand. She begged us to perform a de oy saat (literally, "sewn to be pretty"), cosmetic surgery to narrow her vulva. She hoped a renovated vagina would reinvigorate her husband's interest in her. But it had to be done in secret when the husband was not there.

It was a simple and fairly common procedure. When I worked for MSF many years later, I noticed that the sex workers we treated often had this procedure done by midwives so they could be marketed as virgins. And it wasn't uncommon for young wives to have the de oy saat in hopes of keeping their husbands from straying. It wasn't particularly dangerous if performed by a skilled midwife. But it was an unnecessary risk with no medical purpose, done only to please a man.

The following evening, the midwife made the requested cuts and stitches. But the sutured wound would not stop bleeding. The patient went pale and cried quietly; my boss's face went just as white. "Pray! Pray!" she murmured, casting panicked looks at the bleeding woman.

Pray?! my mind raced. *If we are busy praying, who will stop the bleeding?* That's when I realized that my boss had no idea what she was doing.

Finally, the bleeding stopped. The next day, I returned to check on the patient but found the door locked. I slipped down an alley to try the back door and caught sight of three Thai men through a window. One of them, I guessed, was the child's father: His dark skin and features resembled those of his newborn son. The men were spooning white powder out of a big plastic bag onto a scale. I flattened myself against the wall and stole back down the alley.

The mother, probably no older than twenty, had nearly bled to death to enhance the pleasure of a heroin smuggler who cared nothing for her. I ached for her and her child, and for the illiterate brothel girls and their mothers. And even for the ruthless brothel owners, and for my miserly boss whose scant medical know-how did more harm than good. Every one of them just trying to survive any way she knew how.

I ached for all of us women in this miserable shantytown, fighting for one more day of rice, at the mercy of anyone with a shard of power. None of us Koh Kong strivers had any real control, but the women among us had even less. I wondered how long this era of fighting for daily rice would endure in this town, this country, this star-cursed and forgotten corner of Asia. I wondered how long women would remain the poorest of the poor, in a great sea of poverty. We'd heard so much about our *Chbab Srey* responsibilities—and were often expected to fulfill them, even in this merciless time and place. I wondered what the *Chbab Proh*, the "Rules for Men," had to say about men's responsibility to not exploit teenage girls for their own gratification, or about how not to abuse or abandon their wives and children.

I walked back to the clinic and prepared a very nice soup. It was all I knew to do.

AFTER A FEW months of working at the clinic, I informed my boss that we planned to try for Thailand again. She was sad to see me go, but I was not sad to leave.

Chan had put together a smaller group this time, with a smaller boat. This one was a tiny wooden fishing boat—long and thin, with no covered area. The hull was no more than three feet wide at its midpoint.

This time, we took no chances with the Big Water. We merely crossed the estuary and hugged the dark coastline. We came ashore in a village. By that time I had learned a few words of Thai. We found a taxi driver, and I pronounced some syllables that I hoped meant "Take us to Trat."

Instead of taking us to Trat, he reported us to the police.

At the station, the Ministry of Interior (MOI) policeman demanded that I speak to him in Thai. I told him that I didn't know Thai; I knew French. "You told the taxi driver, 'Take us to Trat,'" said the policeman in a tone of accusation. "In Thai."

"Yes, but that's all I can say," I explained, in a mix of Khmer, French, and execrable Thai. We went back and forth like that for an hour and a half, with him interrogating me about my supposedly covert knowledge of Thai, as if I were some kind of spy.

Finally, he put me in a cell with the others. We waited there for many hours, locked up, with only rice and fish sauce to eat.

Under the circumstances, I shouldn't have looked sideways at a gift of rice. But try to see things through a refugee's weary eyes. You have fled war, occupation, and countless miseries and washed ashore somewhere peaceful. Surely the decent people of the world know what you have endured. Surely, they wait for you on some free shore, offering smiles, blankets, and steaming bowls of soup! It's an absurd wish, of course. I suppose even the civilized and decent have a breaking point, when faced with a tsunami of need.

Still, as we waited in our cell, wondering whether we'd be driven back to Cambodia again (or worse), I found myself wishing for the Thai marines' spicy beef soup—a warmer welcome by far than this rice-and-fish-sauce dish, which gave off a powerful flavor of distaste. Its message was clear: *Go back where you came from. We don't want you here.*

I have never mastered the subtleties of that dish, but the recipe, in theory, is very straightforward.

Recipe: Go-Home Rice

Bring rice to a boil using the heat of your contempt. Lower heat and simmer resentfully.

Smack the boiled rice into a bowl as aggressively as you can; this is where the real artistry lies, in the noisy theatricality of your rice-smacking technique. Practice this to get it just right.

Squirt subpar fish sauce across the rice mound in a single, surly wrist-flick. The idea is to take great care in imparting a sense of carelessness.

Serve with a side of loathing.

13. Land-Mine Chicken

Run away from a tiger and face a crocodile.
—Thai proverb

AFTER THREE DAYS in the village jail cell, a Thai representative of the United Nations High Commissioner for Refugees (UNHCR), the UN refugee agency, loaded us into a pickup truck and drove us to a nearby temporary holding camp. Behind a corrugated metal fence, a few open-air shelters had been slapped together with bamboo frames and topped with thatched roofs that pattered like rain when the wind riffled the leaves.

The camp was a waypoint for several dozen people who, like us, had made it to Thailand by boat. Many came all the way from Vietnam over water and under horrific circumstances. More arrived every day. Each group received two cooking pots, and someone from the UN brought fresh meat and vegetables every morning. We cooked the rations in the big pot and prepared rice in the small one. Everyone ate together around low bamboo pallets, which became our beds at night. We chattered gleefully about what came next: another camp, interviews with UNHCR, new homes for us all.

In my memory, the stilted structures were simple but cheerful—elevated high above the earth and washed with sunlight and salt breezes. But maybe it was our anticipation that bathed the shadows in light and sweetened the air. My mind surged with excitement. We were weeks from being resettled in a new country, some earthly paradise where hard work would be rewarded with safety and full stomachs. Although I had relatives in Europe, most refugees had their hearts set on America. I imagined the place as an exuberant nation of dazzling color and clamor. Confident people with wide-open faces and big laughs. No reeducation camps or Year Zero extermination projects.

Mountains of good food, anything you wanted, and no citizen allowed to starve.

AFTER SEVERAL WEEKS, we were moved to Phanat Nikhom, a large camp in Chonburi Province where new arrivals were processed. We waited in a hot office full of bewildered families and weary-looking officials filling out forms. The chaos of many languages filled the room, as new arrivals struggled to understand what was happening and functionaries repeated questions in ever-louder voices.

In a practical sense, Chan and I had been living as husband and wife for months, so we registered as a couple. We had never discussed love or marriage. There was no room in our lives for romance. We had simply thrown in our lot with each other and faced our troubles together. We filled out a mountain of documents, and then the bleary-eyed representative told us some disquieting news: being resettled would not be as simple as we thought. He said that some kind of deadline had passed. I still don't understand what he meant, or what changed. We had believed that all we had to do was select a country and go.

From the moment our feet met the solid ground of Thailand, America had felt so close. Now we would have to wait for a lengthy screening by UNHCR to determine our status—in other words, whether we could be defined as genuine political refugees with "a well-founded fear of persecution," and not mere "economic migrants" or "displaced persons." These murky distinctions reeked of Cold War politics.

It was difficult to know what to believe. For some reason we could not understand, someone in charge of our fates had closed the doors of the world to us. We were not bound for France or America. We were bound for nowhere.

We tried to remind ourselves that we were lucky to have made it to Thailand at all. Our lives here might be austere, but at least we were relatively safe and would not starve. In the meantime, our transition would take a bit longer than we had imagined, while UNHCR determined whether we were fleeing in good faith or had merely become displaced. It seemed like madness that a tiny difference in terms should exert so much influence over a person's future. But according to the rumors that shot through camp—via the fog of information that passed from mouth to desperate mouth—policy toward refugees was constantly being revised. If the winds had shifted against us, surely, they would rotate again in our favor.

News of our nonimminent departure dampened our excitement. But we stayed, hoping and waiting.

AGAIN, A UNHCR official issued us two cookpots. This time we also got a small wood-burning cook stove, two blankets, a mosquito net, a spoon, and a plastic plate. Someone showed us to a long, narrow structure with concrete floors, tin roofs, and thin cement walls on three sides. "This is your house," the man said.

The shelters were designed for forty people, so each person was allotted a rectangle of concrete about the size of a single bed. At night, some families hung makeshift walls of plastic sheeting, converting the dark dormitory into a synthetic beehive of plastic-wrapped cells. But the sheeting was not standard issue—we would have to buy it from the Thai traders who ran shops in the camps.

We had no money, so we did without bedroom walls for the time being. We slept on concrete under a mosquito net, shared one blanket, and used the other one for a pillow. There were no electric lights. The only illumination came from kerosene lamps, which had to be out by the 10 p.m. curfew.

The sleeping shelters were arranged into squares of four around a center courtyard; 160 people shared four toilets and a septic tank, which was emptied every afternoon. By then, sewage was usually overflowing onto the ground. Wading in sewage so disgusted me that for several weeks, I ate as little as possible so I would not need to use the toilet. Once, I went two weeks without defecating. When Chan found out, he shouted that it was dangerous and stupid to starve myself, and he made me start eating a normal amount of food again.

Our section strung up plastic sheeting around five shower stalls to give women some privacy while they washed. During the dry season, a line of water buckets in front of the showers signaled how long the wait would be. We didn't shower when it rained—there was no way to keep our clean clothes dry while we were bathing.

Phanat Nikhom was vast—a city of exiles separated into smaller zones by corrugated tin and razor wire. Because we spoke Vietnamese, we were placed in a section designated for Vietnamese and Khmer Krom (ethnic Khmers living in southwest Vietnam). We were not allowed to leave camp or to venture into the Khmer, Lao, or Hmong areas. Our section had six blocks of twelve shelters each; blocks were named by letter and buildings by number.

Our first home was called F7.

The camp's rat population was of unknown national origin or refugee status, but they moved freely, and with no apparent shame. Judging from their size, they were the best-fed residents of the camp. Many nights, I woke up screaming as something scuttled across my face in the darkness. I never got used to the disgusting creatures, and I hate them still.

Everything about camp life was a shock to us: the rats, the rules, the constant guard patrols. We had somehow expected to be treated like guests here for a short stay; instead, we felt like prisoners. Those first nights, I slept poorly on the hard floor, enveloped by the night's thick heat, our bunkmates' gentle murmurs, and my unease about the future unfolding for us in this dreary place.

Inside me there lived the shadow of a soft little girl, whose mother had fed her by hand and rocked her to sleep in a hammock. That ghost still shuddered with revulsion at the rats and the sewage, and ached from sleeping on cold concrete. It was time for the pâté-de-foie girl from Battambang to toughen up, for this camping expedition was to be no brief interlude.

It would be two years before we were granted a screening interview. And two more years to learn the results.

In the end, we would wait for a decade for the result we hoped for. And that result would never come.

THREE TIMES A week, we received our rations:

Monday: 50 grams of chicken (slightly less than two ounces, bones and all); ½ kilogram of vegetables.
Wednesday: 50 grams of pork; ½ kilo of vegetables.
Friday: 50 grams of fish; ½ kilo of vegetables.

The food was dropped off in front of each housing block and chopped up into portions right there in the road, so everything was encrusted with a crisp layer of dirt and gravel. But even before the dirt layer was added, these rations were of lower quality and freshness than the food we'd received from the UN at the temporary camp. Apparently, at Phanat Nikhom, supplies filtered through the Thai authorities' hands first. We assumed that a certain percentage of that food aid never made it to us inside the wire. That missing percentage, we figured, came out of the choicest rations.

The vegetable rations rotated among three or four varieties, usually bok choy, a leafy green we call spei kror nhanh, and eggplant—all of which we used to prepare cha dishes: Khmer-style stir-fries. For flavor, we added a little garlic and MSG from the camp store.

There was one season when we received nothing but eggplant for months on end. People became so sick of eggplant that a few people actually picked it up at the collection point and threw it straight into the trash. I didn't mind the eggplant—it could be made tasty without too much effort. Usually, I cut the long, slender vegetable into five-centimeter pieces, soaked them in salt water for a few minutes to remove the bitterness, stir-fried them, and added water to make a thick soup.

The meat rations were more difficult to salvage. We nicknamed them Grandmother Chicken and Grandmother Pork because of their advanced age and extraordinary toughness. The meat was so rubbery, you had to cook it for hours to render it edible.

I used a technique Mae had taught me, searing it and adding water little by little until the meat was tender. When I could get my hands on garlic and shallots, I added them to the pan. The cooking oil, chicken fat, and simmering water thickened into a gravy, and the shallots and garlic flavored it nicely.

Mae's slow-braise method required many hours of cooking. This wasn't a problem: time was one thing we had in abundance.

WATER WAS A more limited resource. Every afternoon, fellow internees delivered twenty liters per person for cooking, drinking, showering, and washing clothes, which meant we had to plan ahead and use it sparingly. First, I used five liters to wash the rice, then I saved the rice water to wash the vegetables and reused it again to soap up the dishes after dinner. I rinsed them in clean water. That left less than five liters to wash clothes—which I did every other day—and ten for bathing, drinking, and brushing our teeth.

Each month, we received nine kilos of good rice, cooking oil, salt, and firewood. The rice ration was more than enough—so much that we sometimes sold half our portion to a Thai merchant who came into camp to trade with us. That paid for plastic sheeting, soy sauce, eggs, and extra vegetables to supplement our rations. It soon became clear that the economics of camp life were not so different from anywhere else. Money could ease the starker discomforts. We saw that people who had financial support from relatives in America or Europe lived easier and ate better. They had bedroom walls and good Thai soy sauce.

Privacy and flavor: two commodities we craved beyond measure.

THE THAI CAMP authority had allotted office space for two Buddhist monks and two Catholic priests; they held mass and Buddhist prayer services every week and were available to help refugees locate families abroad. A few weeks after we arrived in Phanat Nikhom, I visited the priest and asked him for an aerogram and postage. And then I swallowed my pride and wrote to Caritas (an alliance of Catholic relief organizations) to ask them to help find my sister Yen.

I was still angry with Yen for her cold letter cutting ties with me after Mae died. And now I was crawling back like a beggar. But in camp, being supported by a relative abroad didn't make you a beggar; it made you a king. When a neighbor in the dormitory spied me writing an aerogram, I suddenly became important in her eyes. She offered to loan me a little money until I received a reply.

Keeping secrets in camp was impossible.

A month later, an envelope arrived from Europe. It contained a money order for $100 and a promise to send another one every month. Sometimes the money was from Yen, and sometimes from Caritas. That money was a huge relief to us. I was torn about turning to her, but her help made our lives more comfortable—and later, made it possible for us to improve our situation considerably. Yen also did her best to help us get to Europe, but her letter of invitation had zero effect on the screening officer.

One new comfort we could afford now, thanks to Yen, was a kerosene cooker, which was cleaner, easier to use, and safer than a wood fire. Some ingenious refugee had invented a compact prototype using scrap metal from an aluminum drum and a cut-up blanket as a wick; the entrepreneurial spirit did the rest.

In 1984, we paid around fifteen dollars for our kerosene burner. The thing still worked more than a decade later, when we moved into our first house in rural Cambodia.

YEN'S MONEY ORDER gave us choices. Now we could shop at the camp store, which sold everything from tarps and clothes to shampoo and toothpaste. But the prices reflected a cynical understanding that we were a captive market. Everything was wildly inflated. The most affordable items were eggs, chicken knees (which smelled old and nasty), instant noodles, and lank poultry that we referred to as "land-mine chicken." The pitiful birds looked like they had reached the camp by crossing a minefield—skeletons whose legs, wings, and breasts had been removed by means of explosion.

This was not a delicious chicken. Still, the weekly rations didn't quite add up to seven days of sustenance. So we were happy for anything to supplement our food allowance, even if it had been previously detonated (or so we joked). I have no idea how families managed on the camp rations alone, but plenty of people did.

We soon learned that goods from the camp store cost many times the price of the same products obtained from outside the wire. Thai tradesmen from a nearby village would cut a hole in the corrugated metal fence and push kerosene or noodles through the gap to smugglers inside camp, who resold the contraband for a small profit. It was one of the few ways for refugees with no outside support to make money. But the smugglers were taking a big risk. Anyone caught with illegal goods could be beaten and jailed by Thai MOI guards.

Many of us felt the risk was worth it. Our money fed us far better if we shopped through the hole in the fence.

Unfortunately, the guards would sometimes search our sleeping shelter for contraband—easy to identify because the colorful camp-shop label was absent. Once, guards confiscated a twenty-liter drum of kerosene and a thirty-pack box of instant noodles from us. We were not beaten, but I was sick about losing a month's supply of cooking fuel and our instant noodles. Those noodles were one of our few luxuries.

I laugh when I think about it: in Battambang, my mother would never have let an abomination like instant noodles into her kitchen. The first time I ever tasted them was in Vietnam—they were made of cassava and very cheap. My mother refused to touch them.

And now, here I was slurping instant noodles for breakfast every chance I got. And liking them. When the world whittles down your choices, even a mediocre comfort food can become a sumptuous indulgence. If you can't imagine it, try eating eggplant for ninety-seven days in a row, or a thin soup made of land-mine chicken for a decade. Then you'll find out how delicious instant noodles can be.

The "Mama" brand noodles were my favorite; I still eat them sometimes—a shameful secret pleasure. Try the tom yum shrimp flavor— it's the best one. You probably won't have to enlist a smuggler to obtain them.

Recipe: How to Prepare Instant Noodles in a Thai Refugee Camp
Serves 1

Ingredients:
Smuggled Mama noodles
Smuggled kerosene
Cooking oil
Chili
1 homemade kerosene stove, bought in secret from its creator
1 empty beer can
EXACTLY 330 milliliters (about 1⅓ cups) of your water ration

Using your quietest voice, order a 30-pack box of "Mama" instant noodles from a smuggler. (Noodle packs will be slid under the door; payment will be handled later.)

Quickly tear the box up and throw it away, keeping only the noodles, so the damning absence of the shop's stamp will no longer be obvious to the guards. (Noodles need to appear to the authorities as if you bought them legally inside the camp for many times the smuggled-noodles price.)

Order kerosene separately. Divide the 20 liters into 4 plastic jugs; return empty drum to stove maker/smuggler so that guards cannot determine where you acquired it.

Measure 330 milliliters of water into the pot to boil. (Note: Use no more than 330 ml of water, otherwise you won't have enough water left to brush your teeth that night. You can use an empty beer can to measure.) Don't forget to put the lid on for quicker boiling, to conserve water and kerosene. Ignite homemade camp stove . . . carefully. When water begins to boil, shut off the fire immediately to save kerosene *and* to make sure water doesn't evaporate too much.

Put noodles into a bowl, add flavoring, oil, and chili, and pour boiling water over everything. Cover the bowl for 1 minute before serving. Eat dutifully.

In order to avoid beatings and/or incarceration, *do not* feel hungry after mandatory lights-out curfew at 10 p.m. Guards will see the cooking fire, and your dinner will end abruptly.

Maybe it sounds ungrateful to grumble about wan poultry and repetitive nightshades when you're a ward of the world, eating donated rice and living on borrowed land. But we refugees had escaped war and repression only to find ourselves in a purgatory between painful histories and vague futures. It didn't help that we'd come looking for freedom and landed in a sort of prison, where time had ceased to advance. Waiting for a life to become unpaused, with no meaningful work to do and nothing to strive for, can drive a person mad.

And still, we waited and dreamed.

Hope can be dangerous when you have no power to enact the thing hoped for, when you are merely waiting. To be of use, optimism needs to set something into motion. Hope without enterprise ages poorly, leaving an aftertaste of bitterness and apathy.

We could see our hopes personified through the gaps in the fence, where there was a transit center for people who'd been granted asylum. There they were, just across the wire, free to come and go as they pleased.

Our nightmares also resided there, as the camp jail was housed in that same facility. Whereas the UNHCR screening was a lengthy and complicated process, the camp guards could lock you up very quickly. The guards patrolled the compound day and night with swaggering menace. They could punish us with impunity, a privilege they exercised frequently. The guards beat anyone who broke the rules—both the rules we knew about, and the ones they invented on the spot.

Because our quad block was near the fence, I saw many people caught smuggling by the guards and beaten right where they stood. The police would raise a thick bamboo pole over their heads and bring it down hard, again and again, until the person lay unconscious. I suspect that some people did not survive those beatings. Once, I looked on helplessly as they beat an older woman so hard that the bamboo sticks snapped.

One of the guards was particularly cruel, a tall policeman we called Hua Na—"The Boss." He came around every few days and augmented the guards' enforcement activities with great zeal. If anyone was caught sneaking noodles or kerosene through the fence on his watch, he would beat, kick, and stomp the person until his foot became tired of kicking.

His power was absolute. He could demand anything he liked. One morning, when I was shopping at the camp store, I saw a pretty girl of fourteen or fifteen walking back from his quarters. She looked exhausted, pale, and terribly sad. Her family lived near us, and I noticed that for many nights after that, the girl left in the evening and returned in the morning.

Of course, the family had no choice. If Hua Na wanted someone's daughter, the family had to send her.

WE REFUGEES WONDERED whether the Thai police's brutality was part of a strategy to make camp life so miserable, we would give up and go home, and rid the Thais of their refugee problem. In fact, the Thai Ministry of Interior did adopt policies to discourage asylum seekers, by making the camps very austere refuges, at best. Those policies were known as "humane deterrence."

One day, after we had been in the camp for a few years, a neighbor invited us to join a demonstration. Our refugee camp was boiling over. We were furious with the guards' cruelty, and with the incomprehensible resettlement screening, which seemed to have ground to a halt for many of us.

For several weeks, thousands of internees sat together in peaceful protest by the corrugated tin fence. Protesters had broken down the fence in many places. Every morning before first light, we would step just outside the compound and sit all day in silence. We returned to our shelters after dark to sleep.

One evening after the protest had ended for the day, a group of us gathered by the fence to eat ice cream we bought from an outside seller. Suddenly, everyone was jumping over the ditch in a panic, fighting to get back inside the fence.

We knew what the guards could do to us, so we scattered. I had no idea what was happening, but I ran, ran, ran to the far end of camp, where no refugees lived. The fence was intact there, and I was stuck on the wrong side of it.

Five big soldiers chased me. I ran like I had never run before, toward a small hole in the fence—the kind that people cut for passing smuggled goods through, about the size of a half-Chantha. As I dove toward the opening, I felt a bamboo stick hitting me and a boot kicking me through the gap. The world slowed as I hurled myself through the wire. A shard of metal tore into my wrist, and I rolled down a slope and into a ditch. Once the soldiers saw that I was back inside camp, they turned and strode away.

I had reentered in a deserted area at the far end of camp. Blood soaked my trousers as I struggled to find my way back to our shelter. And then I passed out. I have no idea how long I was unconscious. It was lucky that I woke up at all. Nobody had any business in that part of camp, so I might have bled a great deal before anyone found me.

When I got to our building, Chan and our neighbors gaped at my blood-soaked clothes. They had been searching frantically for me.

We went to see a friend, Mr. Linh, who worked as a small-surgery nurse at the camp health center. He sutured my wound. For a month, I couldn't move my hand—Chan had to do all the cooking and washing. And the three fingers that were cut by the wire never healed properly.

It's strange: You'd think they would have lost all sensation. Instead, those fingers feel everything acutely, even now. If a mosquito bites there, the pain is extra sharp.

That irony makes me laugh. Don't people say that what doesn't kill you makes you stronger? Could be. Or it may be that what *tries* to kill you does harm that can never be fully repaired. Perhaps they are the same thing: the strength and the damage.

I have prayed many times for numbness, but even now I feel everything too much. Decades later, tears flood my eyes whenever I recall the darkest moments of my life: fleeing one home after another in defeat, my desolation after Mae's death. Those memories still burn like a raw slash that will not seal.

Whereas Chan never speaks about any of it. To him, it never happened; he is focused on the future. So I wonder, without answer, which one is a greater strength: feeling too much, or allowing yourself no feeling at all?

WITH ALL THIS bitter philosophy, I should offer a dose of sugar to take off the edge—a silver lining to my dark-cloud story. This brush with death and resulting injury helped launch my life's work.

As I watched Mr. Linh close my wound with a needle and thread, an idea came to me: I wanted to learn his healing art. I was so intrigued, I asked him to teach me to sew up a wound. Days later, he brought me to the clinic, showed me what he knew, and made me practice until I could do it by myself. Soon, Chan and I were working at the camp clinic. We became nurses, and then medical translators.

LATER, IN OUR first years back home, we would turn to those skills again and again for survival and purpose. That training led us to our first good jobs in the new Cambodia, at Médecins Sans Frontières. And from that work, our very own small nonprofit was born, first as a hospice, and then as a weaving center for women in rural Cambodia.

What began with a needle and thread suturing my torn wrist grew and bloomed into a fleet of wooden looms, shimmering with colorful silk threads.

The Saigon fortune teller had told me so: He predicted that cooking and sewing would lift me somehow. I hadn't taken him seriously. Those skills were a poor woman's work.

But of course, I had become a poor woman.

As I learned to close a wound with needle and thread, and found useful work inside the camp, I wondered: How had the fortune teller known?

He had been right about everything so far. He knew from the start that sometimes, sweetness and bitterness are too tangled to separate. A hated task like sewing can turn into a life-giving skill and a livelihood like suturing and weaving. A lost mother's lessons can nourish a daughter for a lifetime.

A wound can become a source of power. Pain into strength.

The best recipe I know for capturing that tangled taste of bittersweet is bánh flan, a dessert of velvety darkness that, to me, evokes the unhappy, complicated marriage of colonizer and colonized.

Crème Caramel (Bánh Flan)

Most countries of the former Portuguese, Spanish, and French empires adopted some version of this custard dessert with its slightly bitter, caramelized sugar topping. In North Vietnam, it's known as bánh caramel or kem caramel; South Vietnamese call it bánh flan or kem flan. You can even incorporate strong Vietnamese coffee into the caramel topping.

My mother and sister made this often in Battambang—it was a
family favorite.

Serves 4 to 6 (makes 1 round flan, 6 to 8 inches in diameter)

Ingredients:
10 egg yolks
½ cup whole milk
½ cup full-fat, unsweetened coconut milk, whisked
½ cup sweetened condensed milk
½ cup granulated sugar (or however much you want to caramelize)
2 tablespoons strong coffee or water

For serving: fresh fruit, mint

Set up a steamer large enough to hold a 6- to 8-inch glass or
ceramic dish. Fill the bottom half of the steamer with water.

In a large bowl, whisk together egg yolks, milk, coconut milk,
and condensed milk until mixture is smooth. Strain egg mixture
through a fine-mesh sieve, then let it sit for 30 minutes to allow the
bubbles to disperse.

Make the caramel: In a small, heavy-bottomed saucepan, heat
sugar over low heat. Add a few drops of water. Don't stir until the
sugar starts to turn yellow and liquefy around the edges, then stir
constantly until caramel turns golden brown. (Watch closely, as
this will happen quickly!) Remove from heat. Add 2 tablespoons
strong coffee (or water) to the melted sugar and stir quickly. Be
careful—the caramel will boil vigorously when you add the liquid.
The darker the caramelized sugar, the more bitter and complex the
taste will be.

Working quickly, add caramel to the glass or ceramic dish,
and swirl to coat the bottom. Slowly add custard to it and pop any

bubbles with a paring knife. Cover the dish tightly with aluminum foil.

Bring the water in the steamer to a gentle simmer, place the foil-covered flan inside, and cover with the steamer lid. Steam until the flan is set around the rim and the surface jiggles just a little when you gently shake it, 30 to 40 minutes. Remove flan from steamer.

Let flan cool on a wire rack for a half hour, then refrigerate for at least 4 hours (or overnight, if possible).

Use a paring knife to separate the flan from the edge of the dish. Set a plate over the top of the dish and invert carefully. The bottom of the flan, which is now on top, will have a lovely caramel color. To serve, cut into wedges and top with fresh fruit or a sprig of mint.

14. The Life Aquatica

Big chickens and small chickens are alike:
They all eat grain.
—Khmer proverb

AFTER MR. LINH'S suture lessons, I trained as a small surgery nurse at Phanat Nikhom's health-care center. I found it satisfying to clean, suture, and dress a patient's wounds and then watch them heal. Mr. Linh said that I made clean and beautiful stitches.

Perhaps I had learned something from the sewing course after all.

One afternoon, a woman brought in her five-year-old son covered in blood. The father had beaten him with the sharp edge of a bamboo stick. The child was covered head to toe in lacerations and needed more than a hundred stitches. This wasn't the first time I'd seen families taking out their frustrations on each other. From dawn to curfew, you could hear couples fighting—shouted arguments and, sometimes, violent altercations. Mental illness was rampant in the camps, and with it came anger, resentment, and sometimes, violence.

It was little wonder. Vietnamese, Cambodian, and Laotian refugees had been starved, bombed, brainwashed, raped, or tortured. They had seen family members executed, worked to death, or kidnapped by pirates. Some had been combatants and executioners themselves, by choice or under duress. Now here they were, packed together like stinking river fish in a basket, with nothing to do but wait.

Unrelenting trauma. Overcrowding. Boredom. Helpless dependency. It's a recipe for anxiety, depression, and far worse ailments of the mind.

One of my best friends at Phanat Nikhom was a boat person from Hà Tiên, a pretty coastal town in Vietnam near the Cambodian border. Her name was Vân. We became very close, and over time, she told me her story. Pirates had raided the craft she was crossing the Gulf of Thailand in, robbed everyone, and raped the women. She could no longer bear small, enclosed spaces. For her, going to the toilet or bathing brought the memories rushing back. "I just can't close the door," Vân explained. I guarded the entrance so she could leave it cracked open.

In return, Vân asked the Chinese man who ran the Thai camp store to teach her to make you char kway, the Chinese-style fried crullers that I liked. Street food would always be in demand, and I wanted to learn it all. Vân taught me to make the fried dough. That's just how she was—despite her trauma, she always helped people and shared what little she had.

Camp life was full of such paradoxes. Brutality coexisted with kindness, destitution with generosity. We refugees had nothing, but many of us drew close and found ways to ease one another's suffering. That was a lovely surprise after the betrayals of my last months in Saigon. Here in camp, we were *all* poor and full of loss. Often, that united us. And while some minds took refuge in madness, others found inspiration in scarcity. What we lacked provided a creative limitation that drove people to concoct the things we needed, like a Chinese fried doughnut made on an ingenious oil-drum kerosene stove.

OUR AFTERNOON WORK in the clinic filled the days with something besides waiting. During our time off, we distracted ourselves any way we could. In the mornings, I fried leftover rice for breakfast and ate it with eggs and soy sauce, then I shopped for food—usually, morning glory, land-mine chicken, and eggs. Strange cravings wormed their way into my belly; one fixation was rich, velvety duck eggs. I promised myself that one day, when I had a real home and could afford good food, I would devour twenty boiled duck eggs in one go.

Better ingredients—like duck eggs, chicken wings or legs, and carrots or cabbage—were beyond our means at Phanat Nikhom. We used most of the aid money from Yen and Caritas to pay for English classes. After class, I cooked and washed clothes. Occasionally I bought fabric and stitched myself a new shirt. In camp, clothes got filthy and would not come clean.

In the afternoons, I cooked lunch, and then we worked at the clinic. After work, we played Scrabble with Mr. Linh and his wife while we waited for the water delivery. We carried the water to our shelter, then did our English homework, and I reheated our lunch for dinner right after sunset. That was the shape of our days.

Chan was a more dedicated English student than I was, initially. I fought with doubts: What use was English in a place like this? Why spend money on a thin hope of betterment when we could eat better food right now?

Or if not better food, at least a tasty packet of instant noodles?

There were many times I wanted to give up on the classes—most of our classmates dropped out within weeks—but Chan wouldn't let me. For him, learning English was simple practicality: here was a skill that would prepare us to become citizens of somewhere else. At one point, when I threatened to quit after several years of lessons, he whipped out a pencil and scribbled something on a slip of paper. "This is how much we have spent on English lessons so far," he said, pointing to a large figure. "If you want to throw that money away, go ahead."

I stuck with the lessons, and my English gradually improved. And sometimes, the act of studying even tricked my brain into believing that the skill would one day be needed.

SEVERAL MONTHS AFTER the camp demonstrations, we were finally granted our screening interview. The American interviewer had cold, silver eyes and spoke flawless Khmer with no inflection. Everyone called him "Iron Face" because his expression never changed.

He asked why we had run from Vietnam, and why we didn't stay in Cambodia after leaving Saigon. I told him that I wanted to live somewhere

I could practice my religion freely. The reasons were more complicated, but this seemed like the answer most likely to define us as "refugees."

Still, we walked out of the interview sensing that our answers had not been correct. For two years after this, we heard nothing. And then we received a note from the UNHCR office saying that we had not passed the screening. I cried all day and could not stop. Four years we had languished in this camp, with not an inch of progress to show for it. Even Chan was somber.

Soon after the message from the UNHCR, we were moved to Sikhiu, a camp in northern Thailand. Rumor had it that the Thais were consolidating and closing the refugee camps and moving people eastward, into camps closer to the frontier. This move east from Phanat Nikhom, a camp established as a stepping stone to resettlement, did not bode well for us. It felt like we were moving backward—closer to Cambodia, and further from our dream of America.

We were part of a great mass of leftovers, people who had failed the screening and stubbornly continued to wait. We didn't want to repatriate. We had already *ex*patriated and wanted to move forward with our lives. And to us, forward meant West.

IN THE MEANTIME, we did our best to make a life in this new camp, however temporary it might be. Thanks to a letter of recommendation from Mr. Linh, we were accepted to work in the small surgery room at the camp's health center, operated by Médecins Sans Frontières. Our surgical-dressing department saw more than a hundred patients a day: patients with skin diseases, burns, and lesser injuries that needed sutures and dressings. Some of the patients I will never forget. One little girl came in on Christmas Eve after falling onto the barbed wire. It took fifteen catgut stitches to close the deep gashes in her palm and fifty to close the outer skin. Another was a toddler who was terribly burned when a pot of boiling water spilled onto his back. For months, I dressed his wounds with paraffin gauze treated with antibiotics. New, pink skin grew back little by little, and the boy's smile grew back, too. Since then, I've always found satisfaction from treating burn patients. They require extra patience and love. And the job allowed me to resurrect my grandmother's magical burn cream.

My colleagues said I had the hands of a healer because my patients' wounds never became infected. The real reason is that I devoutly followed the protocols of hand-washing and using disinfectant, but the belief persisted. One day, I arrived at work to find a row of people sitting on the bench outside the small surgery room. My coworkers explained that the patients had insisted on waiting for me because I was the one they trusted most to change their dressings.

I waved this off but smiled to myself. I was happy to think that maybe the ghost of my maternal grandmother lived in me, guiding my hands in their healing work.

SIKHIU HAD A notorious police chief equal in cruelty to "The Boss" of Phanat Nikhom. He was a small man named Cho, but he made everyone call him Anh Hai or Bong Thom—Vietnamese and Khmer, respectively, for "Big Brother." He carried a retractable metal baton and snapped it to full length whenever he felt that someone needed punishing. I once saw him whack a man across the back without any warning as the man strode by. "You are ill-mannered!" Bong Thom shouted, by way of explanation. The man's offense was leaving his top shirt button unfastened.

No one could predict what behaviors would qualify as unmannerly.

At Sikhiu authorities did introduce one policing innovation we had not seen in Phanat Nikhom: The Ministry of Interior (MOI) recruited refugees for their police force and ordered them to patrol the camp and bring any "ill-mannered" internees to Bong Thom. These recruits didn't wear uniforms, but they had power, and they abused it to their advantage.

The health center was next to police headquarters, so we often heard the cries of prisoners being punished in the night by Bong Thom. The punishments began after the foreign NGO employees left camp for the evening. One rainy, chilly night, Cho beat a prisoner brutally, then commanded his underlings to throw the man into a fishpond and make him stand there until his feet went numb. Then they pulled him out and hit him some more. We witnessed this kind of torture many times. Sometimes the same prisoner was beaten for several nights in a row.

For Bong Thom, this was more than a job. It was an avocation.

I had to pass by the police headquarters every day as I walked between our shelter and the health center. Whenever I passed the guard tower, I stared straight ahead and made my face a blank page.

One night I left work to find the gate closed. Dozens of Thai policemen sat stiffly at the station, as if they were being reviewed by a visiting delegation. Standing near the gate was a frequent patient of ours, a refugee who worked for the MOI. "Could you open the gate for me?" I asked him.

"No," he said.

"Really? Come on! We are friends."

He opened the gate with a sneer and grabbed my hand. "Come with me," he said loudly, performing for the audience of guards. He took me straight to Bong Thom.

My life is about to end, I thought, shivering.

Bong Thom glared at me. "Why did you insult my soldier?" he shouted.

"Sir, I did not," I said.

They put me into a concrete cell and locked the door. I was there for less than an hour, but a month of thoughts shot through my head. *What will happen to me? How can my flesh bear the kicking?* I went numb, fearing the worst.

A slat of light crossed my face as the door opened. The "friend" had been ordered to let me go, but he wore victory on his face. His arrogant smirk said, See my power?

I had spoken to him as an equal. That was my mistake. And the hate in me bloomed like a flame.

THE PRESSURE TO voluntarily repatriate was intensifying. Thai authorities and the UNHCR made little secret of their wish for us to go back to wherever we came from. They might not force us to return to our countries of origin, but they were willing to make us feel unwelcome enough to view going home as a good alternative. The unpredictable orders to move shelters or camps, the worsening rations, and the abuses of power produced a feeling of helpless limbo, a "nowhereness" that urged people to move on.

I often wondered whether the camp had exuded hopeless, dreary impermanence from the beginning. Surely it was born of a more high-minded spirit. A sculpture by the old camp gates seemed like evidence of some earlier, loftier intent; it was a concrete bas-relief image of a boat, with two giant hands lifting it from the waves. I wanted to believe in the ideal it represented—that humankind would unite to save its brothers from drowning.

Later, as our burning hopes for resettlement in the West dimmed to an ember, we joked that the hands weren't lifting the boat after all; they were pulling it down into the sea.

One day, I saw an article in a Vietnamese-language newspaper that someone's relatives had sent. Beneath the headline, CHARITY GETS TIRED, was a story about how dispiriting it was to pour support into refugee camps for years, as the ocean of need only deepened. People were sick of sending money to their families in camp, while their lives remained in limbo. Countries grew weary of resettling a storm surge of humanity that never seemed to abate.

The years have softened my bitterness. With the decades of distance, I can almost understand the world's impatience. People want their help to change things for the better; otherwise, they'll turn to less futile-seeming ventures. Charity gets tiring. It was inevitable that the doors would close eventually.

We had hoped they would close *behind* us.

EVEN AS OUR hopes faded, we refugees struggled against the disorder of camp existence. To give our days meaning and stay sane, we invested in our lives as best we could—in our case, with nursing work and English classes; with friendships and laughter; with dreams and books and songs.

In this rootless place, we tried to establish roots. We doctored our rations with our mothers' seasonings (the ones we could acquire). And occasionally, when we found bare patches of ground, we cultivated the tastes of home.

In Sikhiu, the authorities allotted detainees small garden plots where we could grow herbs and vegetables—healthy, fresh food to augment our rations. A popular favorite among Khmer refugees was the morning glory, a tenacious weed and a nutritious culinary treasure.

There are more than a thousand varieties of morning glory; this edible one, so beloved by Cambodians, is *Ipomoea aquatica*, a floating vine that goes by many aliases: water spinach, kangkong, ong choy, swamp cabbage, and water convolvulus, to name a few. It is a stubborn survivor, native to Asia. In Khmer, we call it trakuon.

In Cambodian villages, *I. aquatica* is life itself, a fast-growing leafy green vegetable you can grow year-round in a tiny village garden, rich in vitamins and minerals, and excellent for supplementing diets of rice and river fish. It thrives in irrigation canals and drainage ditches, invades waterways, snarls boat traffic, flourishes under neglect, and quite simply refuses to die.

It is as stubborn in clinging to life as the villagers themselves are.

And like us refugees, *I. aquatica* also endured setbacks.

The gardens were flanked by a canal flowing with raw sewage, and a few enthusiastic gardeners poured the sewer-water over the tender new shoots—water and fertilizer all in one. Those fertilized greens spurred a cholera epidemic in Sikhiu. The sickness was so widespread that we heard Bangkok ran low on oral rehydration solution (ORS). As an emergency measure, MSF taught us health workers to mix homemade ORS: twenty parts water to one of salt and seven of sugar. Many emergency truckloads of water rolled into our camp during the worst of the epidemic. After that, the Thai MOI police destroyed the gardens.

No more morning glory.

THE STORY OF the morning glory is the refugee's story. When you must flee and can carry only one thing, what will it be? What single seed from your old life will be the most useful in helping you sow a new one?

Unlike Chan and me, the morning glory achieved refugee status. The plant crossed an ocean, reached for the American dream, and won.

I. aquatica was an immigrant in America, only recently naturalized. Someone quietly introduced it to Florida sometime in the 1970s: "Sunshine State, please allow me to present *I. aquatica*," declared some penniless refugee in Vietnamese or Khmer or Lao, casting the precious seeds into a subtropical bog, imagining the delicious soup garnishes that would rise from the murky water.

The plant was a successful expatriate, providing sustenance and income for refugees in subtropical southern pockets of the US. After the wars, a few dozen Khmer families settled south of Houston and turned morning-glory farming into an industry, selling *I. aquatica* to Asian markets and restaurants all over Texas.

Eventually, Texas parks and wildlife managers discovered *I. aquatica* infiltrating the area near Galveston Bay. They added the plant to the USDA's Noxious Weeds List and declared it illegal to cultivate, a mortal threat to native flora. But one man's noxious weed is another man's stir-fry—or a refugee's survival strategy. After several heated town council meetings, officials deemed *I. aquatica* a "low-risk exotic species," one that could coexist peacefully with Texas plant life, if growers avoided seeding it in the wilds and waterways.

Other states, like Florida, California, and Georgia, have recognized the culinary usefulness of this resilient plant and allowed it to be cultivated—carefully. It offered a generation of new Cambodian-Americans (and other Southeast Asian immigrants) a way to convert the recipes of their past into their own American dream—a big accomplishment for a humble vine.

American Dream Morning Glory, Stir-Fried

Note to American readers: Do not tear the morning glory vine off your neighbor's arbor. This is not the morning glory you want. You can find morning glory and other excellent greens in Asian groceries across

America, thanks to the entrepreneurial spirit of the refugee. But because
I. aquatica is invasive in the wild, it is federally regulated—and even
illegal in some states. So if you can't find it, try this recipe by substituting
watercress, kale, spinach, or mustard greens.
Serves 4

Ingredients:
1 large bunch morning glory
1 tablespoon neutral oil
2 cloves garlic, roughly chopped
1 Thai red chili, diced (optional)
2 tablespoons oyster sauce
¼ cup chicken or pork stock (or water)

Rinse morning glory thoroughly and drain in a colander. Remove
bottom inch of stem and older leaves. Chop into 2-inch pieces.

In a large skillet, heat oil over medium-high heat. Add garlic
and fry until golden. Add greens and chili (if using) and stir-fry
until cooked through but still crisp, a couple of minutes at most.
Stir in oyster sauce and a splash of stock or water, then remove
from heat. Serve with jasmine rice.

━━━

THE MORAL OF the morning glory is this: For plants or humans, making
yourself indispensable is the key to survival. It took many years for me to
learn that lesson, but my mother had given me the recipe. And a Saigon
fortune teller had provided me with a hint of how I might do it.

As it turned out, I would have to deploy my hard-won usefulness back
home in Cambodia, where we were faced with not only rebuilding our lives,
but with resurrecting our ruined society. Where civilization was still in the
process of being reseeded, in ground sown with salt and poison.

We had hoped to sow our new lives on a patch of real estate in America;
the rest, we could sort out later. Here is what happened instead:

In 1989, a decade after the Vietnamese army ousted the Khmer Rouge, Vietnam withdrew their troops.

In 1991, the Paris Peace Agreement officially ended the war in Cambodia.

In 1992, the United Nations Transitional Authority in Cambodia (UNTAC) became the temporary government of Cambodia. Their mandate was to keep the peace, restart the country's destroyed institutions, and oversee free and fair elections.

Cambodia's first elections were scheduled for May 1993. The planet was united in their desire for Cambodians to go home and vote. In 1992–93, UNHCR sent more than 350,000 Cambodians home.

Repatriation was nominally voluntary.

In 1993, after almost ten years in the camp, we volunteered to go back.

We were tired of charity. The misery of Sikhiu had become intolerable, and UNHCR was constantly broadcasting messages on loudspeakers, appealing to Khmer refugees to register for repatriation. So one day, we walked into the UNHCR office and put our names on the list. We gave up the certainty of dead-end camp lives for an uncertain future in whatever was left of Cambodia.

When our names were announced on the loudspeaker and we boarded the bus to leave Sikhiu, Bong Thom shook our hands and wished us luck. For an instant, we were human in his eyes. And then we were gone, outside the razor wire, heading east.

15. No Thanks for the Frog Soup

The tiger depends on the forest.
The forest depends on the tiger.
—Khmer proverb

AFTER A FEW weeks at Site Two, a huge transit center near the border, we boarded an overnight train to Cambodia. I cried for most of the trip. I could see only a very black future for us. In the camps, at least, rice and cooking oil were guaranteed. No guarantees awaited us in Cambodia. How would we earn the money to feed ourselves? The question was a dark hole in my mind.

It was shattering to have hoped and waited for nearly a decade, only to return to the place we had fled so long ago.

We arrived at a camp on the outskirts of Phnom Penh—a cluster of raised houses, where thousands of other newly repatriated refugees were staying. We saw our own anxiety reflected in their faces. A tall, slender Ghanaian UNTAC representative took an interest in us, perhaps because we were fellow Catholics, and dropped by for daily chats. Those visits helped pass the time, and our apprehension began to transform into something like relief: the Thai camps were behind us, and we were hearing rumors that people who spoke English could find work.

After a week or so, someone came to our hut and described the terms of our repatriation. If we chose to resettle in Battambang, we would receive a

small plot of land, some plastic sheeting and tools to build a house, and a
year's supply of rice. If we stayed in Phnom Penh, we would receive $50 each
and a year's supply of rice.

We had to make our decision on the spot.

We chose the $100.

This was our first taste of freedom—the right to choose one shadowy
future over another.

WE COLLECTED OUR $100 and the rice coupons, walked out of the last
refugee camp we would ever see, and hailed a moto into the city. I asked
the driver what kind of work I might find, explaining that I could do many
things: clean houses, cook meals, sew clothes, translate from Vietnamese,
French, or English. "I don't believe you," he said. "All those things in one
person? You can't be good at all of them."

The infusion of more than a billion dollars of foreign aid, many thousands of UNTAC employees, and a multitude of international NGOs had
breathed new life into Phnom Penh since we last saw it, but the capital
still didn't measure up to my prewar memories. The city was wary, like an
invalid recuperating from a long, debilitating illness. Many houses stood
empty. Electricity was a rare resource. The Vietnamese soldiers were gone,
replaced by expatriates working for UNTAC and aid organizations. Trucks
full of UNTAC soldiers seemed to occupy every road.

We rented a dark little room on a wide, rutted street. The landlady's
daughter invited us to a nearby coffee shop; it had a generator and a big,
loud TV, so we went there with her a few times in those first weeks to watch
shows from Hong Kong and ask about possible work. Like us, the other
Cambodian returnees we saw looked lost, without purpose, sitting in the
broken streets.

We checked in at the local Médecins Sans Frontières headquarters
and found temporary work as radio operators. From 6 p.m. to 6 a.m.,
we relayed calls to and from MSF stations in the provinces. Every
morning, we ate a spicy fried chicken after our shift was over. We slept

during the day, then woke up and made a vegetable-and-pork cha before our shift.

Phnom Penh and the surrounding areas felt much safer than they had nearly a decade ago, in 1984, but we heard rumors of chaos and violence in other provinces. The Khmer Rouge still controlled around 20 percent of the countryside, especially in the north and west near the Thai border and in Kampong Thom, a central province north of Phnom Penh; in their strongholds, the Khmer Rouge guerillas sabotaged infrastructure, raided villages, and attacked aid workers. As the 1993 elections approached, there were reports of political killings and attacks on ethnic-Vietnamese enclaves. Apolitical banditry and lawlessness were also rampant, rural roads were abysmal, and the land exuded silent menace—it was still seeded with millions of antipersonnel mines.

When our two-month MSF contract was up, we searched job listings. There were lots of postings for MSF translators left unfilled. We deduced that no Khmer–English speaker wanted to be stationed in Siem Reap or Kampong Thom, areas still hot with fighting. We'd heard stories about UNTAC employees and aid workers in remote areas being kidnapped or murdered by the Khmer Rouge. It was widely understood that MSF employees took these war-zone postings at their own risk. We opted out.

Meanwhile, some friends from Sikhiu had heard that you could make good money mining for gold and rubies in Ratanakiri, a far-flung province tucked into the northeastern corner of Cambodia, by the Laotian and Vietnamese borders. *Ratana-kiri* means "gem mountain" in Khmer, and those two features summed up everything I knew about the place— except that the Khmer Rouge had set up their headquarters there in the 1960s. The northern forests were supposedly quiet now, but to get there, you had to pass through lawless and mine-strewn Kratié and Stung Treng Provinces.

Here we were, facing another choice between bad and worse: We could work for an aid organization in a war zone or become treasure hunters in a remote forest. Choose your own peril.

Digging for rubies in the jungle was the kind of madhouse plan that people with nowhere else to go would formulate. So of course, that's exactly what we did. We had bought a moto earlier, which we now sold for seed money. Then we redeemed one last rice coupon and gave the rest of our vouchers for the year to a kind woman who'd driven us for free to the rice collection point on her moto. Her face opened into a big, grateful grin as she waved goodbye.

BANDITRY AND BOMB craters had made the road impassable, so Chan and I and a friend from Sikhiu climbed aboard a cargo ship up the Mekong River northbound for Kratié. We strung hammocks among the boxes piled on deck. By day, the ship chugged up the middle of the Mekong River, staying far from shore. At night, we stopped in villages for meals of rice and dried fish, pickled cucumbers, and salted eggs—typical village fare of simple foods that don't spoil easily.

Passengers and crew alike were too jittery to enjoy the scenery. Concealed in all that lush greenery were cadres of unvanquished Khmer Rouge combatants, who funded their revolutionary activities by raiding, kidnapping, and looting. Sometimes they set ships afire and left the burned-out exoskeletons as a ghostly reminder of the war's ongoing threat. People joked that if you survived that trip up the river, you had been born again. It took us three days and two nights.

In Kratié Province, we climbed onto a truck piled high with goods, sat atop the tarp-covered merchandise, and rode in the rain to Stung Treng Province. We carried very little with us: the money from UNHCR plus our MSF earnings, and two plastic bags containing secondhand shirts, two pairs of pants, three sarongs, and our homemade kerosene burner from Phanat Nikhom. Our improvised taxi stopped every hundred meters or so at security checkpoints, where fees or bribes were extracted. From Stung Treng, we hired a military Jeep. The road was a constellation of mud-filled craters connected by ribbons of solid ground. By the time we got to

Ratanakiri Province, my head was covered in lumps from jouncing into the Jeep's roof.

In Banlung, a town painted with red mud, we formulated a plan with a man named Mao who bought the mining machinery we would need for grinding stone. We joined forces with seven men from the Jarai minority, native to Vietnam's central highlands, who crossed the border during the rainy season when they couldn't work the fields. Our contribution was our labor and the responsibility to feed ourselves and the Jarai men. The Jarai were willing to work for food and to split whatever the group found in the mines with us and Mao.

While Chan and Mao left to scout mining spots and deliver the equipment, I stayed with Thi, a Vietnamese girl whom Mao had introduced to us. A few days later, Mao picked me up on his moto and carried me into the jungle.

OUR GROUP ARRIVED in Ratanakiri near the end of the monsoon season, as the rains were tapering off. The forest canopy was so dense, I could barely hear the rain pattering the leaves high above. We built a hut on stilts near a stream. The hut had a palm-leaf roof and a floor of palm stems with pointy, ridged edges. We had brought plastic sheeting, so we rolled the plastic down as walls when the rain slanted in. We made cooking fires on the ground under the shelter; I became adept at building fires, even when the wood was wet.

The area of forest where we set up our camp was occupied by the Tampuan, an ethnic minority indigenous to the Ratanakiri forests and mountains. They call themselves Khmer Loeu—"Highland Khmer."

For eleven months, I lived among the Tampuan people.

The Tampuan lived as they had done for a thousand years, subsisting from hunt to hunt, harvest to harvest. Every three years, they tore the trees from a new patch of earth, using only machetes, shovels, and flames. They didn't farm with water buffaloes or irrigation like lowland Khmer ("Khmer

Krom") farmers. They planted rice on dry plots during the rainy season and erected temporary dwellings by their farms. When the rice exhausted the soil, they moved on and started again somewhere else.

When the Tampuan weren't planting or harvesting, the men went into the forest to hunt. They carried a knife and gun, a lighter, a tube-shaped rice bag worn around their necks, and a rucksack containing a cooking pot, spoon, plate, salt, and chili. Their daily food was whatever they shot or trapped that day: lizards, birds, porcupines, snakes, or any small animal. If their hunting was unsuccessful, they dined on the rice, salt, and chili they carried.

Scoring bigger game, like a wild pig or a deer, was an occasion to celebrate. The small hunting crew couldn't haul the entire carcass home by themselves, so they'd cut off just enough meat for the "immediate party" and carry it home. Chan was sometimes invited to join this celebration: The men passed plates of meat and jugs of rice wine around a fire while the women and children watched from outside the circle. The next day, a larger team of men would fetch the entire animal and divide it among the families in the village. The men stayed home until the meat was eaten, and then another hunting party would disappear into the jungle.

Tampuan women's work was to help clear the land, gather water and vegetables, crush rice with a mortar, make rice wine, care for children, prepare meals, and keep the fire going. Hot coals in the middle of the low-ceilinged bamboo-and-leaf huts gave off constant smoke and helped ward off mosquitoes. Hanging over the coals were baskets filled with drying chilies, slow-smoked meat, and bamboo threads for weaving the tall kapha baskets the Tampuan carried by long straps on their backs. The kapha were strong and durable but also exquisite and intricate, woven of bamboo threads dyed red, black, and gold with leaf and bark pigments and dried over the fire. I learned that weaving one could take months, and that the work was usually done by elder Tampuan who could no longer hunt or work the fields.

When it was time to cook, the women blew on the coals and stoked the fire, then simmered rice in a pot suspended over the fire from a pyramidal wood stand. After the rice was done, they cooked soup or meat in the same pot. The Tampuan had two main cooking methods for meat: boiled with salt over the fire or roasted over the fire. They knew what leaves to add to make the soup sour, and they gathered bitter-tasting ones to treat diarrhea and malaria. I didn't learn the names of those leaves, only how to recognize them.

Vegetables were plentiful during the rainy season, so we ate fairly well. During the day, Chan and the Jarai worked in the gold mines, grinding rock and rinsing it in the stream using the machinery Mao had bought and delivered. When he had time, Chan caught small fish in the stream using a bamboo basket he had made, and we planted morning glories. The men shot peacocks, jungle fowl, and other wild game I had never seen before. I tasted all kinds of birds. Once, they came home with a gorgeous little white owl, which was delicious—much better than the foul-tasting black bird with a long, yellow beak.

The forest was full of beehives, and the Jarai workers sometimes harvested honey. They squeezed it out into a single shared spoon; we took turns licking the spoon clean. That's how I discovered that I was allergic to honey: a rash erupted all over my body, head to toe.

The nearest village was five kilometers away. I walked there every day or two to trade something with the Tampuan for rice and fruit or vegetables: bananas, purple taro, and a sort of gourd that was dried and used as a water vessel. I exchanged my sarongs for some chickens, so we had eggs to eat (and the occasional chicken s'gnao). And there was an abundance of purple, crunchy eggplant that tasted wild and very bitter. In the camps, I had learned to cook eggplant a variety of ways, to create the illusion of variety—and choice. This skill served us well in the Ratanakiri forest.

Ratanakiri Forest Eggplant, Three Ways

These small, round eggplants were pale yellow and very bitter—I had to soak them much longer in brine to remove the bitterness. They grew wild in Ratanakiri but were also cultivated by the Tampuan. I have never seen them anywhere else.

1. Stir-fry it: Quarter the eggplants. Salt pieces well and let them sit for a half hour while the salt does its work—leaching out the bitterness. Then rinse salt away and chop eggplant into thumb-size pieces. Stir-fry eggplant with whatever seasonings you can find: garlic, salt, chili, MSG.

2. Make samlor: Do the stir-fry steps above, and then fill a pot with water from a stream. If you have a bit of fish, pork, or chicken (or even just the bones), add that. Throw in some onion or any other vegetables or greens you can lay hands on, then simmer the vegetables (and meat scraps) until tender. If you are lucky enough to have prahok or kroeung on hand, use it! Otherwise, add lime, tamarind, or a handful of edible sour leaves from the forest. Top with chili.

3. Make pickles: Wash and cut eggplant into half-inch slices. Salt well and let sit for 1 hour, then rinse. Stir in a lot more salt and a little bit of sugar and let eggplant sit for 5 minutes more. Fill a small Tampuan basket with the salted eggplant and add garlic and chili. Cover eggplant completely with water and press down with washed stones. Leave sealed in a cool place to ferment for 3 to 4 days, unsealing twice daily to release gases. Serve with soups.

―――――

I HAD MY first experience of malaria within a week of our arrival. I thought I was dying. I had a high fever and shivered uncontrollably. Electric waves of pain coursed through my head, body, and joints.

The illness flared up again every few weeks. Whenever I had a bout of malaria, Chan implored me to eat a bite of banana or papaya. Sometimes, I felt too weak to chew the fruit. "I can't," I told him. "Just let me sleep." After several months, I was so skinny, I had to tie a string around my waist to keep my pants from sliding to the forest floor.

Banlung was more than fifty kilometers away. Chan and the Jarai made the two-day trek every two months and brought back supplies: salt and

sugar, emergency glucose ampules, quinine, and antibiotics. Quinine carried me through the fever but gave me excruciating diarrhea and left a disgusting taste in my mouth. That foul aftertaste made me desperately thirsty
for sour fruit. I fell into deep, underwater malarial sleeps and dreamed of
lime juice with ice and sugar. Once, I woke up to see Chan's face full of
worry. "If you can't eat banana, would you like some sugar?" he said. The
word "sugar" woke me up immediately. Chan broke open an ampule of
glucose, and it hit my bloodstream like a lightning bolt.

The closest we got to quenching our thirst for iced limeade was green
tamarind. We could sometimes find it in the Tampuan village market. But
when Chan and I were both too sick or too tired to make the journey, we sat
under a tamarind tree and waited for the tiny, sour pods to drop. If one fell,
we scooted toward the fruit on our bottoms. The memory of us dragging
our butts across the ground to chase the fallen fruit still makes me laugh.

I craved sweetness and sourness, day and night. At times, I ached so
desperately for sugar that I swallowed the honey, knowing I would soon be
swollen with itchy hives. The Tampuan took pity on me one day, seeing how
thin I was and how I cried for sugar. They brought me a piece of sugarcane.
I broke three teeth trying to chew it.

THE DRY SEASON gave Chan and me a taste of real hunger. As the stream
dried up, there were no more fish to catch. Vegetables became scarce or
nonexistent in the closest village, so I provisioned in a village eight to ten
kilometers away. After a few weeks of this, I thought nothing of the long
walks in flip-flops. At first, the bamboo slashed my skin, but my feet soon
toughened. And my shoulders got stronger from hauling food and water
in kaphas.

Fortunately, Chan and the Jarai always brought a few packs of cheap
instant noodles from Banlung, for making soup when we had no vegetables. The Tampuan had taught us which wild leaves were nutritious and
which were poisonous. We gathered long, grasslike leaves that grew along
the stream and filled the pot with them, then crushed the instant noodles

into boiling water. The young leaves added bulk and nutrition (if not flavor) to the soup.

Chan also carried one pack of Mama-brand noodles back for me every trip. I looked forward to that extravagance every eight weeks with a ferocity I can barely imagine now. The Mama noodles dulled the taste of hunger, at least for a day.

On my journeys to market, I made friends with several Tampuan women, who were tougher than me by far. One walked as many as twenty kilometers a day fetching water. (As the dry season wore on, many streams disappeared, so water sources were often farther away.) She carried a kapha water basket on her back and a baby wrapped in a krama scarf in front of her. She had to make twice as many trips because she could not carry both the baby and two water kaphas.

This stoic woman had most likely carried many children on her back, only to see them die in infancy. Few Tampuan children survived to adulthood. One of my first memories of Ratanakiri was entering a hut to find a tiny skeleton with huge eyes blinking up at me. After I recovered from the shock, I saw that the skeleton was a sick, emaciated little boy.

Once I came to know the Tampuan better, I learned that the women often bore ten or eleven children, but malaria, diarrhea, and malnutrition usually stole all but one or two. Some of the Tampuan's animistic rites and food taboos undermined the health of baby and mother alike. One family asked me to help a young mother who was still too weak to stand after giving birth a month before. That's when I learned about the Tampuan's superstition that breastfeeding mothers must not eat anything but rice and salt until they were strong enough to resume their work carrying water or crushing rice. Otherwise, they believed, the mothers would transmit leprosy to their babies through breast milk. I wondered how the mothers could grow stronger without any nutrition besides rice. Husbands would answer that angry spirits were punishing their wives with sickness and must be appeased.

"You have to eat," I told the exhausted mother. "Surely the spirits will let you have an egg." The mother-in-law turned a blank face to me. "We are Khmer Loeu, not Khmer Krom like you," she said.

The young father explained that he had already sacrificed all their chickens to the spirits, but his wife had still not recovered. "The spirits must want a pig instead," he said, "but we do not have one." I wanted to suggest that he feed some chicken and pork to his wife instead of to the spirits, but I kept quiet. For probably a thousand years, they had sacrificed an animal when a loved one fell ill; I wasn't going to change that practice. Instead, I promised to give the mother some medicine if they fed her an egg every day. They agreed, and she recovered.

ALTHOUGH MY BODY was strengthening, a few soft-girl fears remained. I was terrified of poisonous snakes. I dreaded the dark nights alone in the forest. But Chan protected me from a horror that might have paralyzed me, had I known about it. Years later, he told me that when the Tampuan buried their dead, they hollowed out a half log, placed the corpse into it face-up, then sank the open coffin into shallow ground, with only a scatter of dirt over the top—so that the faces looked out upon the sky.

I had seen the Tampuan carving out the log-caskets, and for days after a burial, my nose detected death—the smell of prahok permeated the forest air. It did not occur to me that the prahok aroma might be human in origin.

Chan knew that I was unlikely to walk into the jungle alone to gather water or wild greens if I knew there was some chance I might accidentally stumble upon a face. He warned the Tampuan to omit mention of the unburied corpse-faces: "If you tell her, you will have to carry her water from then on."

In retrospect, I'm grateful that Chan kept me in the dark about Tampuan funerary rites.

THOSE DRY-SEASON MONTHS in Ratanakiri, I was the poorest I have ever been—truly "white hands," in the fortune teller's parlance. I will never forget those eight weeks when I had nothing to eat but rice and salt.

Years later, when I was in Stung Treng working with Volunteer Service Organization (VSO)—an agency that sends development volunteers into villages all over the world—I sat in a meeting with wide-eyed new volunteers. "How do we define poverty?" the instructor asked the trainees.

"No electricity?" said one. Another: "No TV?"

For them, this was an abstract question. For me, it was not.

"Maybe you are poor in America, if you don't have a TV," I said. "But if you eat nothing but rice and salt for two months, you will understand what poverty is."

Silence took hold of the group. Everyone had suddenly lost their taste for academic discussions of who is poor and who is not.

If you want to experience the flavor of poverty for yourself, here is a recipe. I've had only the briefest taste of it. For the full experience, you should duplicate this recipe every year during the dry season, as the Tampuan have done for generations.

Recipe: A Taste of Poverty

This dish is easy to prepare, but the regimen is very difficult to maintain—unless you must.

Ingredients:
Rice
Salt
Chili (optional)

Preparation:
Smash the chili, stir in some salt, and mix with cooked rice. Serve warm or at room temperature. ("Room" is not necessarily literal, especially if you are living in a refugee camp shelter or a jungle hut with no walls.)

Repeat daily for eight weeks.

For Chan, the memory of hunger had a different flavor. It was still the dry season, and for weeks, we had eaten only rice with salt. So he and two of the Jarai men joined the hunting party, hoping to find some meat for us. On the second day they shot a large lizard, then boiled it right there in the jungle for dinner with sour leaves and salt. The famished men devoured it instantly. Chan told me later that it was the best meal of his life.

A few years later, after we had settled in Stung Treng Province, Chan bought a wild lizard and asked me to prepare it the way they had in the forest. When it came time to slaughter it, I hesitated—just long enough for the big silver-black reptile to dart out of my kitchen and flee into the village. Chan and a friend managed to capture and slay it. He was craving the Tampuan's lizard recipe: Capture, boil, eat. I opted for a more refined preparation: marinated in salt and kroeung and slowly braised.

When it was time to eat, Chan and I both felt queasy—slaughtering and dressing the poor beast had destroyed our appetites. We gave the braised lizard to the neighbor who had helped us catch it, so I never learned what the best meal of Chan's life tasted like. I doubt we could have reproduced the flavor. The most important ingredients were Chan's hunger and exhaustion, which made even a lizard boiled in sour leaves taste like heaven.

I ONCE ASKED my Tampuan friend, the one who carried her baby twenty kilometers every day: "What is it like to have such a hard life?"

"What is it, a 'hard life'?" she said.

I immediately saw how absurd the question was.

I cried for her as I walked back to my forest hut: Her life was so hard, she had no word to describe its hardness. But then I remembered, *I am currently living the same life.* And that turned my tears to bitter laughter.

She was content with her future: I will plant rice; I will harvest; I will live my life by the cycles of rainfall. But this was not a future I could accept.

Life in the jungle was actually very peaceful. It's a simple life. You work on the rice field. You don't have to earn money for things that have no purpose except to prove your status and good taste. You don't compete to show off your success. The forest is quiet, and the mind matches its rhythms. But the twin promises of malaria and hunger are always there, waiting to pay you a visit. Stillness never stays; the storms always return.

WE HAD $50 left and had run out of items to barter with the Tampuan. The only thing we had left worth trading was the Seiko watch Chan's mother had given him. An older Tampuan woman we called Yiay Le had her eye on it as a present for her favorite grandson. This was the only family memento Chan had left, so he negotiated hard for it. He asked for 200 kilos of rice and a grown pig. She refused, and we returned to our hut.

Early the next morning, Yiay Le appeared. Her grandson would kill himself if he could not have the watch, she explained. She would have it at any price.

Chan's watch trade fed nine of us for a month or more—the rest of our time in the gold-mining area. If it pained Chan to convert it into sustenance, he never said so. The Jarai killed the pig, and we wore down our tiny knives to nubs cleaning, skinning, and cutting it into pieces. I used the bones, blood, and organs to make bobor. That night was festive. We sat together slurping the rich porridge, fine dining after six months of foraged jungle meals. There was plenty left for breakfast.

I caramelized the pork belly with sugar to prepare a huge batch of khor—it lasted for about ten days in a tightly sealed jar. I used the pork fat as cooking oil and fried the lean fillet meat, then crushed it into thin strands and roasted it over the slow heat of a dying fire. For weeks, we added the dried, shredded pork to our soup and vegetables every day, a little boost of protein and flavor.

AFTER SEVEN MONTHS of digging, Chan and the Jarai had found no gold. Mao, the investor, gave up and left with his moto, so we had only our own money to spend on prospecting—and no transport. One of the Tampuan hunters told Chan about an area where, he said, Prince Sihanouk had launched a ruby mining project forty years earlier, when he was head of state. The mines were inactive but might still be worth the digging.

Here was another wild scheme, formulated based on very little information. But we had no other plan and no forest-exit strategy. We just chased any idea we heard out of sheer desperation. So we hired an elephant; loaded our cookpot, 500 kilos of rice, and the digging equipment onto its back; and pushed deeper into the Ratanakiri forest.

I was just getting over another malarial fever and this time craved something sour. We passed a big mango tree and gathered some wild, under-ripe mango. The pungent fruit flooded my mouth with relief. A few hours later, we passed the mango tree again. The Jarai hunter who guided us had marked trees with his machetes as we walked; I saw the cut-marks on trees we passed. And then I started to see them again. "Chan, we've been here three times already," I said quietly.

"Shut up!" the Jarai guide shouted. "You're a woman!" They were right about that. But *I* was right about the fact that we were walking in circles with an elephant, covering kilometers of forest but going nowhere.

After a very long day of walking, we finally found the reported location: an old, disused ruby mine from the 1950s near a fifty-year-old mango farm. A smaller Tampuan group of six or seven families had recently set up a new settlement there and was preparing a field to farm. We built huts nearby. The men dug for rubies by day and hunted at night.

By then it must have been April or May, I think. Soon there would be lots of ripe mangoes to eat, and another rainy season was about to begin.

ON THE FIRST day of the rainy season, the whole settlement came out to catch frogs. Each family filled a big sack full of them. I watched, fascinated, as one woman boiled a pot of water and poured it into her teeming sack. The croaking went quiet. Then she brought another cauldron of water to a boil, emptied the frogs into it, and added a little salt. She turned out some frogs into a smaller pot and handed it to me. "I want you to have some food today," she said kindly.

My mind raced with ideas for how to evade her good deed. "Please keep it for your own family," I said. "You haven't had meat for so long, I can't take it from you." No matter how hungry I was in those months, I was never hungry enough to try the vile-smelling Tampuan frog soup.

Throughout our time in Ratanakiri, the Tampuan were very kind to us. They let us live among them, even though they couldn't see the point of ruby- and gold-digging. In the Tampuan's world, nothing had value but rice and fish, or the edible greens that grow along the river. They did not use money, only trading one useful thing for another. And there was no time to plan for tomorrow. Most of them were illiterate. In the jungle, what was the point of learning to read? With no banks or currency, what was there to save?

These were the idealized "Old People" in whose name Pol Pot claimed to fight their agrarian revolution: subsistence farmers who worked together in informal collectives, unsullied by education, capitalism, or even Buddhism. But even they had not been ideologically correct enough to escape the forced labor and mass relocations; the starvation, tortures, and executions.

I don't know whether the Tampuan believed the Khmer Rouge's lies, but it hardly mattered: Believers and nonbelievers were rewarded with death, just like the heretical "New People," with their wristwatches, eyeglasses, and television sets—items few Tampuan had ever seen.

IN THE EARLY weeks of the monsoons, the rain was sometimes so heavy, we could barely see more than a few dozen feet into the forest. The second worst memory of my life is from that second rainy season in the Ratanakiri forest. I was covered in a honey-rash and weak from malaria. The men had gone digging in the ruby mines, so I was alone in our little hut, not a soul around. Torrential rain had set in; lightning ignited the silver threads of water in spasms of blinding light, and thunder rolled across the mud like ocean waves. The noise was deafening and seemed only to heighten my isolation.

I screamed into the wall of rain like a madwoman, begging for help, cursing God, crying out for anyone who could hear me. *How had this jungle life become* my *life?* I screamed and screamed until I could not scream anymore. My voice disappeared into the rain and thunder, swallowed by the wind in the leaves. That was the second time I wished for death. The first time was in the weeks after my mother died. There has not been a third.

RUBIES PROVED TO be just as elusive as gold had been. We had pushed forty kilometers deeper into the forest, on the word of a Tampuan hunter, and found nothing but holes in the ground.

We decided it was time to go "home," wherever that might turn out to be.

Not long before we left, the Jarai shot a big deer. The rain was ceaseless, so they built a fire on the ground under the hut and smoked the meat for five days. The smoke rose up through the floor and filled the hut with oily deer-meat smell.

The Jarai threw the deer hide on a tree far enough away to keep it out of stench range. When the meat was completely dry, they packed it into large sacks with the rest of our things, and we headed toward Banlung. Shortly after setting out, we stopped in a Tampuan village, and they invited us to stay in an empty hut for the night. When one of the men heard we had deer meat, he asked excitedly where we had discarded the deerskin, then ran off.

Several hours later, the man returned to the village in triumph. He threw the week-old deer skin over a small tree. Families came to cut off pieces and bring them home for their soup pots. The hide was white with wriggling maggots and smelled like prahok.

Chan and I fell into crazed laughter: *We tried to leave the smell behind, but it followed us here!* we gasped. We laughed until our ribs ached. For two decades, our bad luck had followed us like a foul odor. And still, we weren't as impoverished as our gracious Tampuan hosts, who were happy to have a sliver of rotten hide to flavor their soup.

The absurdity of it—all of it—engulfed us, as our howls spun up into the black jungle sky.

WE HAD FOUND no gold or rubies, only a few garnets. But the Tampuan had carved out a place in my heart. "Stay here and live as our children," said the chief of the small settlement near the ruby mines. We treated him for tonsillitis once, and ever since, he had been kind to us. He even offered to give us his farm to live on and work.

I wish I could remember the village chief's name. But although the Tampuan spoke to us in Khmer, I did not know their Tampuan names. We addressed each other by honorifics.

His offer left me in awe. But we wanted to return to a place where creature comforts were more readily available. We wanted to find out whether civilization in Cambodia had begun to exist again, and to learn whether it might offer us an opportunity to eat more regularly. In particular, I wanted limes, ice, and sugar. And maybe, one day, I could have real noodles again, the slow kind made by hand.

Or even pâté de foie.

We gave everything we had left to the Tampuan—"I will keep it for you until you return," the chief said—minus our cash, the smoked deer meat, the garnets, and a few weeks' supply of rice, and walked toward Banlung. We marched out of the jungle like soldiers retreating from a lost battle. All the same worries as before awaited us in Phnom Penh: no jobs, no money, no future.

In my despondency, I lagged farther and farther behind the men. Finally, I asked Chan if we could rest. "You are not the First Lady," he said, turning and walking on just as fast.

I knew he was right. If I had learned nothing else in Saigon, Koh Kong, and the camps, it was this: When you have nothing, weakness can destroy you.

No one would carry me out of the jungle. I would have to carry myself.

Chan's wisdom was often bitter like this: Hard to swallow, but ultimately, medicinal in nature. "You have to be equal now," he told me, urging me forward. I walked faster. It turned out that I could keep pace with the men if I chose to. And I so chose.

For our ten years together, I had tried to be Chan's silver moon-shadow, as the *Chbab Srey* instructed. But I discovered that obedience could not be exchanged for rice and was therefore of little use. That was all over now. He was right: I could not use my femaleness as an excuse. I had to be equal.

And from that moment forward, I was sunlight—strong and fierce.

"You are not a proper Asian woman at all," Chan told me once, years later, smiling his half-joke smile.

I've often wondered why, in a poor country where women must work as hard as men just to feed their children, feminine "softness" is so highly prized. I no longer consider it a valuable attribute.

The year was 1994. I was thirty-three years old, and as "white hands" poor as I have ever been, just as the fortune teller in Saigon had predicted. As we hiked toward mud-red Banlung, I remembered how the fortune teller had foretold that we would build our own house high in the air when I was thirty-seven. I wondered how our lives could change so drastically in only four years, and I smiled at the sheer impossibility of it.

But by then, the impossible had happened so many times that it no longer surprised me much. I had been a brothel chef, a surgery nurse, and an assistant midwife. I had owned a bar and operated a kuy teav stand. I had feasted on pâté de foie and roasted jungle snake, and everything in between. As a girl, I had turned up my nose at the very idea of instant noodles, but later, particularly in Ratanakiri, it had become a delicacy I treasured.

I had faced my worst fears and tasted hope and despair enough for two lifetimes. We had run from the Communists, to the camps, to the Ratanakiri highlands, always running and wandering, hungry and hoping. We wanted to stand still long enough to grow roots, to plant ourselves somewhere safe and quiet, where the soil was conducive to cultivating a life.

We were tired of waiting for our lives to begin. It was time to restart our own clocks.

In Banlung, we took the garnets to the market to sell. The buyer offered us $50 for the whole lot. Chan refused the pitiful sum and split the garnets with the other men.

We had not managed to enrich ourselves, except in life experience. Years later, I took the biggest stone to a shopkeeper in Phnom Penh. He polished it to a deep crimson shine. Suddenly, its value was evident—he offered me $200 for it. Instead of selling it, I had it set into a ring for Chan, and I made myself a ring with the smaller stones.

I still wear it sometimes, to remind myself of how far we have come.

PART III

Restocking the Khmer Pantry

16. Instant Noodles

*Only several thousand Kampucheans might have died
due to some mistakes in implementing our policy
of providing an affluent life for the people.*
—Pol Pot

IN BANLUNG, WE stayed again with Thi, Mao's Vietnamese friend. She bought me breakfast, a wondrous bobor. The delicious rice porridge warmed me from head to toe and restored my senses. I tried to pay her back, but she refused. She urged us to seek out her parents in Stung Treng on our way back to the capital.

Thi's father, whom we called Pou Ba ("Uncle Ba"), was a fisherman. He and his wife, Ming Ba ("Aunt Ba"), lived on a floating house on the Mekong River and invited us to stay. My legs quivered as I stepped onto the rickety wooden bridge between the house and the riverbank. Midway across, I sank to my knees and clung to the planks, looking into the murky water with fear. His wife's big-hearted laugh punctured my terror. "You won't die!" shouted Ming Ba, her voice deep and smoky. "It's only knee-deep."

I lowered one leg into the water and scraped bottom without wetting my knee. My laughter merged with hers.

The sun had set, but the sky still shone silver-blue. A delicious breeze carried the scent of lush greenery from across the wide river. Another of the couple's daughters, a girl of eleven or twelve, was grilling finger-sized river fish on a charcoal fire—my mother's grilled trei riel, come back to life. Chan squatted to watch the fish, his chin resting in his hand. I will never forget that image of him, gazing at the grilling fish without blinking, his face aglow in the firelight.

Whenever my children complain about something I cook for them, I tell them that story—of the dreamy hunger in their father's face after eleven months in the Ratanakiri highlands. Once, when they were young, I made the grilled trei riel for them. I went to the Sekong riverfront and bought the still-hopping fish right off a fisherman's boat. We gathered around a charcoal fire, just like when I was a child. For hours they sat in the darkness, listening to my stories about my mother's trei riel and tamarind dipping sauce, as we grilled and ate one crispy fish after another.

They can never know their grandparents, but I want them to know the tastes of old Cambodia.

———————

Grilled Fish with Tamarind Dipping Sauce

Clean grill grates and lightly brush a little high-smoke-point, neutral oil onto the fish and grates to prevent fish from sticking. Buy smallish whole fish (or larger fillets) and ask your fishmonger to gut and scale them. Whole fish with skin on is easier to keep whole on the grill and also crisps up better. If you are using fillets (especially thinner ones), consider cooking them in an oiled cast-iron skillet on the grill. Opt for a charcoal or wood fire if you can. A long metal fish spatula is great for turning.
Serves 4

Ingredients:
4 pounds whole fresh fish or fillets with skin on, such as red snapper, trout, tilapia, sea bass, branzino, or even sardines
2 to 4 tablespoons neutral, high-smoke-point oil, such as vegetable or canola

¼ cup sour tamarind paste
¾ cup fish sauce
1 teaspoon sugar
4 cloves garlic, minced
4 Thai red chilies, thinly sliced
Salt

For serving: 4 lime wedges, 4 sprigs cilantro

Wash fish and thoroughly pat dry. Give it 20 minutes to come to room temperature. Clean and oil grill grates.

Make the dipping sauce: In a small bowl, combine tamarind paste, fish sauce, and sugar, then add garlic and chilies.

Lightly brush oil onto the fish and sprinkle with salt. Gently lay fish diagonally across the grill over hot coals. Cook until fish is crisp and slightly charred and releases from the grill grates, about 6 to 8 minutes (depending on size). Turn fish and cook for 4 to 6 minutes more, or until it's firm, opaque, and flaky, or when it reaches an internal temperature of 145 degrees.

Serve fish whole, with jasmine rice and lime wedges on the side. Serve the tamarind dipping sauce in small ramekins or drizzle it over the fish. Top with fresh cilantro. This pairs well with American Dream Morning Glory, Stir-Fried (p. 212).

———————

THAT NIGHT ON the Mekong, I knew we were finished wandering. It was a gorgeous evening: the sweet breezes, the river's slow crawl, the quiet pulse of life in that floating village. *This is what home tastes like*, I thought, as Ming Ba's easy laugh rolled over the water and we filled our bellies with that heavenly fish.

We told the couple our story. When they heard we had been nurses and translators in the refugee camps, they told us we would surely find work in

Stung Treng and invited us to live with them while we found our footing.
I have never forgotten their kindness. And the memory of trei riel—and
that bobor breakfast their daughter bought when I needed it most—still
lingers on my tongue.

WE COLLECTED THE few possessions we'd left in Phnom Penh with
friends, who cried at the sight of us. "We thought you were dead!" they
said. After hearing nothing from us for nearly a year, they were planning a
small memorial service.

Back from the dead, we said our goodbyes and made the three-day "born
again" journey up the Mekong River and back to Stung Treng. We rented
a room for $25 a month and survived by rolling cigarettes for a woman
who sold tobacco in the market. And because we spoke Vietnamese, many
of the local Vietnamese fishermen's families came to us for treatment of
everything from minor infections to typhoid and cancer.

Theoretically, health care existed in Stung Treng—there was a provincial
health center of sorts. But the quality of care was poor, even dangerous—
especially if you had no money. I saw doctors allow patients to die when
they couldn't pay.

Private pharmacies were another lucrative business venture and public health menace in Stung Treng. If a person had the cash, it was easy
to buy a certification permitting the sale of drugs and medical supplies.
Expertise was harder to come by. Untrained "certified" pharmacists often
sold liquor, insecticides, and other merchandise on one side of the shop and
drugs (many of them expired) on the other. Antibiotics and valium, too,
could be purchased in the town market. Nobody checked for a prescription.
More than once, we prevented someone from taking the wrong medicine or
treated them after they already had. We weren't doctors, but we had enough
medical training to keep people from taking drugs that might kill them.
And we would not hesitate to tell a patient when a treatment they needed
was beyond our expertise.

Meanwhile, I asked around for job openings with NGOs. I soon learned that Médecins Sans Frontières was planning a project in Stung Treng. A Frenchwoman named Fabienne, the regional MSF representative, read my letter of recommendation from the camp clinic and said, "I want you, but I can't hire you until September." This was July. "What will you do until then?"

I told her we were barely scraping by.

"Cook for me," she said. "Just until September."

So I reached into my memory and started to cook.

FOR THE FIRST month, I tried to make a new dish every day without repeating. It had been more than a decade since I made my mother and sister's recipes, but somehow, I still remembered dozens of them. Maybe hundreds. And when I craved a dish my mother had never taught me, I learned to replicate it by relying on my puppy-nose memory of how it smelled and tasted.

One recipe I was especially eager to reconstruct was Mae's fried spring rolls. I've never tasted any as delicious as hers. She mixed bean sprouts with seasoned ground pork, rolled everything in rice papers, then fried them perfectly. For our family when I was growing up, this wasn't everyday food, like soup or rice; it was a treat for a special occasion. We children had only been officially allowed to eat one spring roll before dinner, but the alluring smell of frying always drew us back into the kitchen for more. We could not resist Mae's spring rolls, and she could not resist our begging. By dinnertime, we were always too full to eat anything else.

Fabienne loved my fried spring rolls so much, she asked for them every week. It was the one dish I repeated often in those first few weeks of cooking.

Her other favorite was Mae's pâté de foie. I was overjoyed by the chance (and funding) to resurrect that one after so many years. The aroma of fatty pork and liver, steaming over a charcoal fire, brought me nearly to tears.

Word of the pâté de foie and other delicacies spread quickly. Expatriates trickled into Stung Treng to work on new development projects, and they took turns hiring me to feed them home-cooked meals. One aid worker from Hawaii paid me $30—a month's salary—to cook dinner for her colleagues. She invited forty people and requested specialties from four countries.

Chan helped me conjure the sophisticated dishes, special ones we had prepared for weddings back in Vietnam. I cooked the fried spring rolls, Khmer fried red curry, and chả lụa, a Vietnamese steamed pork roll. We crowned the evening with a delicate crème caramel dessert. I had the idea to pour the flan into beer cans cut in half; the convex bottom of the cans made a pretty shape for the desserts.

Soon the foreign aid workers all wanted me in their kitchens—my mother's home cooking seemed to soothe their homesickness—but Fabienne made them stand down. "Chantha already has a job!" she said. And in September, Chan and I started jobs at MSF, work that gave us safety, hope, and soon, a life's calling.

Mae's Fried Spring Rolls

Makes about 12 spring rolls (serves 5 to 6, but this varies according to greed)

Ingredients:
4 to 5 large dried wood ear mushrooms (optional)
1 pound ground pork (or finely chopped belly meat, which has a nicer texture)
1 small shallot, minced
1 clove garlic, minced
½ teaspoon salt
½ teaspoon freshly ground black pepper
12 (16 or 22 cm) rice paper wrappers

¼ pound bean sprouts, broken into ½-inch pieces
½ cup neutral oil

For serving: Teuk Trei Pa'em Dipping Sauce (see recipe for Mae's Memory-Lunch of Wrapped Fried Shrimp, p. 129)

Soak mushrooms (if using) for 30 minutes, then cut into slivers. Transfer to a large bowl, and combine with ground pork, shallot, garlic, salt, and pepper.

Line a baking sheet with parchment paper. Working over a flat, clean surface, brush water onto the rough side of the wrapper with your fingers, and let sit until the wrappers are soft enough to fold (but not too sticky), 1 to 2 minutes.

Combine about 2 tablespoons of the pork mixture with a teaspoon of sprouts. Form the pork-sprout mixture into a finger-size log and place on the softened wrapper, about an inch from the nearest edge. Roll toward the center one complete turn, then fold the sides in, pressing out air bubbles. Continue rolling tightly and seal. Let spring rolls sit, seam side down and not touching each other, on the prepared baking sheet for at least 30 minutes before frying.

In a large skillet, heat a half-inch of oil over medium heat until it shimmers but is not smoking. Carefully place the rolls into the hot oil—it will splatter and sizzle at first. Don't crowd the skillet, as the wrappers can stick together and tear when pulled apart.

Fry rolls until golden brown and crisp, 8 to 10 minutes, then transfer to a paper towel to drain.

Serve with teuk trei pa'em dipping sauce. (Or serve with Banh Sung of Forgiveness, p. 263.)

CHAN WAS HIRED for the MSF logistics section. His job was to make things happen, everything from construction to hauling off waste. He could get anything the doctors needed, and he saw to every detail of setting up surgery and treatment rooms to the standard we had learned in the MSF camp clinic.

After Fabienne left, I became assistant to the new coordinator, Jean-Philippe. One of my first tasks was treating sexually transmitted infections (STIs) and teaching people how to prevent sexually transmitted diseases. I also tried to ease the suffering of AIDS patients. By the turn of the millennium, Cambodia would be in the grip of an AIDS epidemic, with an infection rate among the highest in Asia. But in the mid-1990s, few Cambodians knew what HIV was, even as people sickened and died. There were no antiretrovirals available, and HIV testing was only done for people donating blood.

We focused our efforts on a hundred or so sex workers in brothels scattered throughout Stung Treng City, the sleepy provincial capital. These were uneducated girls fighting to feed themselves. Some had entered the trade hoping to escape lives of destitution as subsistence farmers or manual laborers. I saw the same sad pattern many times: An illiterate girl leaves a brutal marriage or starving family to work in a garment factory—an exciting job in the city, far away from the village where she grew up. Excitement soon gives way to drudgery. She's a beautiful girl, so a beer company recruits her to sell their product in the bars. She wears nice clothes and rides in a limo. After a few months, she is replaced by a "new face."

She becomes a bar girl. Officially, she is hired to chat up patrons and charm them into buying drinks. But it's an open secret that many bar girls offer extracurricular services. Now she's crossed a threshold. For a while, she makes decent money selling sex. Then she turns nineteen, twenty, twenty-one, and the fee she can command steadily declines, until the bar clientele moves on to younger prey.

Sex work in Stung Treng is the end of the line. By this time, the farm girl is considered past her prime back in Phnom Penh. She heads to some backwater where nobody will know her and serves truckers and riverboat drivers for 2,000 riels (fifty cents) per client. Too late, she realizes she has run out of choices; she can see no escape. She dreads going home, where she will be ostracized. And too often, by this time, she is also sick with a dreadful illness no one dares to name.

Some of my coworkers grew angry and hard as they watched this cycle repeat itself. "They didn't listen to us, and now they are dying," said one colleague, her eyes tired. I shared their frustration, and sometimes their cynicism. But I could not judge the young women. Jean-Philippe and I had gotten to know many of them personally; we visited them in the brothels sometimes. Once, we called on a young sex worker who had given birth three weeks before. Her baby was sick, and she was starving. She asked if we wanted the baby. "I cannot work with a baby to feed, but I have nothing to feed him," she said. I was ready to take the infant home, but Jean-Philippe explained that this was not allowed. The memory of that abject woman and her starved little son weighed on me for weeks. I could not be consoled.

Another patient came to us paralyzed from the waist down. That afternoon, she disappeared from the hospital. A friend had carried her on a moto back to the brothel, where she continued serving customers—in denial that she was dying, until she became too sick with pancreatitis to continue. That's how most of them succumbed: an agonized death of pancreatitis, TB, or some other infection, with severe abdominal pain, diarrhea, and sores that refused to heal.

I watched a dozen of those young women, all between nineteen and twenty-two years old, die in the Stung Treng hospital. There was little I could do for them except try to ease their pain and cook them something nice. Jean-Philippe gave me money to spend on good food from a local restaurant. When the girls were still well enough to eat solid food, I bought them a beefsteak or grilled fish and fed them a few bites. In their final weeks, all they could bear was rice, soup, or a sip of coconut water.

I offered to inform the patients' families, but they always refused. I could not fathom why these tormented young women did not want to go home. Surely their mothers would understand! Surely they would cradle their daughters in their arms and feed them rice and s'gnao. But the young women preferred to die alone rather than to admit to their families what they had done to survive.

Those young women's bravery brought me to tears many times. Most had numbed themselves to the abuse and contempt they suffered by encasing themselves inside a thick cocoon. As a defense, some became very rude, but I understood. I felt honored to care for them. They reminded me how lucky I was to have work, an education, a full belly. But for some small turn of history, I might have been in their situation myself. In Saigon, I had narrowly escaped such a life. I still believe that my mother's voice in my head was the only thing that stopped me when I worked in the bar with Nga.

I don't know what it means to die with dignity, but I could at least keep my young patients from dying in the street. And with each moment I spent in the presence of their suffering, I felt my own wounds healing.

MY OTHER JOB during this time was with MSF's mobile health-care project. This team visited remote areas, feeding starving babies and mothers too emaciated to lactate. We saw patients coughing up blood who refused to believe they had tuberculosis, which was considered shameful and would result in their isolation. We treated sick toddlers whose parents would let a child die rather than attempt the arduous journey to a hospital. Many had never left their villages. And if they did make the journey, who would feed the chickens while they were away?

My favorite job was feeding severely malnourished children in the Stung Treng hospital. In the severest cases, when the children's bellies were swollen with edema, I gave them milk with sugar and oil, to bring them back to life. Then, as their bellies filled and color returned to their faces, I cooked them bobor with chopped pork. It was a more hopeful sort of work. In this, at least, we had the power to actually save lives.

On the weekends, I roasted coffee beans using my mother's recipe. She roasted the beans over a low fire until they turned caramel-dark and smelled of cocoa. She added a little sugar and water, then roasted them again. Last, she stirred in butter and cognac, let the beans cool, then packed them in thick fabric or paper bags to age. I sold Mae's coffee to a Canadian VSO volunteer named Thierry for a good price. Soon I had more expat customers, who ordered many kilos at a time.

The MSF jobs gave us our first taste of security since leaving Cambodia as children—we were no longer "white hands." Chan and I began considering whether our newfound security was reliable enough to start a family. "I want a perfect baby," I explained to my MSF boss, Jean-Philippe, as we drove the rural roads of Stung Treng.

"What is a 'perfect baby'?" he asked. We drove past a mud-filled crater in the road, where an emaciated toddler sat belly-deep in the watery mud.

"*That* is not a perfect baby," I said, pointing to the mud hole.

"I see what you mean," he said.

Of course, all babies are perfect. What's less than perfect are the lives they are born into.

IN 1996, AFTER working at MSF for almost a year, I gave birth to our daughter, Clara. She was a perfect baby.

And then, four years after leaving Ratanakiri as failed ruby miners, we built a small house overlooking a great sweep of Stung Treng rice fields, just like the fortune teller said we would. I was thirty-seven years old. Finally, I had a kitchen of my own, a place to bring my childhood memories to life.

In addition to lifting us out of poverty, those MSF jobs gave us a chance to do something meaningful for Cambodia's recovery. We could see that the journey would be a complicated one. The obstacles were overwhelming; every institution had to be rebuilt from the ground up. The experts had been murdered or had fled. How do you revive schools without teachers, banks without bankers, or theaters without musicians and dancers?

Other varieties of loss were more difficult to quantify. A collective memory of hunger and horror lay buried within the survivors' psyches, like millions of land mines, silently waiting. That trauma could detonate in a hundred ways—in violence or despair, paralysis or odd fixations. People might hoard food or dread the darkness. But the most common aftereffect I saw was that people had lost their initiative. Ingenuity and bold action—survival tools of poor people everywhere—lay dead and buried. One of the strangest symptoms of this newfound timidity was a phrase that pervaded my interactions with people: "I don't know." I heard it constantly, even when the answer made no sense.

I might ask someone in the market, "What vegetables do you put into your samlor proher?"

"I don't know" would come the reply.

I was bewildered by this. Of course she knew! She had made that soup twice a week for her whole life, minus the four years immediately after Zero. And then I began to see: Pol Pot's brutal reign had made people fearful and stunted. The victims were burdened with a tragic knowledge of human barbarism, and that had transformed their ideas of the world. And being enslaved and tortured had profoundly damaged their ability to see themselves as human beings with dignity and agency.

Before the war, it was safe to try, to take risks, and to fail. But under Angkar, any action—and especially any presumed failure—could cost you your life. People were so frightened of making a mistake, they could not even commit to a straight answer about vegetables in a samlor, because it could be the wrong one.

Here are the vegetables I prefer in my samlor proher. It's a beloved village dish made from a fragrant paste of lemongrass and fingerroot (similar to ginger) and whatever vegetables and greens you can forage. I use chili leaf, sleuk ngub (*sauropus androgynus*, a leafy green), bok choy or gai lan (Chinese broccoli), kabocha squash, and our native eggplant, which is long, thin, and purple. It is a dish best served with rice and a dash of resolve.

ANOTHER PSYCHOLOGICAL BARRIER to decisive action was this: For many of the traumatized survivors, the future had ceased to exist. Angkar had taught them too much about endings. They had forgotten everything else and focused only on surviving. In my work with MSF and other aid organizations in the early years of recovery, I asked people, "What are your dreams? We will work with you to make them come true." They answered with blank looks. Or they said, "I am dreaming of a sack of rice."

Survival mentality cannot see further than today's meal. Under Pol Pot, the victims had worked their entire lives only to witness everything going up in flames. Pol Pot had taken everything from them, including belief in their own power to better themselves. Why plant a tree, if you will be punished for harvesting the fruit—or if you will never live to see it reach maturity?

It is understandable, but also a poor recipe for transforming a ruined society into a resilient one.

The big foreign aid groups did their best, but they had no idea how to reshape a civilization from nothing. Who does? Donors, NGOs, and politicians want speedy, tangible progress. The natural bias is, Hurry up and heal. We have other emergencies to attend to.

The resulting infrastructure is precarious. The facade can appear robust, but the walls will crumble at the first gust of wind. The cracks aren't always visible, but I saw signs of rot beneath the surface. More than once, I checked on an outreach worker whose job was to teach villagers AIDS prevention, vaccinate children, or deliver rice and cooking oil to tuberculosis patients in remote areas—only to find that he had collected his per diem without performing any outreach, then sold the rice or meds and pocketed the profits. Or I would ask some local official to do his job and sign the documents to certify our nonprofit to operate in the province, only to be charged a large, unofficial fee.

Or a provincial teacher would collect a paycheck for years without ever showing up at school.

Or, of course, those doctors I had watched let destitute patients die of treatable injuries.

I call this Instant Noodles Mentality: a zero-sum game of plunder and temporary betterment, every person for himself.

We Cambodians had gotten a taste of the Dollar, and suddenly we wanted to be paid to help each other—or in some cases, paid not to bother. It was disheartening to see people squander the chance to build something lasting. Selfishness was an infection that resisted treatment. What had happened to our community spirit of sharing and helping each other? Had Pol Pot killed it, with his rhetoric about the Greater Good? Had it ever lived, or was it only a childish ideal that I chose to believe in? Perhaps I had been spoiled by seeing Chanthu and Mae lower dinner out the window to our neighbors. I, too, had been the recipient of the unpaid generosity of strangers, both in Battambang and in Stung Treng. Maybe this wasn't normal behavior.

I didn't care. I wanted generosity to *become* normal. Instead, greed, slapdash aid, and dependency were so common, people simply shrugged them off as inevitabilities: *That is how things are.*

I could not accept that answer. I realized that, one day soon, charity would get tired in Cambodia, just like it did in the refugee camps. We were in danger of becoming addicted to foreign aid. Chan and I began to think hard about how we, and a whole nation of mourners, might come to rely on ourselves instead. It would take a giant shift in thinking. We couldn't rebuild our shattered country in five or ten years. It would take generations to restore what we had lost and to begin advancing the clock again from one minute before Year Zero.

We needed a Slow Noodles approach. Like my mother's bánh canh noodles, rolled out one by one, deliberately and with love.

Hồ Chí Minh once said that it takes ten years to grow a tree and a hundred years to grow a person.

How long does it take to reseed a devastated civilization? That remains to be seen.

EVEN TODAY, AS poor Cambodians are too busy surviving to remember the future, the new generation of rich, educated Khmers wants to forget their prahok past. To them, it smells of the poor village life they left behind.

Perhaps you are reading this, dreaming of a simpler time and place: of wide-open skies, shimmering rice fields, a long-tail boat on the river. I, too, feel wistful—especially about my first nine years of life, which I choose to remember as perfect, a little-girl heaven.

But perfection doesn't exist, and nostalgia in Cambodia is a many-headed serpent. A farmer's life has never been easy. And any Cambodian of my generation recalls those four harrowing years when rice farming was not voluntary.

For survivors of Pol Pot Time who built prosperous new lives in the city, the memory of rice fields will always be linked to starvation and enslavement, mass graves and murder by farm implement. Is it any wonder that many rich Cambodians would rather put village life behind them? Some don't want their sons and daughters to speak Khmer. They push them to study in English, to leave home and live abroad. They want to bury the past and start from scratch, so they refuse to pass on their memories to their children, often for fear that the trauma will trickle through.

But the past never goes away. The fear and pain are still there, buried in our brains like mines. It is better to defuse them than to leave them entombed, quietly waiting for a single misstep.

That is why I am telling my story.

In 2000, four years after we had Clara, our son, Johan, was born. That year Médecins Sans Frontières ended the Stung Treng project. The crisis phase in Cambodia had passed, they said. It was time to move on to more urgent disasters. I told my colleagues that I hoped to continue working with HIV/AIDS patients, who still needed our care.

"There's money available," said the MSF country director. "You just have to knock on the right door." I hoped for some indication of which door that might be. I knocked on a great many of the wrong ones.

And then I met the man behind the right door.

There's so much more to the story than I have room to tell here, but the beginning and middle belong to David Wright, a veteran of the aid world and (at the time) coordinator of a global antipoverty NGO. Between his initial donation of $500 and the introductions he made to other patrons, Chan and I were able to rent a building in Stung Treng town and renovate it, buy beds, and open a very small hospice facility—called the Destination Center—for terminally ill patients, most of them former sex workers, policemen, and ex-soldiers.

That $500 was the beginning of the next phase in our story. Our lives would never be the same.

17. Rice and Golden Mountain

You don't have to cut a tree down to get at the fruit.
—Khmer proverb

CHAN AND I embraced the uncertainty of opening a small nonprofit. The realities were daunting: There would be no salaries for us, nor any guarantee of steady funding. But we wanted to invest in this quiet place where we felt we were needed.

Stung Treng, always a remote and very poor province, had become even more isolated after the war. Even by the early 2000s, getting there was still a "born again" adventure. The local ex-Khmer Rouge cadres had put aside ideology in favor of nonpartisan banditry. The roads were unusable. Mines and unexploded ordnance (UXO) were stealthy killers. We sometimes heard the low thunder of explosions at the disused airport, where old bombs were taken for detonation.

Most of the population subsisted by farming—mostly rice, but also cashews, cassava, and rubber. Stung Treng farmers worked the fields by hand—unimaginably hard labor—and most barely raised enough rice for their own families. A few people got rich by illegal logging or drug trafficking. But most people lived in dire poverty, one bad harvest away from starvation.

Education was a low priority, especially for girls, who were expected to stay home and help with the housework, then marry young and start families—which, with no birth control, quickly grew large. Stung Treng women lived on the edge of catastrophe. If a husband fell off a roof or contracted typhoid, how would they pay for a doctor? If the father died or disappeared, who would feed the children? And if a provider turned out to be an abusive drunk, where could a dependent wife turn for help?

The women of Stung Treng needed everything. Most had never been to school. Few had any education or skills to fall back on, and no way to pull themselves out of poverty. They were expected to live by the old *Chbab Srey* code and depend on men to survive. That strategy often failed.

I took a job with UNICEF to keep us fed while Chan volunteered his labor for our hospice project. He had a gift for making big things happen with small amounts of cash. He did renovations himself and scrounged leftover pipe or lumber from bigger NGOs where we had friends. Almost every month, we ran out of money and had to ask our patrons for more. I wondered how long we could go on like that, surviving on a trickle from one or two loyal donors. I loved the work but hated the begging.

The Cambodian government had announced a new initiative called *Neary Rotanak*—"Women Are Diamonds"—focused on women's literacy. I was glad to hear that we had been promoted from fabric to gemstones. More important, it seemed that women's literacy was something philanthropists (and our government) were willing to fund. So no matter how much I loved our hospice work, financial realities meant we had to find ways to serve women who needed us and call it literacy training.

When we launched our women's literacy and health education project upstairs from the hospice, the classes filled immediately. Most of the students were farmers, and many were young wives with many children. They sold vegetables in the market while their babies played in a nearby trash heap. Some cleared garbage or washed dishes in a food stall for around a dollar a day.

I was ecstatic! Here were fifty women putting aside the "I don't know" mentality and acting on their own behalf. But within a few months, many began to drop out of class. I asked myself, how can one year of reading and writing classes change their lives? A taste of literacy wasn't enough. These women needed a skill that would feed their families.

The more need I saw, the more my focus shifted. Our hospice work mattered. If only in a small way, it helped ease people's pain. But I began to apply the Slow Noodles logic to these issues and think longer term: What if we could help prevent women from contracting HIV in the first place? What if we could offer an alternative to subsistence farming, garment-factory drudgery, or the brothels? Economic independence was a superpower the women of Stung Treng desperately wanted.

That's how the weaving center idea was born.

David Wright had once asked me to head up a weaving project in a village near the Laotian border. Although that job didn't last long, I learned about silk dyeing and the basics of weaving. I had the idea that a silk-weaving center could bolster the hospice and the literacy training. Women would learn a trade, and we could pay them a decent wage and fund our social services by selling silk. I hoped this could be a way for Chan and me to become self-sufficient, and to help Stung Treng's women to do the same.

David loved the idea and promised to help us find the money.

ARMED WITH A $3,000 donation, four hand-built looms, and a batch of raw silk, we opened the Stung Treng Women's Development Center (SWDC) in early 2002, at the site of our former hospice. More than a hundred applicants applied for our weavers' training regimen. Choosing only five was agonizing. We brought in a weaver from Takeo Province to train the first class and kept the literacy and health education program running in tandem.

Money was still tight, so when my UNICEF contract ended, I freelanced as a translator and took part-time jobs with the UK's Volunteer Service Overseas (VSO) and other NGOs. The fortune teller's words about my future husband had also been prescient: I was never his financial dependent. I relied on his resourcefulness and dedication to SWDC, but it was an interdependence as equals.

Still, we often asked ourselves whether trading security for a sense of purpose was the wisest choice.

And then David Wright helped us find a miracle. He urged us to write a funding proposal to the Allen Foundation, an American family philanthropy that supported development projects all over the world. In answer to our proposal, they sent $50,000—an unimaginable sum.

With that money, Chan bought a piece of land a few kilometers out of town, built a modest compound of open-air wood structures, and constructed more looms. Eight months later, we reopened the Stung Treng Women's Development Center in Sre Po village and had money left over to operate for a year. Slowly, we added services: a midwife and clinic, a kindergarten, free lunch every day. The money Chan set aside for his own salary was just about enough to cover his cigarette budget.

In my time off from the NGO work, I helped Chan at SWDC. He had built a small open-air café on site, but there was no staff to keep the charcoal fire burning. I often had to drop everything and run to the café if a group of tourists or foreign NGO employees stopped in. I steamed fish amok, fried chicken with ginger, or grilled pork ribs and fish for the aid workers, who enjoyed lingering in the quiet café until very late. On those nights, Chan fed the kids, and I fell into bed well after midnight.

On Sundays, I trained women who did not want to be weavers to clean and cook for the growing expat community in Stung Treng. I taught them fancy wedding and festival dishes, like my mother's special-occasion tamarind stew. I didn't expect rural cooks to possess my mother's culinary skills—she was a middle-class wife with the money and leisure to prepare sophisticated fare—but some of the women had little grasp of what I considered the basics of Khmer cooking.

I wondered if Pol Pot had erased our culinary past, too. I was determined to remember.

Chan and I scarcely had any rest, even on Khmer New Year or Pchum Ben, when every other Khmer was offering food to their ancestors. If there were customers in the café, the ancestors had to wait their turn. Often, I barely had time to feed myself. One morning as I rushed to get ready for work, I hastily slid a fried egg into a bowl of leftover rice and dribbled on some Golden Mountain seasoning—my favorite soy sauce. In the refugee camps, we splurged for it in the camp store and always had it on hand.

The first bite of my no-thought breakfast that morning shot me back to the refugee camps like a thunderclap. I had nearly forgotten that egg and rice with soy sauce had been my breakfast nearly every day in Phanat Nikhom and Sikhiu—and sometimes, my lunch and dinner, too. I wept over my bowl of rice and could not finish it.

As I said before, in Southeast Asia, rice is what you eat when you have nothing and when you have everything. That day, the careless breakfast rice tasted of the former—a powerful have-nothingness, the squalor and deprivation of the camps.

For me, the simplest taste can trigger a memory. That was one that I preferred to keep interred. There were far more delicious tastes, and memories, to resurrect.

THE EARLY TRAINEES at SWDC feared me, at first. But I sat beside them, ate with them, listened to their stories. As they chatted to each other, I learned things—about sick mothers, violent husbands, teenagers pressured to marry, pregnant girls whose boyfriends had run off and whose families had kicked them out. Once I knew, I could help. The exiled girl could have her baby at SWDC. The sisterhood of weavers would help care for mother and child. The frightened wife could hide with us from a drunken and dangerous husband.

As we worked through problems, the women saw that we were equals. They wanted to know what I had learned about digging out of poverty. "If you want the fruit, you have to climb the tree," I told them. "You will fall many times. But the fruit tastes sweetest when you pick it yourself."

And then we zoomed in on how the thing was done: First, show up. Every day. Sit still and learn, even when it seems impossible. Focus on worthwhile dreams, like becoming a weaver and sending your children to school. Marrying a rich man? Not a worthwhile dream, I told them. He will soon cast you aside for a fresher fish.

But education for the kids—that is possible. We opened a kindergarten on site for our employees' children, and when they graduated, we supported them through the rest of their schooling by paying for school supplies, class fees, and a bicycle to get them there. Maybe our weavers couldn't dream of finishing high school, but their children could.

I was often their translator, a bridge between the village and the modern world. I taught them to talk to imperious doctors. "They are not gods," I explained. The women learned to decide how many children to have and how to protect themselves from STIs.

It took a lot of translating to convince the weavers to use the Western-style toilet we built at the center. Some women, ashamed to ask how it worked, sneaked off to use the forest instead. First, I had to explain that you don't stand on the seat. Then I had to convince them to take turns cleaning it. "I'm a weaver now," they protested, "not a toilet cleaner!" I told them that they were neither lower than doctors nor higher than toilet cleaners. Status didn't matter; what did matter was work and independence, and giving their children a chance to live well.

"Don't be a dependent housewife," I told them. The voice I heard speaking sounded a lot like my mother's. I smiled at the paradox: Here I was, delivering a lesson about self-reliance that I had failed to fully absorb before my mother's death—and had learned the hard way thereafter.

The weavers watched me closely, saw how I worked for myself and my family and spoke up with confidence. They saw Chan treat me as a partner. And then they saw me take my turn at scrubbing the toilet.

They wanted the things I had, so they worked very hard. And that has made all the difference. They climbed the tree. We only offered a very small boost.

THE JOURNEY TO Stung Treng is now much safer. You can drive there from Phnom Penh in seven hours. (I have done the trip many times—I moved to Phnom Penh when Clara was ten, so my children could go to better schools in the capital, while Chan stayed in Stung Treng to run the center.) The gravest danger on that route now is facing an oncoming truck as you're passing an oxcart. Other things have not changed as much: Poverty and illiteracy. Illegal logging. Desperate girls making desperate choices.

But in Sre Po village, we have carved an island of self-reliance out of the lush greenery. There's a faded sign by the entrance, hand-lettered in English and Khmer: STUNG TRENG WOMEN'S DEVELOPMENT CENTER. And although the weaving center went quiet when the pandemic struck, SWDC still serves women and their families. I want you to picture an ordinary day there, back when the place was at its peak of pre-Covid bustle: a kindergarten teacher leading children in song; cooks peeling carrots and daikon in an outdoor kitchen while a calico cat vies for scraps; women threading brilliant silk threads on wooden looms in a breezy structure bathed in sunlight.

Many of the women at our center still don't read much—one year of literacy classes is only a beginning. But the women we trained as weavers learned to produce exquisite silk scarves. The work requires intense concentration and patience. They must fold the warp across a beam and then count their trips back and forth as they weave the weft. It takes more than a week to create a single scarf this way, and intricate patterns like ikat and jacquard can take even longer.

Dyeing the silk is also a complicated process. The measurements and proportions are not easy for someone who has never been to school. The dyers worked hard to master the calculations, but the foreign color names stumped them: Words like *ultramarine* and *scarlet* mean nothing to a rice farmer's daughter. So I renamed the dye colors after things they see in their everyday lives: Bright orange is "shrimp paste." Deep red is "chili." Dark blue is "night sky," and pale green is "young rice stalk." The familiar names are easy to remember, and the dyers perfected the recipes for dozens of brilliant colors.

We named our brand Mekong Blue Silk. The scarves won UNESCO awards and have been sold all over the world, at international art festivals and in museums like the Smithsonian. Our weavers are still amazed by the fact that people in Japan and America are wearing their creations. And so am I.

WHEN A GIRL named Nuon Srey Nim came to us more than a decade ago, she was living a no-lights life. Her parents died, leaving her to care for three younger siblings and her aunt's three children. She had one useless brother, who hit her whenever he drank, and one diligent brother, who planted rice and helped her care for the younger ones. The good brother was struck by lightning and killed in the rice field. Nim had inherited the house, but the rotten bamboo poles were sinking into the mud. She was eighteen years old and had no one to help her feed the children or repair her house.

The lights in Nim's life had been extinguished, one by one. But even with her bad luck, she learned fast and laughed easily. Nothing defeated her, which made me want to protect her all the more. When her aunt tried to make her marry an older man, we hid her in the center until the aunt relented. And when her house finally collapsed, we emptied the donation box and organized a village house-raising. The weavers chipped in a few thousand riels, and I cooked a massive pot of samlor machu kroeung and fried pork ribs for the builders.

If you feed people, they will come.

Nim finished the literacy and medical education classes, then became one of our best weavers. She went to work every day and earned a good salary, a turn she never expected her life to take. She sent her siblings to school and saved her earnings to buy a cow, and then another one. Now she lives in a sturdy house that keeps her family dry when it rains. She makes a living buying a cow every year and selling it two years later for three times the purchase price. She grows vegetables by the river and sells them in the market. She is prosperous and free. Her face is always smiling.

I love to see women change their lives that way.

I learned in Saigon that there is no such thing as utopia. But what's wrong with creating a community of safety, where softness will not prove fatal? Where we Stung Treng women can help each other turn our pain into strength? Where freedom is there for the taking, for anyone who wants to climb the tree?

ONE AFTERNOON SEVERAL years ago, I spoke too sharply to the women at our center. They were sitting down to their daily free lunch, chattering and complaining. "We are sick of s'gnao sach mouan," they griped.

"Charity gets tired," I chided them.

And then I smiled: *They are in a position to take chicken soup for granted*, these women who had survived on rice and river fish, or sometimes, on much less. Young girls who'd gone hungry, who'd begged for a job as a silk weaver.

They have become women who can support themselves and their families. They have enough to eat. They don't have to leave their children behind for the garment factories—or the bars and brothels. They can be picky about soup, and also about husbands. Some of them hold out for a good man or choose no man at all. They have children *if* they want to, and usually only one or two, and they send them all to school.

Together, we are learning that it's better for a woman to cast her own light, like a sun that nurtures others. We are, I hope, a new kind of Cambodian woman—both strong and soft, and terribly improper.

I'm glad my children grew up among the weavers at SWDC. I want them to understand the hard work of climbing out of poverty, so they will always remember to help and to share. Those village childhood memories, I hope, are their own recipes for Little-Girl and Little-Boy Heaven. And I hope they never lose their taste for trei riel, bobor, and even prahok.

THE STUNG TRENG market, more than any other place, reminds me of my parents' neighborhood in Battambang. The place pulses with the smells and tastes of old Cambodia: pickled fruit and prahok, sweet potato cakes and rice/mung bean dessert, num banhchok, and bai sach chruok, a popular Khmer breakfast of BBQ pork and rice. And of course, kuy teav. So long as Cambodians still walk this planet, kuy teav will abide—the eternal Teochew-Chinese-Khmer breakfast.

I love strolling the market at first light, when the vendors are just arriving on small wooden boats from their villages, climbing the steep riverbank, and spreading blankets with garden vegetables or fresh fish to sell. I wind my way into the maze of covered market stalls and sit on a wooden bench, where my favorite vendor offers tea to a makeshift shrine and spoons steaming bánh canh out of a cauldron, into my bowl. That one is the most delicious. Or I might buy a bánh xèo, the Vietnamese crepe, or Khmer xiu mai—a steamed pork meatball dripping with delicious juices, served with a baguette.

Or a bowl of banh sung, my mother's making-amends dish, the one she bought for me after she had raised her voice in anger. Of course, I always forgave her.

I don't know whether Cambodians can ever forgive what was done to us in the catastrophic years after Year Zero. The old Khmer Rouge cadres live quietly among us, pretending that nothing was ever amiss. The mass graves prove otherwise. How do we truly make peace? The joint UN-Cambodian Khmer Rouge war crimes tribunal (ECCC) spent sixteen years and $300 million to convict three geriatric defendants. Then—like so many ambitious, expensive aid projects here—the whole thing just ended, was left unfinished.

Pol Pot was never tried. In 1997, he told a journalist that his conscience was clear. He died the following year without ever expressing any remorse.

There can be no easy reconciliations, only complicated truths, told without shame.

The murderers among us would have us believe that history is slippery and unknowable. Insisting otherwise is an act of defiance.

The taste of banh sung contains my own history—a powerful, sensory proof that it all existed: my mother and sister, the Providence school nuns, my father's winding clock, and the banana sellers and noodle-makers of 1960s Battambang. I did not invent those memories. In the absence of

yellowed family photos or priceless keepsakes, let these noodles serve as a
memorial. Whenever I eat them, I imagine my mother, silently asking my
forgiveness for everything.

But of course, there is nothing to forgive.

———

Banh Sung of Forgiveness

Like the many popular Vietnamese bún dishes (such as bún chả),
Cambodian banh sung is essentially a noodle salad, topped with pork,
spring rolls, or anything you like; lots of fresh greens and herbs; and two
sauces. The main differences are the additional coconut milk sauce and
the thicker, springier noodles.

Serves 4

Ingredients:
1 pound pork (belly meat, skin removed, or pork chop), cut into
4-inch strips about ½ inch thick
2 shallots, diced
4 cloves garlic, minced
1 teaspoon salt
1 (14- to 16-ounce) package round, thicker rice noodles,
approximately the thickness of spaghetti (you can usually find
packages labeled "bún bò Huế")
Pinch of sugar
2 tablespoons toasted rice (see "Notes on Ingredients, Techniques,
and Supplies" for prep tips)
Mae's Fried Spring Rolls (see p. 242) and Teuk Trei Pa'em Dipping
Sauce (see p. 129)

For the coconut-milk sauce:
1 (13.5-ounce) can full-fat, unsweetened coconut milk
1 tablespoon sugar

½ teaspoon salt
1 tablespoon all-purpose flour
2 scallions, thinly sliced

For toppings, any assortment of the following: 1 cucumber, cut
into 2-inch matchsticks; ½ head leaf lettuce, roughly torn into
bite-size pieces; ¼ pound bean sprouts; 1 bunch Thai basil; 2 to
4 scallions (green and white parts), thinly sliced

In a medium bowl, combine pork with shallots, garlic, and salt,
and let sit for at least 30 minutes.

Cook noodles, drain, rinse with cold water, and set aside.

In a skillet, add a pinch of sugar to pork and sauté over
medium-low heat until partially cooked, about 10 minutes. (The
sugar produces a nice caramel color.) Add ¼ cup water, reduce
heat, and simmer until pork, shallots, and garlic are golden brown.
Add additional water if needed. Transfer pork (with all those crisp
garlic and shallot bits) to a bowl and stir in toasted rice.

Make the coconut-milk sauce: In a small saucepan, heat
coconut milk over medium heat. Stir in sugar and salt, then mix
flour with 1½ tablespoons water and add the flour slurry. Bring
to a boil momentarily to thicken, then turn off the heat and add
scallions.

Place noodles in one half of each bowl and crowd in the
herbs and greens on the other half. Cut spring rolls into bite-size,
diagonal pieces and layer pork and spring rolls on top. Pour the
sauce over everything and toss like a salad before eating.

Serve with contrition.

18. The Elephant Fish

When you eat fruit, remember who planted the tree.
—Vietnamese proverb

MY STRANGE LIFE taught me to speak many languages and wear many faces: I can Buddha-smile for an ambassador, laugh with a street vendor, or curse in a bar like a workingman. A refugee must learn to be anything people want her to be at any given moment. But behind the masks, I am only myself—a mosaic of flavors from near and far. Pâté de foie. Grilled prahok. Poor Grandmother's pickles. Land-mine chicken. My mother's slow bánh canh and instant Mama-brand noodles.

A powerful craving for sugar and lime.

Actually, let's consider the lime: I told you that my mother trained me to peel it so the bitter rind would not corrupt the juice. But another impulse has overtaken the first. Now I remove the peel and roll the soft, skinless lime against a tile so I can squeeze out every drop of juice. As if this were the only lime for thirty kilometers of rain-choked forest.

My son, Johan, rolls his eyes at my refrigerator, stuffed with ancient leftovers I can't throw away. "You're not starving anymore," he says, worried for me. On the outside, I wear a mask of reassurance. But inside, I cannot relax my vigilance: I know that hunger can always return. Luck can run out anytime, so I always have a plan. Is this PTSD? Or is it déjà vu, paired with practical action?

The answer is yes.

Which leaves me wondering, which Chantha is the one who *must* peel the lime: the diligent chef with a puppy's nose or the compulsive saver, driven by lime-thirst memories? Perhaps the two are chemically bonded, as impossible to separate as rice flour and water once they are rolled into noodles and cooked.

I sometimes wonder how different my life would have been if my mother had lived for ten more years. Would I have ended up in refugee camps or the Ratanakiri forest? Or at a women's weaving center in Stung Treng?

For so long, I was consumed by the idea that Mae had failed to toughen me for the world outside her kitchen. In my twenty-fourth year, when I was newly alone (and dreaming of a sack of rice), I needed an Instant Noodles strength—a thief's ingenuity that would feed me right away. Instead, my mother gave me a Slow Noodles recipe, with ingredients that would need years to simmer and meld. Little-girl heaven tempered with Buffalo Girl luck. A healer's hands and a puppy's nose. A silken rebel's patient resistance, behind a mask of diplomacy. A toolkit for transforming something rotten into deliciousness—lemongrass fish.

A decades-long recipe for cooking pain into strength.

I had believed that once I fell into poverty, I had to cast aside Mae's values. But every day, they are with me. When I sink into sadness, I soothe myself with her Vietnamese hymns. The charcoal smoke in my Phnom Penh courtyard calls forth her ghost, as I squat over the grill and simmer a samlor. And the stories she told me over lunches in Saigon will stay with me forever. I tell them to my children when we are eating together.

Chanthu was right: Struggling hard to squeeze something out of nothing is my Buffalo birthright. Finally, it has borne fruit. I marvel at my luck these past twenty-five years. When I leave one good job, I immediately find another. And I proved the fortune teller right once again: by making a living with my words. I am a translator—part wordsmith, part diplomat. A bridge between two worlds: Cambodia and America. Rich and poor. The past and the future. My mother and my children.

I feel like a lucky Buffalo.

MAE USED TO tell me a Khmer fairy tale called "The Elephant Fish"—a children's story, like the Cambodian Cinderella. A rich man and his wife give birth to a daughter with a pure heart. But a conniving widow wants the husband for herself, to provide for her and her daughters. She seduces the man, and he takes her as his second wife. Quickly she plants in him a dark suspicion—that his first wife has a lover.

The husband confronts his first wife in a rage and strikes her. She falls into the river and drowns, her spirit entering the body of an elephant fish.

The child goes to the river and calls for her lost mother. As her tears fall into the water, the elephant fish speaks to her. "I am your mother," the fish says. "I am hungry."

The daughter promises to bring her a bit of rice to eat every day.

The mean stepmother soon notices the missing rice and follows the girl to the river. When the daughter has gone, the stepmother catches the fish, cooks it, and serves it to the child.

The little girl recognizes the cruel trick, sneaks her bowl outside, and buries the elephant fish in the garden. From that spot a tree grows, which bears a perfumed yellow fruit, bursting with seeds. When she cuts the seed in half, there in the pod is the face of her mother.

The daughter spreads the seeds to the wind.

Her mother's face is everywhere.

Mae and Chantha's Pâté de Foie

This rustic, country-style pâté is delicious served as an appetizer with crusty bread, or as a num pang pâté (sandwich) with a Khmer baguette and any combination of pickled vegetables—such as carrot and daikon— cilantro, cucumber, mayonnaise, and even sliced chả lụa.
Serves 6

Ingredients:
1 pound chicken livers
1 cup brandy or cognac (or enough to cover the livers)

6 ounces pork fat

2 Khmer baguettes

6 large cloves garlic, chopped

1 teaspoon black peppercorns, freshly ground, plus more for serving

4 to 5 whole cloves, freshly ground

Rinse livers and pat them dry. Trim off the fat and veiny, tough connective tissue. In a bowl, soak livers in brandy or cognac for at least an hour (or overnight, if possible).

Cut fat into 1-inch squares. In a food processor or blender, blend liver, fat, and about ¼ cup of the soaking liquor until very smooth.

Soak one of the baguettes in water to soften it, squeeze out the excess water, and add it to food processor. Add garlic, pepper, and cloves and blend again until smooth.

Press the pâté into a Pyrex or other steam-safe container (such as a large ramekin) about 4 inches wide. Cover with a steam-safe lid or aluminum foil, and place in a steamer. Steam for 1½ to 2 hours on high heat; add water to steamer as needed.

Open lid and test pâté with a toothpick or paring knife. If it comes out clean, the pâté is cooked. If not, add more water to the steamer and steam for 15 to 30 minutes more, or as long as needed.

Grind more black pepper over pâté and serve with a Khmer baguette.

EPILOGUE

by Clara Kim

WHEN I WAS five years old, my parents carved a clearing into the Cambodian forest and built a dream. I grew up at the Stung Treng Women's Development Center and played with the kids at SWDC's kindergarten. We ran together on the paths between rice fields and fished in the Stung Treng streams. I shadowed the weavers as they worked, pretending to weave the shiny silk threads before I was tall enough to see over the looms.

I watched how my mother fought for poor women who had never been to school, and I watched how she fought for their children. One day an emaciated woman brought two severely malnourished little boys to the center. Since birth, they'd had no milk, only liquid porridge and sugar to drink. The boys had swollen bellies and could barely speak or walk, although they were four and five years old. They came back to life under my mom's care. My brother and I took them home sometimes to share lunch with us. I saw the light return to their faces, and I felt a leap of joy when I heard them laugh for the first time.

In Stung Treng, hunger was all around us. There were lots of kids with empty stomachs at my primary school. I often felt powerless against this river of need, but at least I could share my breakfast money. In third grade, a few of us organized a committee to raise money for students who had less than we did.

My mother taught me that when you feel powerless, you can always find at least one thing to do, however small it may be.

Living at SWDC reminded me every day that I was luckier than most of the girls in my country. My parents ignored the old Khmer saying about gold and cloth and treated my brother and me as equals. They never taught me the *Chbab Srey*, but my female classmates studied it. Most of them left school when they were preteens to take care of younger siblings and help with the housework. They learned to be "proper" Cambodian women—obedient, demure, and dutiful.

I had no talent for following such rules. My friends and elders often criticized me for being an improper girl. I fought for my own beliefs; I competed; I challenged; and I laughed out loud—things a proper Khmer woman should never do. But my mother didn't want me to be proper. She wanted me to be strong, educated, and ready to face the world. When I was ten years old, she moved to Phnom Penh with my brother and me so I could attend one of the best public schools in Cambodia. Scraping together the money and moving to the capital was a sacrifice many Cambodian families might not have made for a daughter. But my mother happily did this for me, breaking the cycle of so many generations, in which eldest daughters inherit a life of selfless drudgery and eldest sons inherit education and freedom.

My mother's sacrifice has added fuel to my own dreams of self-reliance. After high school, I earned a math and economics degree from a university in the US, worked for several years at a global investment banking firm, and went to graduate school in London. My mother says that knowledge will always carry you. So I keep reaching as far as I can in my education.

I love going home to Stung Treng, where my father still lives and runs SWDC, but the visits are sometimes painful. Many of my childhood friends became teenage mothers. They never really learned to read or write. And I have become an outsider to them, a stranger transformed. No other girl from my town has ever gone to the best public high school in Cambodia, let alone studied at a university in America. As it was for my mother all those years ago, that dream is as dim and distant as the stars for the women I grew up with in Stung Treng.

Still, I see hope. A few years ago, I visited my primary school again and saw that the student committee I started is still raising money for the poorest kids. I saw the confident faces of female student-leaders, and I saw myself in them. I left Stung Treng promising myself that once my education was done, I would find some way to help them build lives of their choosing. I am still working out the best way to keep that promise.

DURING MY TIME away, I have longed for my mother's dishes—not only the flavors, but the act of cooking and the togetherness. As a child, I loved helping her roll handmade noodles for bánh canh and crank the meat-grinder on holidays when she made her delicious pâté de foie. That dish tastes like Christmas to me—my friends always begged her to make it. And whenever she grilled pork ribs on the charcoal grill, I sat next to her and hoped she would feed me the first bite. I had to argue with my brother for it, of course. Johan loves them just as much.

During these meals together, my mother—I call her "Mak" in Khmer—tells us stories of her childhood, her mother, and her time in Vietnam. I never met my grandmother, but Mak's stories paint a vivid picture of her: a beautiful, tiny woman whose kindness was her greatest strength.

I'm so glad my mother told me about her past lives. But if I'm honest, I was not always fond of hearing her stories when I was little. Whenever a taste triggered a memory for her, it was hard to predict whether the story would come out as laughter and hope or as tears and heartache: a bowl of instant noodles might prompt a laughing story about resourcefulness—how my parents made black market deals for instant noodles and sugar. Or the same dish might spin into a dark tale of hunger, powerlessness, and desolation. Even now, I can't fully understand the immensity of my mother's grief or the intense emotions that pour out with those stories. I don't know what it's like to be hungry, or to be alone in the world as a young woman. I cannot imagine losing Mak. The thought leaves me sick with worry.

That, too, is part of my Cambodian inheritance: the collective trauma, anxiety, and guilt so many of us children and grandchildren of survivors share. As I approached my twenty-fourth birthday, I developed an intense fear that my mother would die. Many nights I jolted awake from nightmares of losing her: an accident, a fall, an illness. I counted the days until my next birthday and felt a huge relief when it came. To me, twenty-three was a cursed year. It was the year my mother lost her Mae—who, to her, was everything.

I often think about what I would do if I became a refugee, with no home or family to turn to. Would I be as resourceful as my mother? Did she raise me to be useful and tough enough to survive? Would the cooking skills she taught me help carry me through catastrophe? It may seem strange to think that way, but growing up in Cambodia, we're never far from reminders that the worst things can and *do* happen anywhere. As a child in Stung Treng, I didn't need the stories to know about Pol Pot Time. Everyone knew where the mass graves were—people in the village sometimes excavated those makeshift tombs, hunting for valuables. Ex-Khmer Rouge soldiers lived among us—we knew who they were and left them alone. Land mines were hidden dangers children learned about in primary school. Our teachers trained us to avoid areas marked with red or skull-head signs and to recognize unexploded grenades and bombs so we wouldn't play with them. I remember hearing a loud boom one day when I was out playing with friends. The sound of sirens followed. A girl who lived a few houses down the street had stepped on a mine while she was herding cows near the old airport.

Whenever I tell this story to my non-Cambodian friends, their eyes widen in shock. But these were the kinds of hazards and tragedies that came to seem normal to us in the early 2000s in rural Stung Treng.

MAK STILL CRIES sometimes when she talks about the past. She says that during her years of hunger and loss, her soul was floating. But her painful history has given her two powerful gifts: she understands what it's like to have nothing, so her empathy is ocean-deep; and she isn't really afraid of anything—she's just prepared.

After the wars were over, her soul found solid ground in Stung Treng, where she re-launched her life by helping other women to launch theirs. Now, I am launching my own life, building myself into the kind of person a poor country needs most. These are my years of gathering. I am collecting skills and experiences like gems, to carry back home. I want to be useful. I want to help change how people think about poverty and the value of women's lives. I want to help women achieve financial independence and equality. I want every girl to finish school. And I want to help build a society where girls and women will be respected as productive citizens, because only then will they truly be free.

Maybe it's an impossible task, but impossible tasks don't scare me. Fifty years ago, my country lost everything. But if there's one thing I learned from my mother, it's that losing everything is not the end of the story. She taught me that lost civilizations can be rebuilt from zero, even if the task will require many generations of work.

So here I am, the next generation, ready to begin. Mak taught me the Slow Noodles ways, in the kitchen and in the world. I love to prepare the dishes she taught me to make, the dishes her mother taught her to make, and so on—an unbroken line of mothers past. Those recipes are my inheritance, and they remind me that even when you lose everything, you can fight hard and win it back again—if you are patient and stubborn enough.

These are my years of gathering. My mother is here to help. When I Skype with her, I am collecting her stories and recipes. I hate to hear her cry, but I love to cook with her. I've been assembling a book of her favorite dishes—noodles of varying speeds, for cooks of all skill levels. That cookbook is growing all the time, a treasure box that is always filling. These are treasures I am happy to share. Unlike gold, they become more abundant and valuable the more you pass them on.

Mee cha—a medium-fast noodle—is an easy and delicious place to begin.

———————

Mak and Clara's Stir-Fried Egg Noodles (Mee Cha)

You'll want to gild these noodles with an insane quantity of fried garlic—2 whole heads, or ½ cup minced, would not be too much. Try to mince garlic into uniform pieces, so it'll brown more evenly. You can speed the process by buying packages of peeled garlic sold at many Asian groceries. Pulsing garlic in a food processor is another time saver.
Serves 4 to 6

Ingredients:
½ cup neutral oil
2 heads garlic, minced
½ pound boneless pork, chicken, or beef, cut into bite-size strips
¼ teaspoon salt
Freshly ground black pepper
1 to 2 (14- to 16-ounce) packages flat egg noodles
1 pound bok choy or baby bok choy, roughly chopped
6 to 8 eggs
Golden Mountain Seasoning Sauce (or your favorite soy sauce)

For serving: ½ bunch fresh cilantro, roughly chopped; 3 scallions, thinly sliced; chili sauce or paste

In a small skillet, heat oil over medium heat. Set aside 2 tablespoons of minced garlic; add the rest to the skillet. Fry garlic, stirring constantly, until light golden, about 2 minutes. (Watch closely—garlic can burn quickly.) Reduce heat to low and continue stirring until garlic turns deep golden and crisp. Remove from heat and strain, setting aside fried garlic and reserving the garlic oil.

In a medium bowl, combine meat with reserved 2 tablespoons garlic. Season with salt and pepper.

Cook, drain, and rinse noodles (about 3 to 4 rolled bundles of noodles per person) with cold water. Drizzle with a little garlic oil and stir with chopsticks to keep noodles from sticking together.

In a large skillet or wok, sauté bok choy over medium heat in the reserved garlic oil with a pinch of salt until it has softened slightly, a minute at most. Remove and set aside.

Add meat to the skillet and sauté in garlic oil until cooked through and just beginning to brown, about 2 to 3 minutes; set aside meat.

In a small bowl, beat 2 eggs and season with salt.

Add noodles to skillet and stir-fry for a minute or so. Make a well in the center of the noodles, pour in beaten eggs, and mix well with noodles. Stir in a tablespoon or so of Golden Mountain, or more to taste. Remove skillet from heat, add bok choy and meat, and stir everything together while you complete the last step.

Fry one egg per person. Over easy is nice—runny yolks taste wonderful mixed with the noodles.

To serve, place the noodles on a large platter. Top with fried garlic, more black pepper, cilantro, scallions, and fried eggs. Serve with lots of condiments: Golden Mountain (or soy sauce), chili sauce or paste, dried chili, and more fried garlic.

NOTES ON INGREDIENTS,
TECHNIQUES, AND SUPPLIES

⚊⚫⚊

THIS BOOK IS not intended as a scholarly treatise on Cambodian gastronomy. These recipes and food descriptions reflect my own experiences and are not the final word on how Cambodians cook and eat. Cambodian recipes are traditionally passed down informally from one generation to another in home kitchens and are rarely written down; so think of my recipes as fluid and customizable. And like any national cuisine, ours is a shifting blend of influences—from multiple ethnic groups (we are not all Khmers) to the travelers, traders, neighbors, and former occupiers/subjects of empires past, all of whom have contributed ingredients. That's why you'll find not only Khmer recipes in these pages, but also French, Teochew Chinese, and Vietnamese dishes, and regional specialties with Thai or Laotian overtones. In so many dishes, tastes and techniques cross over. You can see this linguistically in the Khmer word for bread, *num pang*—"num," meaning cake, and "pang," from *pan*, the French word for bread. (Num pang dak sach, which means "bread filled with meat," and num pang pâté are classic Cambodian iterations of bánh mì.)

Still, Cambodian cuisine has its own distinctive character—irreplaceable flavors that we crave when we're away from home. I hope this book will spark curiosity and entice you to experiment with Cambodian cuisine(s) in your own kitchen. Keep in mind that there's no definitive way to transliterate Khmer words into English, so as you research, you'll encounter multiple spellings of food terms like *kuy teav* (e.g., katiew, kathiew, or k'tieu, or hủ tiếu in Vietnamese). Most Vietnamese words in this text come equipped with their diacritical marks, but you may see some inconsistencies: note the accented spellings of bánh canh, a Vietnamese dish, versus accentless num banhchok ("Khmer noodles") and banh sung, a Cambodian take on Vietnamese noodle salads like bún chả giò. For dishes that I think of as primarily Cambodian, I've written the names in transliterated Khmer (i.e., without diacritics), in an attempt to give each culture and language its due. But this is not an exact science.

As you cook, this guide can help you find and prepare ingredients. If you're not shopping in cities with large Southeast Asian diasporas, you can order some ingredients online—or make creative substitutions. There are more resources at slownoodles.com.

annatto seeds—Brick-red seeds from the achiote tree; also called achiote. They have a mild, nutty flavor and give foods a red-gold color. Stir annatto seeds in hot oil for less than a minute—just enough to redden the oil—and then remove oil from heat and discard seeds. Any longer, and the seeds may burn and make the oil bitter. You can find packages of annatto seeds in the dried chili section of Asian or Latin American groceries.

Asian eggplant—Either the round, green-and-white Thai eggplant, about the size of a golf ball, or the long, slender purple Japanese (or Chinese) eggplant. Soak sliced eggplant in salted water for two minutes and rinse before cooking to keep it from turning the curry an unappetizing brown color. You'll find these eggplant types in Asian groceries.

banana flower—Long, conical purple blossoms that grow from the end of banana bunches. We Cambodians use them in salads and as soup toppings. To prep banana flower, mix two cups water, a pinch of salt, and the juice of one lemon in a small bowl. Peel away the reddish outer leaves and petals of the flower to expose the inner white leaves (bracts). Roll and thinly slice the white leaves crosswise. Submerge slices in lemon water as you go; otherwise they will turn brown and taste bitter.

banana leaf—Inedible leaves used for wrapping, steaming, grilling, and/or serving certain dishes, such as fish amok. If you want to make the optional banana leaf bowls for steaming amok, you can usually find banana leaves in the freezer or produce section of Asian, Latin American, or international groceries. Thaw and rinse the leaves and cut them into circles about ten inches in diameter. Take two leaf circles and fold four pleats, one at each cardinal point. Secure the pleats with toothpicks to create a four-cornered bowl. Store extra leaves and use them later to decorate a serving platter or as a wrapper for leftovers.

bean sprouts—(mung bean sprouts) Germinated mung beans with long, glossy white shoots that have tiny yellow ends. Mung bean sprouts add nutrition and crunch to some noodle dishes and soups. Add them to the dish raw or quickly blanched. You'll find fresh mung bean sprouts in the produce section of Asian or international groceries. Keep them refrigerated and serve within a day or two—they don't keep long.

bobor—(borbor, babaw, b'baw) Essentially congee, or white rice porridge. Bobor is inexpensive comfort food eaten at all times of day in Cambodia, often in street stalls. It can be served solo or cooked with meat or seafood and topped with lots of condiments, such as fish sauce, pickled vegetables, chili oil, sliced scallions, fried garlic, or fresh ginger.

chả lụa—A Vietnamese pork roll that's made from lean pork that is pounded, seasoned, tightly wrapped in banana leaves, then steamed or boiled. It's sliced and served atop noodles and soups and is delicious in a num pang dak sach (cold cut sandwich; bánh mì chả lụa, in Vietnamese). You'll find chả lụa in the deli or freezer section of some Asian groceries and international supermarkets.

chili paste (dried)—To make this paste (for amok), use mild, dried red chilies, like New Mexico, ancho, or guajillo. To rehydrate, put dried chilies into a medium bowl and pour 3 cups boiling water over them. Let chilies soak until they're soft, 15 to 30 minutes. Drain. Remove stems and seeds, then grind chilies in a blender until a paste forms. (Drizzle in a little of the soaking water to help chilies blend.) In a skillet, fry paste in 1 tablespoon of neutral oil for five minutes over low heat. Freeze any leftover paste you don't use.

chili sauce or chili-garlic oil—You likely know sriracha. Get to know a wider range of heat delivery systems starring red chilies and garlic; some also have shrimp paste, soybean oil, or vinegar. Clara and I love a fiery Thai product with a gold label called Sambal Bajak Ground Chili Garlic Oil, but it's tricky to find. Browse the chili aisle and discover your new favorite, or experiment with making your own.

coconut cream (canned)—Coconut cream has less water and a higher fat content than coconut milk, and its consistency is thicker, richer, and creamier. Shake cans before opening.

coconut flakes (toasted)—You can buy these flakes already toasted in a gourmet market. Or get unsweetened coconut flakes in the baking section of a supermarket and toast them yourself: Spread them on a large baking sheet and bake at 350°F for 8 to 10 minutes. Stir flakes every 2 to 3 minutes to ensure they toast evenly. Remove when they turn golden-brown.

coconut milk (canned)—Look for unsweetened, full-fat coconut milk. (Avoid "lite"—it's less flavorful.) You want a brand that's rich and velvety and not watery or chalky. We like Chaokoh and Aroy-D—they're available in any international supermarket. But you'll also find workable brands (such as Thai Kitchen) on the "international" aisle of some supermarkets. Shake cans before opening.

culantro (ngò gai, sawtooth herb)—An herb with long, serrated leaves that tastes somewhat like cilantro but has a stronger flavor and can withstand cooking. Find it fresh in Asian groceries or international supermarkets, often labeled "ngò gai." To store, wrap in damp paper towels and refrigerate.

daikon—A large, whitish radish used in soups and stocks, sliced for salads and garnishes, and julienned and pickled (with carrot) for loading many varieties of num pang– or bánh mì–style sandwiches.

egg noodles—(mee, mì) Chewy Asian-style noodles made with wheat flour and eggs, great for stir-frying. For Clara's mee cha recipe, look for Vietnamese or Chinese-produced packages of bundled, flat noodles the shape and size of fettuccine. (In Asian groceries, look for packages labeled "*mì trứng,*" "Canton Style Egg Noodle," or "Chinese Style Noodle.") You can substitute round egg noodles the size of spaghetti.

fingerroot—(rhizomes, Chinese keys, Chinese ginger, lesser galangal; krachai or grachai in Thai; k'jeay in Khmer) A yellowish rhizome resembling long, slender fingers and related to ginger. Sometimes you'll find jars of pickled rhizome in Asian groceries. There's no ideal substitute, so omit it from the kroeung if you can't find it.

fish—These recipes call for white, flaky fish such as branzino, tilapia, catfish, snapper, or bass. In Cambodian cooking, we use lots of freshwater fish and mostly cook it whole with the skin on—the skin crisps up nicely. You can ask your fishmonger to clean and gut a whole fish for you.

fish sauce—(teuk trei, in Khmer) An amber-colored, liquid byproduct of fish fermentation. This vital seasoning ingredient is used widely in Southeast Asian cuisines to add salt and umami—and as a base for many dipping sauces. You'll find many options at Asian groceries. Avoid cheap brands with long, chemistry-lab ingredient lists. My go-to is Squid

Brand—it makes green papaya pickles taste like my great-aunt Yiay Thom's. Red Boat costs more but is full-bodied and complex. Fish sauce keeps for a long time, but if you don't use it often, buy a small bottle and refrigerate it.

galangal—(greater galangal, blue ginger, Thai ginger, romdeng in Khmer) A cream-colored rhizome related to ginger and used as an earthy and citrusy spice in some soups and kroeungs. Not to be confused with fingerroot, or lesser galangal. Peel and slice it as thinly as you can (it's quite tough) before pounding or processing it. If you don't find fresh galangal in an Asian grocery or international supermarket, look for (or order) galangal paste or powder. Substitute 1 teaspoon of galangal powder for 1 inch of galangal root. Ginger isn't a good substitute—the two flavors are different. Slice leftover galangal and freeze for later use.

glutinous rice—(sweet rice, sticky rice) An opaque, short-grain rice that's lower in one type of starch and becomes sticky when cooked (but, despite the name, contains no gluten). Cambodians use it in desserts and snacks like krorlan (roasted rice in bamboo) and num ansom (sticky rice cakes in banana leaf). To cook sticky rice, soak it for 2 to 24 hours, then steam for 20 to 30 minutes (until soft) in a bamboo or metal steamer lined with parchment, or in a fancy rice cooker with a "sweet" rice setting. You'll find bamboo steamers of various sizes, as well as bags of glutinous rice, at Asian groceries.

Golden Mountain Seasoning Sauce—A sauce made from soybeans that is a staple in Thailand (and in my cupboard). It's sweeter and saltier than many soy sauces and is reminiscent of Maggi or Bragg. Be aware that Golden Mountain contains a lot of sodium, so use with care. You'll find it at Asian groceries that stock Thai products.

green papaya—Unripe papayas, dark green on the outside with whitish-green interiors, that are crunchy and rather bland. (Papayas turn orange, soft, and sweet as they ripen.) In the produce section of Asian markets, look for a football-sized, vivid green fruit that's relatively free of spots and firm to the touch. (You can also find shredded green papaya for papaya salad in the refrigerator section.) Peel papaya with a peeler, as you would a cucumber, then cut in half and scoop out the seeds. A whole green papaya will keep for a week or two in the refrigerator.

jasmine rice—A long-grain, fragrant rice cultivated in Southeast Asia and served at almost every meal. Although brown, red, and purple varieties exist, you'll most often see processed white jasmine rice with the bran and germ removed. When cooked, it's soft, moist, and slightly sticky. Suggested portion size is around a half cup (or a little less) of dry rice per person. Before cooking, rinse rice in a large bowl of cold water, then drain in a colander; repeat at least once more. To cook on the stovetop, use a ratio of 1¼ to 1½ cups of water per 1 cup of rice and a thick-bottomed pot with a tight-fitting lid. (Don't fill more than halfway—the rice will expand.) Add water and rice to pot and bring to a gentle boil over medium-high heat. Stir occasionally for 2 or 3 minutes, until small pockets appear in the surface, then reduce heat to low and cover. Simmer until there's no water left in the bottom of the pot, around 15 minutes. Remove from heat and leave rice covered for 10 minutes, then fluff with a fork and serve. (Refrigerate leftover rice and use it to make fried rice!)

To steam rice perfectly with less guesswork, invest in an electric rice cooker. Compact 6-cup models may cost as little as $30, whereas a 10-cup rice cooker with a timer, warmer, and settings for various rice types can be $200. You'll find quality jasmine rice from Thailand and a good selection of rice cookers at Asian supermarkets.

kabocha—(kabocha squash, Japanese pumpkin) A dark green, pumpkin-shaped winter squash with an orange-yellow interior. Use in soups, desserts, and curries. Peel and chop the kabocha as you would a pumpkin. Substitute sweet potato or butternut squash.

Kampot pepper—Prized peppercorns, cultivated in the southwestern Kampot Province for centuries. These are Cambodia's champagne of spices—they even have their own geographic indication (GI). Splurge on an order and grind these over grilled meats, soups, or pâté de foie.

Khmer baguette—Khmer and Vietnamese-style baguettes, used to make the splendid Southeast Asian street food sandwiches that have conquered the globe (num pang / bánh mì). These are softer and airier than French-style baguettes. You can find these small, light baguettes in many Asian groceries, Vietnamese bakeries, or international supermarkets. They freeze well.

Knorr—Chicken bouillon cubes that are a staple in many modern-day Cambodian kitchens, including mine. They're an easy, affordable way to boost the flavor of soups and curries. Omit them if you prefer, or replace some of the water in the recipe with homemade or store-bought chicken stock.

kroeung—A Khmer word, meaning "ingredients," that describes several spice and herb pastes that form the foundation of many iconic Khmer dishes. Traditionally, kroeungs are made by pounding ingredients with a large mortar and pestle, beginning with the tougher ingredients, then adding the softer ones one by one (e.g., lemongrass > galangal > turmeric root > fingerroot > lime leaves > garlic > shallots). You can also grind these ingredients (in the same order) in a food processor or blender. (Processing first, then blending with a drizzle of water, can work well.) Specific kroeungs often take their names from a key ingredient: turmeric gives yellow kroeung its color; lemongrass and lime leaf prevail in green kroeung; and dried chili defines red kroeung. Some dishes have a specific "individual" kroeung, and families have their own recipes. You can order some jarred kroeungs from specialty retailers (such as Angkor Cambodian Food), but fresh is best. Make extra and freeze the surplus in a Ziploc bag.

Lady Finger banana—An edible cultivar of three- to five-inch-long bananas, which grow in large clusters. They are called nam wah in Thai, chek nam va in Khmer, pisang awak in Indonesian, and chuối xiêm in Vietnamese. Smaller and sweeter than the Cavendish bananas sold in the US, they're also called baby or dwarf bananas, or may even be labeled Thai bananas in the store; similar varieties are found throughout Southeast Asia. For ice pops, let bananas ripen at room temperature until they are speckled with dark spots and soft to the touch.

lemongrass—A culinary herb with a citrusy flavor, used in soups, kroeungs, stir-fries, and marinades. Fresh lemongrass stalks resemble long scallions but are tough and woody. Dried, frozen, and powdered lemongrass are inferior backups; substitute 1 teaspoon of ground lemongrass per stalk. To prep lemongrass, cut off ½ inch from the bottom of the stalk (the tough root), and also its top 4 to 6 inches (also dry, fibrous, and tough), using a sharp knife. Remove fibrous outer layers, then bruise stalk with the blunt edge of the knife. For soups, cut stalk into thirds and simmer with other broth ingredients. (If you're lucky enough to find fresh lemongrass with the leaves still intact and green, use them in the num banhchok samlor Khmer recipe.) Some kroeungs may call for only the bottom (white) part of the stalk or the top (green) part. Freeze unused portions. (You can also freeze the outer layers and use them to add a hint of lemongrass to soups. Tie them into a bunch and add to stock, then remove before serving).

Slice thinly with a very sharp knife, and for kroeungs, pound with a mortar and pestle (or process in a food processor) before adding softer ingredients. (A whole stalk will yield around 2 tablespoons of sliced lemongrass.) Find lemongrass stalks in the produce or freezer section of Asian groceries and some supermarkets.

long beans—Green, snakelike beans that stay crunchy when cooked, so they're great in stir-fries. For curries, chop and add them near the end so they aren't in the liquid for too long. You'll find bundled long beans in many Asian groceries, but if not, you can substitute green beans.

makrut lime leaves—Shiny paired leaves from the makrut lime tree that add a citrusy flavor to curries and soups. Fresh leaves are superior to dried. When using for kroeung, remove the central vein and cut into slivers before pounding or processing. You'll find fresh leaves in the produce or freezer section of some Asian groceries. Buy extra and freeze for later use.

morning glory—(*Ipomoea aquatica*, water spinach, Chinese spinach, water convolvulus; rau muống in Vietnamese, trakuon in Khmer) An edible green with long, thin leaves that grows abundantly in waterways or wet soil throughout Southeast Asia. To prep, trim off the bottom inch of stem, remove older leaves near the ends of stems, and cut the rest into 4-inch sections. Blanch before using as a soup topping. You'll sometimes find morning glory in Southeast Asian groceries, in cities where there are large Vietnamese or Cambodian diasporas, but it's illegal to cultivate in some states and can be tough to find. Substitute watercress or spinach.

neutral oil—Some of these recipes call for oils with neutral flavors. Canola and vegetable are good multipurpose oils with neutral flavors and relatively high smoke points for frying.

num banhchok—Lightly fermented rice noodles, also known as Khmer noodles, that are handmade by hardworking noodle makers all over Cambodia and sold fresh. The term also refers to several quintessentially Khmer breakfast dishes sold in street stalls that feature these noodles. Many num banhchok dishes include fish gravy or a kroeung-based soup and lots of local herbs, greens, and vegetables. You can use very thin rice vermicelli (bún) for the num banhchok recipes.

oyster sauce—A dark brown, savory-sweet syrupy condiment made from oyster extract. It imparts powerful umami to stir-fries and is a splendid marinade for grilled ribs. Lee Kum Kee Premium Oyster Sauce is a solid brand—find it in Asian groceries. Or order the velvety Megachef brand online, from vendors such as the Mala Market. Refrigerate after opening.

palm sugar—A caramel-tasting sweetener made from the sap of palm flowers that usually comes in small discs or plastic tubs. If discs are pliable, slice off slivers with a large, sharp knife. As discs lose moisture and harden, break them up with a mortar and pestle. The palm sugar that comes in tubs is initially soft enough to scoop, but as it hardens, you can microwave it briefly to soften it. Store both kinds tightly sealed in the pantry. You'll find palm sugar in Asian groceries. Substitute with light brown sugar or cane sugar. For recipes with a teaspoon or less of sugar, white granulated sugar is fine.

pork belly—A boneless cut of layered fat and meat from the belly of a pig. It resembles bacon or pancetta (but is not cured). We use this inexpensive cut frequently—for braised dishes (khors); in noodle salad bowls and num pang dak sach (bánh mì); or ground and seasoned in fried spring rolls. It's sold in big slabs in the refrigerated or butcher section of an Asian or international grocery, and at some supermarket butchers. You can leave the skin on, or remove it before roasting, braising, or frying. Substitutions depend on the dish.

prahok—A gray fish paste made from salted, fermented fish—usually trei riel, or mud carp. For generations, prahok has been a staple protein source of the Cambodian diet—and an essential, defining ingredient in the national cuisine. A small amount adds intense savory umami to some samlors, kroeungs, and dips. You might find prahok on the condiment aisle of some Southeast Asian groceries. Look for jars of gray paste labeled "mud fish sauce" (or "mắm cá lóc," in Vietnamese). A little bit goes a long way. Be prepared for a powerful aroma when opening the jar. Substitute anchovies or shrimp paste.

rice flour—A Southeast Asian staple, milled from raw, white rice, that is used for making rice noodles, crepes, and pastries. You can find it in Asian groceries, but don't confuse it with *glutinous* or *sweet* rice flour, which makes chewier doughs.

rice noodles—So-called rice vermicelli or rice stick noodles are generic terms for a huge variety of rice noodles of different shapes and consistencies. When facing a wall of noodles, it helps to know what specific kind you're looking for. Bún are round rice noodles of various sizes; use small-to-medium bún for vermicelli salads and to fill fresh spring rolls. (You can also use them for the num banhchok recipes.) Thicker, spaghetti-sized bún works well for bún bò Huế or banh sung. Bánh phở noodles are wide and flat, like fettuccine. For kuy teav, you'll find squared-off noodles of rice and tapioca flour labeled hủ tiếu (the Vietnamese term for kuy teav), or you can use phở noodles or even egg noodles (mì, mee). You can find fresh noodles, such as thick, chewy bánh canh noodles (made with rice and tapioca flours), in the refrigerated section of some Asian or international groceries.

To cook bún (or any rice noodle), take package cooking instructions with a grain of salt: soaking doesn't necessarily work well, and recommended cooking times aren't always enough. Boil just until noodles are soft (but not overcooked and mushy): small bún may only need two or three minutes, while thicker bún may need ten minutes or more. Drain and rinse in cool water after cooking.

rice paper wrappers (bánh tráng)—Edible sheets, usually made from rice flour and tapioca starch, used for wrapping fresh summer rolls and fried spring rolls. (I prefer the lacy crunch of fried rice paper rolls over the wheat-based wrappers, but the rice paper ones don't brown as easily.)

Rice paper wrappers come in various shapes and sizes. I like the Three Ladies brand of large round wrappers (22 cm) for fresh rolls and the smaller ones (16 cm) for fried spring rolls and, cut in half, for Mae's wrapped fried shrimp. (For the latter, you can also use the 22-cm wrappers cut into pie-shaped thirds). Moistening the wrappers makes them pliable enough to roll, but too much water makes them sticky and unmanageable. You can quickly submerge the wrappers, but I prefer to brush warm water with my fingers onto the rough side of the wrapper and lay it out flat, dry side down. Within a minute or two, it's pliable enough to roll. (For efficiency, alternate by moistening one and rolling a second one while you wait for the first to soften.)

To roll the fried pork spring rolls, mold the pork and bean sprout mixture into a compact, finger-sized log and place it in the middle (laterally) of the wrapper, about an inch from the edge nearest you. Roll away from you one full turn, until the filling is encased. Flatten both sides and press out air, then fold the sides toward the middle and seal. Continue rolling away from you, pressing out air bubbles, until you're out of wrapper. Store spring rolls (not touching—they will stick and tear), on a sheet pan lined with parchment, in a cool, dry place for 30 minutes to one hour before frying.

samlor—(somlor, samlah) A category of thicker and more complex soups and stews that may contain kroeung, coconut milk, and/or prahok; samlor machu is a beloved subcategory with a prevailing sour ("machu") taste, often imparted by tamarind.

shrimp (dried)—In a Cambodian market, you'll find a gorgeous bounty of dried seafood for snacking and to use as a condiment for soups; in the US, you'll have to make do with vacuum-packaged dried shrimp (or squid) found in Asian groceries. Soak for 20 minutes and rinse before using.

shrimp paste—A Southeast Asian staple made with fermented shrimp and salt. A small amount of shrimp paste packs a concentrated umami punch in dishes like amok. Look for small jars of pink or brownish paste labeled "shrimp paste" or "shrimp sauce" in the condiment aisle of Asian groceries. If you can't find it, substitute 1 teaspoon of shrimp paste with 2 teaspoons of fish sauce. Keep refrigerated.

s'gnao—(s'ngao, sgnor) A Khmer verb meaning "to boil"; as a noun, a category of (usually) clear broth-based soups with a few simple ingredients.

soy sauce—A condiment made with fermented soybeans, wheat, and brine. My favorite is a Thai product called Golden Mountain (see separate entry), which isn't technically soy sauce, but I use it the same way—to add salty umami to certain dishes. Use your favorite regular soy sauce (i.e., not "dark" or "sweet") from the supermarket, or taste-test something new from an Asian grocery. Tamari is a decent alternative if you're allergic to wheat.

spring roll dipping sauce—See entry for teuk trei pa'em.

tamarind paste—A concentrated reddish-brown paste made from the sour fruit of a tamarind-tree pod. Tamarind is one of the sources of that famous sourness in some Khmer soups, stews, and sauces. Find small jars or plastic packages of sour (not sweetened) tamarind paste at Asian or Indian groceries, gourmet supermarkets, or online retailers.

teuk trei pa'em (spring roll dipping sauce)—A spicy sour-sweet dipping sauce, similar to Vietnamese nước chấm, that is made with fish sauce, rice vinegar, water, sugar, garlic, and red chili. It is used for dipping fried spring rolls and dressing some noodle dishes. (Some versions add carrot and crushed peanut.) Teuk trei Koh Kong, a more concentrated sauce for dipping seafood, replaces the water and vinegar with lime juice.

Other Cambodian dipping sauces may incorporate freshly cracked black peppercorns, tamarind, or prahok, but most include garlic and chili. For an even simpler accompaniment to any Cambodian meal, float sliced chilies in a ramekin of quality fish sauce and spoon some onto every bite.

Thai red chilies (fresh)—Small, slender chili peppers, sometimes called bird's-eye chilies, that are green when young and ripen to become redder and hotter. Think of the chili quantity suggested in these recipes as an opening bid and adjust according to your heat preferences. We serve a small dish of sliced chilies at most meals as a condiment. You can usually find bulk packages of these in the produce section of Asian or international groceries. Refrigerate them for a month or more sealed in a plastic bag; they also freeze well.

toasted rice—Jasmine rice or glutinous rice, toasted and pounded to a coarse powder. It adds texture and a nutty flavor to dishes like banh sung and larb (laab, laap), a minced meat entrée. You can find it at Asian groceries, but it tastes much better freshly prepared. Spread a thin layer (⅓ cup or so) of uncooked jasmine or glutinous rice evenly in a thick-bottomed, medium-sized dry skillet and turn heat to medium. Lightly shake or stir rice frequently until rice turns evenly golden-brown and smells nutty and toasty, around 7 to 10 minutes. (Reduce heat if rice begins to smoke.) Remove from pan and let cool, then pound with a mortar and pestle or pulse in a spice grinder until consistency is like cornmeal (i.e., not too fine a powder). Store in a sealed jar in the pantry—it'll keep for a month or so.

turmeric root—A rhizome and culinary spice that resembles ginger but has an orange-yellow interior. It imparts a saffron color and slightly bitter, earthy flavor to kroeungs and other foods. Peel and grate (or mince) turmeric before pounding or processing for kroueng. (Beware—it stains.) You'll find fresh turmeric root in many Asian and international groceries and in some upscale supermarkets. Substitute one teaspoon of powdered turmeric for one inch (about a tablespoon, grated) of fresh root.

wood-ear mushrooms—(tree ears, cloud ears) Edible fungi that look like crinkled brown ears and are chewy and earthy. You'll find them, dried or fresh, in Asian and international groceries, and the dried version in some supermarkets. Reconstitute dried wood ears in warm water for 20 to 30 minutes before using.

LIST OF RECIPES

———

ACKNOWLEDGMENTS

—————

To ANN WALLING, my longtime friend and benefactor: my life would look very different without your family foundation's support, which helped Chan and me build SWDC and Mekong Blue. This book owes everything to your vision, underwriting, and steadfast belief that my story should be told.

To Joy Tutela, our all-seeing agent and staunch advocate: thank you for believing in this book when the odds were stacked against it, and for guiding us through the stormy seas of publishing.

To Donna Talarico and Steph Auteri of *Hippocampus Magazine*, and to Cheri Lucas Rowlands of *Longreads*: thank you for taking a chance on my story and breathing new life into our hopes for this book.

To Amy Gash, the editor of our dreams, and the talented editorial, PR, and marketing teams at Algonquin Books: thank you for championing this project, and for your hard work to help us make something larger than ourselves. Thanks also to June Park for the stunning cover design.

To Maria Browning, Rachel Rueckert, Cindy Wall, Nancy Mullane, Hal Humphreys, and Faye Green: thank you for reading early drafts and offering brilliant editorial insights. Thanks also to writing-community allies Margaret Renkl, Lisa Donovan, Mary Laura Philpott, Theo Emery, Alice Randall, Pam Colloff, Leigh Stein, Stephanie Pruitt Gaines, Jennifer

Justus, Erin Byers Murray, Taylor Holliday, Daniel Potter, Becca Andrews, Joyful Clemantine Wamariya, Lisa Bubert, M. B. Roberts, and Natasha Senjanovic—and to Susannah Felts and Katie McDougall of the Porch Writers Collective—for practical advice and moral support.

To the skilled team of food-expert friends and recipe testers: thank you for helping us transform word-of-mouth traditions and raw instinct into polished written recipes that can now come to life in thousands of home kitchens. Big thanks to Erin Byers Murray, Delaney Gray, Josh Habiger, Meg Stemmler, Nancy Vienneau, Jennifer Justus, Trisha Boyer, Evi Bruster, Lisa Donovan, Faye Ziegeweid, Nick Kassebaum, Louisa Shafia, Rebekah Turshen, Tabitha Ong Tune, Amy Peterson, Meg Giuffrida, Andrea Miller, and Clara Kim.

To everyone else who backed our play along the way, including dear friends, donors, volunteers, scarf-buyers, and guests at our many fundraisers, Cambodian dinner parties, and cooking lessons: you and everyone listed above are charter members of the Slow Noodles Allies Club (SNAC), and we are grateful to you all.

To ourselves: we (Chantha and Kim) thank each other for being patient and diligent during this long collaboration. It isn't easy to write a book together, especially one so personal.

To Chan: thank you for your survivor's strength and the energy you've poured into helping to build our life's work.

Most of all, to my beloved Clara and Johan: thank you for bearing witness to so many of my stories (and tears). I hoped that writing this would transfer some of that listening burden from your shoulders—and that it might help loosen my grief and finally set it free. I don't know if that's how grief works, but in sending this book into the world, I acknowledge that these stories and recipes are no longer mine alone. Think of them as your gift and legacy, passing through me from Chanthu and Mae and the women who came before them. Watching you learn to cook the dishes they passed on to me has been one of the greatest joys of my life. May these tastes of my history linger on your tongues long after I am gone.